Turkish

sebooks
and
Arzu Kürklü

Turkish phrasebook
4th edition – July 2008

Published by
Lonely Planet Publications Pty Ltd ABN 36 005 607 983
90 Maribyrnong St, Footscray, Victoria 3011, Australia

Lonely Planet Offices
Australia Locked Bag 1, Footscray, Victoria 3011
USA 150 Linden St, Oakland CA 94607
UK Media Centre, 201 Wood Lane, London W12 7TQ

Cover illustration
Çay in red by Daniel New

ISBN 978 1 74104 582 6

text © Lonely Planet Publications Pty Ltd 2008
cover illustration © Lonely Planet Publications Pty Ltd 2008

10 9 8 7 6 5 4

Printed in China

Editor Jodie Martire would like to acknowledge the following people for their contributions to this phrasebook:

Arzu Kürklü for her flexibility and precision in the translation of this book. Born in Turkey, Arzu completed her teaching degree at Dokuz Eylül University (DEÜ) in İzmir, and went on to teach English at the Turkish Air Force Language School, and Turkish-American Association. She now lives in Melbourne, Australia, with her husband and daughter, and teaches English as a Second Language at AMES (Adult Multicultural Education Services) and Turkish at CAE (Centre for Adult Education).

Arzu would like to thank her husband Yücel Kürklü for contributing his knowledge of the Turkish language and culture, and for all his support and patience. She would also like to thank everybody on the team who put this phrasebook together.

Fellow editor Branislava Vladisavljevic for her proofing skills.

Lonely Planet Language Products

Publishing Manager: Ben Handicott
Commissioning Editors: Karin Vidstrup Monk & Rachel Williams
Editors: Jodie Martire, Branislava Vladisavljevic, Francesca Coles, Meladel Mistica & Laura Crawford

Layout Designers: David Kemp & Sonya Brook
Managing Editor: Annelies Mertens
Layout Manager: Adriana Mammarella
Series Designer: Yukiyoshi Kamimura
Cartographer: Wayne Murphy

make the most of this phrasebook ...

Anyone can speak another language! It's all about confidence. Don't worry if you can't remember your school language lessons or if you've never learnt a language before. Even if you learn the very basics (on the inside covers of this book), your travel experience will be the better for it. You have nothing to lose and everything to gain when the locals hear you making an effort.

finding things in this book

For easy navigation, this book is in sections. The Tools chapters are the ones you'll thumb through time and again. The Practical section covers basic travel situations like catching transport and finding a bed. The Social section gives you conversational phrases, pick-up lines, the ability to express opinions – so you can get to know people. Food has a section all of its own: gourmets and vegetarians are covered and local dishes feature. Safe Travel equips you with health and police phrases, just in case. Remember the colours of each section and you'll find everything easily; or use the comprehensive Index. Otherwise, check the two-way traveller's Dictionary for the word you need.

being understood

Throughout this book you'll see coloured phrases on each page. They're phonetic guides to help you pronounce the language. You don't even need to look at the language itself, but you'll get used to the way we've represented particular sounds. The pronunciation chapter in Tools will explain more, but you can feel confident that if you read the coloured phrase slowly, you'll be understood.

communication tips

Body language, ways of doing things, sense of humour – all have a role to play in every culture. 'Local talk' boxes show you common ways of saying things, or everyday language to drop into conversation. 'Listen for ...' boxes supply the phrases you may hear. They start with the language (so local people can point out what they want to say to you) and then lead in to the pronunciation guide and the English translation.

CONTENTS

5

turkish

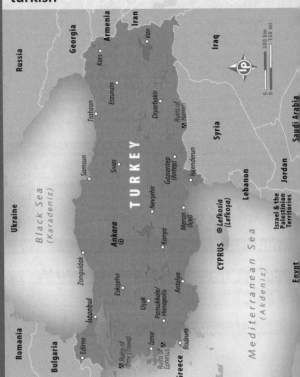

Russia
Georgia
Armenia
Iran
Iraq
Syria
Saudi Arabia
Jordan
Lebanon
Israel & the
Palestinian
Territories
Egypt
Ukraine
Romania
Bulgaria
Greece

TURKEY

Black Sea
(Karadeniz)

Mediterranean Sea
(Akdeniz)

Kars
Van
Erzurum
Trabzon
Diyarbakır
Ruins of
Nemrut
Gaziantep
(Antep)
İskenderun
Mersin
(İçel)
Sivas
Samsun
Nevşehir
Konya
Ankara
Zonguldak
Eskişehir
Uşak
Pamukkale/
Hierapolis
Antalya
İstanbul
Edirne
İzmir
Ruins of
Ephesus
Ruins of
Troy (Truva)
Bodrum

CYPRUS   Lefkosia
(Lefkoşa)

200 km
150 mi

■ official language
■ widely understood

EUROPE
Russia
Turkey
MIDDLE
EAST
AFRICA

For more details, see the **introduction**.

For a language which traces its roots as far back as 3500BC, has travelled through Central Asia, Persia, North Africa and Europe and been written in both Arabic and Latin script, you'll be surprised that Turkish is a highly regular language with no genders, one irregular noun and only one irregular verb. So how did it transform itself from a nomad's tongue spoken in Mongolia into the language of modern Turkey, with a prestigious interlude as the diplomatic language of the Ottoman Empire?

The first evidence of the Turkish language was found on stone monuments, dating back to the 8th century BC, in what's now Outer Mongolia. When their Mongol neighbours took control of the Turks' pasturage in the 8th century AD, the tribe migrated to the south and west. By the 11th century, most Turks in the Middle East had become Muslims. Among them was the Seljuq clan, which invaded large tracts of Asia Minor (Anatolia) and imposed their language on the peoples they ruled. Over time, Arabic and Persian vocabulary was adopted to express artistic and philosophical concepts and Arabic script began to be used. By the 14th century, another clan – the Ottomans – was Turkey's dominant power, and was busy establishing the empire that was to control Eurasia for centuries. In their wake, they left the Turkish language. There were then two levels of

at a glance ...
language name: Turkish
name in language: *Türkçe, Osmanlı* tewrk·che, os·man·luh
language family: Ural-Altaic
approximate number of speakers: 70 million worldwide
close relatives: Azeri, Gagauz, Qashqay, Turkmen
donations to English: baklava, bridge (the game), caviar, horde, kaftan, kismet, khan, sequin, shish kebab, yoghurt

introduction

Turkish – ornate Ottoman Turkish, with flowery Persian phrases and Arabic honorifics (words showing respect), used for diplomacy, business and art, and the language of the common Turks, which still used 'native' Turkish vocabulary and structures.

The Ottoman Empire fell in 1922; the military hero, amateur linguist and historian Kemal Atatürk came to power and led the new Republic of Turkey. With the backing of a strong language reform movement, he devised a phonetic Latin script that reflected Turkish sounds more accurately than Arabic script. On 1 November 1928, the new writing system was unveiled: within two months, it was illegal to write Turkish in the old script.

In 1932 Atatürk created the Türk Dil Kurumu (Turkish Language Society) and gave it the brief of simplifying the Turkish language to its 'pure' form of centuries before. The vocabulary and structure was completely overhauled. As a consequence, Turkish has changed so drastically that even Atatürk's own speeches (he died in 1938) are barely comprehensible to today's speakers of öztürkçe ('pure Turkish').

Turkish is now the official language of Turkey and the Turkish Republic of Northern Cyprus (an area recognised as a nation only by itself and the Turkish government). Elsewhere, the language is also called Osmanlı, and is spoken by large populations in Bulgaria, Macedonia, Greece, Germany and the '-stans' of Central Asia.

This book gives you the practical phrases you need to get by in Turkish, as well as all the fun, spontaneous phrases that can lead to a better understanding of Turkey and its people. Once you've got the hang of how to pronounce Turkish words, the rest is just a matter of confidence. Local knowledge, new relationships and a sense of satisfaction are on the tip of your tongue. So don't just stand there, say something!

abbreviations used in this book

a	adjective	gen	genitive	nom	nominative
abl	ablative	inf	informal	pl	plural
acc	accusative	lit	literal translation	pol	polite
adv	adverb	loc	locative	sg	singular
dat	dative	m	masculine	v	verb
f	feminine	n	noun		

Pronouncing Turkish is pretty simple for English speakers as it uses sounds which are similar to ones you already use. You'll hear some variation in pronunciation throughout Turkey, but this phrasebook is based on standard pronunciation so you'll be understood wherever you go.

vowel sounds

Most Turkish vowel sounds can be found in English, although in Turkish they're generally shorter and slightly harsher.

symbol	english equivalent	turkish example	transliteration
a	father	*abide*	a·bee·*de*
ai	aisle	*hayvan*	hai·*van*
ay	say	*ney*	nay
e	red	*ekmek*	ek·*mek*
ee	bee	*ile*	ee·le
er	her	*özel*	er·*zel*
ew	ee with rounded lips, like 'few' or the French *tu*	*üye*	ew·ye
o	go	*oda*	o·da
oo	moon	*uçak*	oo·chak
uh	habit	*ıslak*	uhs·lak

consonant sounds

Most Turkish consonants sound the same as in English, so they're straightforward to pronounce. The exception is the Turkish r, which is always rolled.

symbol	english equivalent	turkish example	transliteration
b	**big**	*bira*	*bee*·ra
ch	**church**	*çanta*	chan·*ta*
d	**day**	*deniz*	de·*neez*
f	**fun**	*fabrika*	fab·ree·*ka*
g	**go**	*gar*	gar
h	**house**	*hala*	ha·*la*
j	**jam**	*cadde*	jad·*de*
k	**kilo**	*kadın*	ka·*duhn*
l	**loud**	*lider*	lee·*der*
m	**man**	*maç*	mach
n	**no**	*nefis*	ne·*fees*
p	**pig**	*paket*	pa·*ket*
r	**run** (but rolled)	*rehber*	reh·*ber*
s	**sea**	*saat*	sa·*at*
sh	**ship**	*şarkı*	shar·*kuh*
t	**tin**	*tas*	tas
v	**van** (but softer, between 'v' and 'w')	*vadi*	va·*dee*
y	**you**	*yarım*	ya·*ruhm*
z	**zoo**	*zarf*	zarf
zh	**pleasure**	*jambon*	zham·*bon*

syllables & word stress

In the coloured pronunciation guides, words are divided into syllables separated by a dot (eg *giriş* gee·*reesh*) to help you pronounce them. Word stress is quite light in Turkish, and generally falls on the last syllable of the word. Most two-syllable placenames, however, are stressed on the first syllable (eg *Kıbrıs kuhb*·ruhs), and in three-syllable placenames the stress is usually on the second syllable (eg *İstanbul* ees·*tan*·bool). Another common exception occurs when a verb has a form of the negative marker *me* (*me* me, *ma* ma, *mı* muh, *mi* mee, *mu* moo, or *mü* mew) added to it. In those cases, the stress goes onto the syllable before the negative marker, for example *gelmiyorlar* gel·mee·yor·lar (they're not coming).

vowel harmony

Word endings in Turkish need to 'rhyme' with the final vowel in the word they're attached to. This is called vowel harmony. In the examples below, both the endings -*da* ·da and -*de* ·de mean 'at'. The reason they have different forms is because they need to harmonise with the vowel sounds in the root words (in this case, Ankara and Cevizli).

Does it stop at Ankara?
   Ankara'da durur mu?   an·ka·*ra*·da doo·*roor* moo
   (lit: Ankara-at stop *mu*)

Does it stop at Cevizli?
   Cevizli'de durur mu?   je·veez·*lee*·de doo·*roor* moo
   (lit: Cevizli-at stop *mu*)

The rules of vowel harmony are quite regular, and you'll soon get the hang of them as you practise speaking Turkish. We've put the patterns into the table below.

if the final vowel in the noun is …	*a* or *ı*	*o* or *u*	*e* or *i*	*ö* or *ü*
it can be followed by …	*a* or *ı*	*u* or *a*	*e* or *i*	*ü* or *e*

reading & writing

Turkish has a phonetic alphabet with 29 letters. It's the same as the Latin alphabet, except for 'q', 'w' and 'x', and has additional letters which were invented specially or borrowed from German. For spelling purposes (like when you spell your name to book into a hotel), the pronunciation of each letter is provided. The order shown below has been used in the **culinary reader** and **turkish–english dictionary**.

The letter *c* is pronounced like the English 'j'. The letter *h* is never silent, so always pronounce it as in 'house', eg *sabah* sa·bah (morning). The *ğ* is a silent letter which extends the vowel before it – it acts like the 'gh' combination in 'weigh', and is never pronounced. When you see a double vowel, such as *saat* sa·at (hour) you need to pronounce both vowels.

Be careful of the symbols *ı* and *i* – *ı* uh is undotted in both lower and upper case (like Isparta uhs·par·ta), while *i* ee has dots in both cases (like *İzmir* eez·meer). It's easy to read both of these as an English 'i', but you can be misunderstood if you don't pronounce the two sounds distinctly – *sık* suhk means 'dense', 'tight' or 'frequent' but *sik* seek means 'fuck'. Take the same care with *o/ö* o/er and *u/ü* oo/ew – *kızları oldu* kuhz·la·ruh ol·doo means 'they had a baby girl' but *kızları öldü* kuhz·la·ruh erl·dew means 'their daughter died'.

alphabet							
Aa a	Bb be	Cc je	Çç che	Dd de	Ee e	Ff fe	Gg ge
Ğğ yu·moo·shak ge		Hh he	Iı uh	İi ee	Jj zhe	Kk ke
Ll le	Mm me	Nn ne	Oo o	Öö er	Pp pe	Rr re	Ss se
Şş she	Tt te	Uu oo	Üü ew	Vv ve	Yy ye	Zz ze	

contents

The index below grammatical structures you can use to say what you want. Look under each function – in alphabetical order – for information on how to build your own phrases. For example, to tell the taxi driver where your hotel is, look for **giving directions/orders** and you'll be directed to information on **case**, **demonstratives**, **verbs**, etc. A glossary of grammatical terms is included at the end of this chapter to help you. Abbreviations such as nom and acc in the literal translations for each example refer to the case of the nouns – this is explained in the glossary and in **case**.

adjectives & adverbs

Adjectives and adverbs only have one form for singular and plural, and come before nouns and verbs respectively. Most adjectives can also be used as adverbs. See also **articles**.

That was a good concert.
İyi bir konserdi.　　　　ee·*yee* beer kon·*ser*·dee
(lit: good a concert-nom-was)

Did you sleep well?
İyi uyudun mu?　　　　ee·*yee* oo·yoo·*doon* moo
(lit: well sleep-you *mu*)

articles

There is no word in Turkish for 'the', so the word *pazar* pa·*zar* means both 'bazaar' and 'the bazaar'.

Bir beer means both 'a/an' and 'one' and comes before the noun it modifies.

I'd like to hire a car.
Bir araba kiralamak　　beer a·ra·*ba* kee·ra·la·*mak*
istiyorum.　　　　　　ees·*tee*·yo·room
(lit: a car-nom to-hire would-like-I)

There was only one car in the car park.
Otoparkta yalnızca　　o·to·park·*ta* yal·nuhz·*ja*
bir araba vardı.　　　　beer a·ra·*ba* var·duh
(lit: car-park-loc-in only one car-nom there-was)

In phrases where the noun is described by an adjective, *bir* usually appears between the noun and the adjective.

I'd like a local speciality.
> *Bu yöreye özgü bir*   boo yer·re·*ye* erz·*gew* beer
> *yemek istiyorum.*   ye·*mek* ees·*tee*·yo·room
> (lit: this region-dat-to special a meal-nom want-I)

be

The Turkish equivalent of 'be' is a suffix (word ending) added to the noun or adjective. If the final letter in the noun or adjective is a vowel (as for *iyi* in the first example below), you'll need to add the letter *y*, pronounced like the 'y' in 'yes'. The next table gives the suffixes for the present tense.

We're well.
> *İyiyiz.*   ee·*yee*·yeez
> (lit: well-are-we)

I'm English.
> *İngilizim.*   een·gee·*lee*·zeem
> (lit: English-nom-am-I)

For the negative of 'be', the noun or adjective remains unchanged, and the same endings from the table on the next page are added to the separate form *değil* de-*eel*.

I'm not a student.
> *Ben öğrenci değilim.*   ben er·ren·*jee* de·*ee*·leem
> (lit: I student-nom am-I-not)

See also **adjectives**, **negatives**, **suffixes**, **verbs**, and the box on **vowel harmony** on page 13.

'be' – present tense

final vowel in noun/adjective	a or ı (eg avukat lawyer)	e or i (eg öğrenci student)
I	-(y)ım avukatım a·voo·ka·tuhm	-(y)im öğrenciyim er·ren·jee·yeem
you sg inf	-sın avukatsın a·voo·kat·suhn	-sin öğrencisin er·ren·jee·seen
he/she/it	no ending avukat a·voo·kat	no ending öğrenci er·ren·jee
we	-(y)ız avukatız a·voo·ka·tuhz	-(y)iz öğrenciyiz er·ren·jee·yeez
you sg pol & pl inf/pol	-sınız avukatsınız a·voo·kat·suh·nuhz	-siniz öğrencisiniz er·ren·jee·see·neez
they	-lar avukatlar a·voo·kat·lar	-ler öğrenciler er·ren·jee·ler
final vowel in noun/adjective	o or u (eg doktor doctor)	ö or ü (eg gözlükçü optometrist)
I	-(y)um doktorum dok·to·room	-(y)üm gözlükçüyüm gerz·lewk·chew·yewm
you sg inf	-sun doktorsun dok·tor·soon	-sün gözlükçüsün gerz·lewk·chew·sewn
he/she/it	no ending doktor dok·tor	no ending gözlükçü gerz·lewk·chew
we	-(y)uz doktoruz dok·to·rooz	-(y)üz gözlükçüyüz gerz·lewk·chew·yewz
you sg pol & pl inf/pol	-sunuz doktorsunuz dok·tor·soo·nooz	-sünüz gözlükçüsünüz gerz·lewk·chew·sew·newz
they	-lar doktorlar dok·tor·lar	-ler gözlükçüler gerz·lewk·chew·ler

case

doing things • giving directions/orders • indicating location • naming things/people • possessing

Turkish is a 'case' language, which means that endings are added to nouns and pronouns to show their relationship to other elements in the sentence.

nominative nom – shows the subject of the sentence

This bag is very heavy.
*Bu **çanta** çok ağır.*
(lit: this bag very heavy)

accusative acc – shows the object of the sentence

Did you see that bag?
*Şu **çantayı** gördün mü?*
(lit: that bag saw-you mü)

genitive gen – shows possession ('of')

The colour of this bag is very nice.
*Bu **çantanın** rengi çok güzel.*
(lit: this bag-of colour very nice)

dative dat – shows the indirect object with verbs like 'happen' ('to')

What happened to your bag?
***Çantana** ne oldu?*
(lit: bag-your-to what happened)

locative loc – shows location ('in', 'on', 'at', 'with' etc)

It's in her bag.
*Onun **çantasında**.*
(lit: her bag-in)

ablative abl – shows point of origin in space or time ('from')

He pulled the timetable from the bag.
*Tarifeyi **çantasından** çıkardı.*
(lit: timetable bag-his-from pulled)

The forms of the six cases are outlined in the following table, and they're all governed by the rules of vowel harmony (see the box on page 13).

case endings for nouns				
	the vowel in the noun's last syllable is ...			
	a or *ı* (eg *kitap* book)	*e* or *i* (eg *ev* house)	*o* or *u* (eg *okul* school)	*ö* or *ü* (eg *göl* lake)
nominative	no ending *kitap* kee·*tap*	no ending *ev* ev	no ending *okul* o·*kool*	no ending *göl* gerl
accusative (ending in a consonant) *	*-ı* *kitabı* kee·ta·*buh*	*-i* *evi* e·vee	*-u* *okulu* o·koo·*loo*	*-ü* *gölü* ger·*lew*
	* For a noun ending in a vowel, add *y* y before the ending above.			
genitive (ending in a consonant) *	*-ın* *kitabın* kee·ta·*buhn*	*-in* *evin* e·veen	*-un* *okulun* o·koo·*loon*	*-ün* *gölün* ger·*lewn*
	* For a noun ending in a vowel, add *n* n before the ending above.			
dative (ending in a consonant) *	*-a* *kitaba* kee·ta·*ba*	*-e* *eve* e·ve	*-a* *okula* o·koo·*la*	*-e* *göle* ger·*le*
	* For a noun ending in a vowel, add *y* y before the ending above.			
locative	*-da/-ta* *kitapta* kee·tap·*ta*	*-de/-te* *evde* ev·de	*-da/-ta* *okulda* o·kool·da	*-de/-te* *gölde* gerl·de
ablative	*-dan/-tan* *kitaptan* kee·tap·*tan*	*-den/-ten* *evden* ev·den	*-dan/-tan* *okuldan* o·kool·dan	*-den/-ten* *gölden* gerl·den

In this **phrasebuilder**, the case of each noun has been given to show you how the system works. The lists in this book and the **dictionary** are in the nominative case. You can use the nominative case in phrases and be understood just fine, even though they aren't completely correct without one of the endings on the previous page.

demonstratives

giving directions/orders • indicating location • naming things/people • pointing things out

The Turkish words for 'this' and 'that' are listed below.

this (near the speaker)	bu	boo	these (near the speaker)	bunlar	boon·lar
that (just over there)	şu	shoo	those (just over there)	şunlar	shoon·lar
that (far away)	o	o	those (far away)	onlar	on·lar

The concept of *bu* boo and *bunlar* boon·lar is more precise than the English idea of 'this' – in Turkish it means only what is directly in front of you. *Şu* shoo and *şunlar* shoon·lar are just a bit away from you and *o* o and *onlar* on·lar are not between the speakers. To ask a salesperson about their wares, don't ask 'What's that?' – instead, you'd need to say *Bu nedir?* boo ne·deer (lit: this what-is). As in this example, these words can stand alone; they always come before the noun.

have

Turkish doesn't use a word for 'have' as English does. To express ownership, see **possession**.

negatives

For all verb forms except the present simple tense, the negative is formed by placing the particle *ma* ma or *me* me directly after the verb stem before any other ending. When this ending begins with a vowel, you need to use the form *mı* muh, *mi* mee, *mu* moo or *mü* mew instead of *ma* ma or *me* me. A *y* y is added to these negative particles to separate the two vowels. Negative endings function according to vowel harmony (see the box on page 13).

| Come! | *Gel!* | gel |
| Don't come! | *Gel**me**!* | *gel·**me*** |

The bus is coming.
   Otobüs geliyor.   o·to·*bews* ge·lee·yor
   (lit: bus-nom coming)

The bus is not coming.
   Otobüs gelmiyor.   o·to·*bews* gel·mee·yor
   (lit: bus-nom come-not-ing)

The negative in the present simple tense has an irregular form. This is laid out in the table below. See also **be**, **there is/are** and **verbs**.

negative particle in present simple tense			
	I	we	you sg & pl, he, she, it, they
verbs that end in *a, ı, o* or *u*	*ma* ma	*may* ma·y	*maz* maz
verbs that end in *e, i, ö* or *ü*	*me* me	*mey* me·y	*mez* mez

nouns

naming things/people

Turkish nouns have different forms as case endings and suffixes are added to show the noun's role in the sentence. See **case**, **plurals**, **possession**, **suffixes** and the box on **vowel harmony** on page 13.

personal pronouns

doing things • naming things/people • possessing

Pronouns in Turkish change according to their case. This table shows only the nominative case – though not always completely correct, you'll be understood when you use it. The verb form always shows who the subject of the sentence is, so pronouns are only used for emphasis, as in the example below. See also **case** and **nouns**.

I	*ben*	ben	we	*biz*	beez
you sg inf	*sen*	sen	you sg pol & pl inf/pol	*siz*	seez
he/she/it	*o*	o	they	*onlar*	on·*lar*

We booked these seats, not you.

Bu koltukları **biz**	boo kol·took·la·*ruh* beez
ayırttık **siz** değil.	a·yuhrt·*tuhk* seez de·*eel*
(lit: this seats we booked you not)	

plurals

naming things/people

Show the plural of a noun by adding -*lar* ·lar or -*ler* ·ler, depending on vowel harmony (see page 13). Add -*lar* to words with *a, ı, o* and *u* and -*ler* to words with *e, i, ö* and *ü* respectively. The plural suffix is the first suffix added to a noun, and stress moves from the last syllable of the root word to -lar or -ler. See also **case**.

plane	*uçak*	oo·*chak*	**meal**	*yemek*	ye·*mek*
planes	*uçaklar*	oo·chak·*lar*	**meals**	*yemekler*	ye·mek·*ler*

possession

naming things/people · possessing

There are several ways to show possession in Turkish. One of the easiest ways is to use the words *var* var (lit: there is/are) and *yok* yok (lit: there isn't/aren't). See also **there is/are**.

I have a ticket.
  Biletim var.   bee·le·*teem* var
  (lit: I-ticket-**gen** there-is)
I don't have a ticket.
  Biletim yok.   bee·le·*teem* yok
  (lit: I-ticket-**gen** there-isn't)

Another simple way is to use possessive pronouns (the equivalents of 'my', 'your' etc) shown in the next table, plus the noun that's owned. (This isn't strictly correct, but you'll be understood.) These pronouns can also mean 'mine', 'yours' etc.

my/mine	*benim*	be·*neem*	our/ours	*bizim*	bee·*zeem*
your/ yours sg	*senin*	se·*neen*	**your/ yours** pl	*sizin*	see·*zeen*
his/ her(s)/its/ somebody's	*onun*	o·*noon*	**their/ theirs**	*onların*	on·la·*ruhn*

pen	*kalem*-**nom**	ka·*lem*	
your pen	*sizin kaleminiz*-**gen**	see·*zeen* ka·le·mee·*neez*	
backpack	*sırt çantası*-**nom**	suhrt chan·ta·*suh*	
her backpack	*onun sırt çantası*-**gen**	o·*noon* suhrt chan·ta·*suh*	

See also **case** and **personal pronouns**.

postpositions

doing things • giving directions/orders •
indicating location • pointing things out

Postpositions are used in Turkish the way prepositions like 'for' and 'near' are in English, except they come after the noun. For each postposition, the noun takes a particular case ending – in the example below, with *için* ee·*cheen* (for), the noun *çocuklar* cho·jook·*lar* (children) takes the nominative case. Useful postpositions are listed in the **dictionary**. See also **case** and **suffixes**.

for the children
    çocuklar için   cho·jook·*lar* ee·*cheen*
    (lit: the-children-nom for)

questions

asking a question

To form a yes/no question, add the word *mi* mee, *mı* muh, *mu* moo or *mü* mew (depending on vowel harmony, page 13) after the verb.

The bus is coming.
    Otobüs geliyor.   o·to·*bews* ge·lee·yor
    (lit: bus-nom coming)

Is the bus coming?
    Otobüs geliyor mu?   o·to·*bews* ge·lee·yor moo
    (lit: bus-nom coming *mu*)

Another way to form questions is to place a question word (in the next table) before the verb. Note that if the question uses the verb 'be', the question word usually goes at the end of the phrase (see also **be**).

Where's the taxi rank?
    Taksi durağı nerede?   tak·*see* doo·ra·*uh* ne·re·de
    (lit: taxi-nom rank-acc where)

how?	*nasıl?*	na·suhl
how many?	*kaç?*	kach
how much?	*ne kadar?*	ne ka·dar
what?	*ne?*	ne
what kind?	*ne tür?*	ne tewr
what size?	*kaç beden?*	kach be·den
when?	*ne zaman?*	ne za·man
where?	*nerede?*	ne·re·de
which?	*hangi?*	han·gee
who?	*kim?*	keem
why?	*neden?*	ne·den

suffixes

doing things • giving directions/orders • indicating location • pointing things out

Turkish uses case endings and suffixes to show how elements in a sentence are related. It's an agglutinative language, meaning that the endings are added to the root word. *Düşünemedim* dew·shew·ne·me·deem means 'I was unable to think' – *düşün* (think) + *e* (able) + *me* (un) + *di* (was) + *m* (I). When several endings are added, the plural comes first, then the case marking, then possessive and other suffixes. All suffixes change according to vowel harmony (see page 13). In the table below are some useful suffixes. See also **case**, **postpositions** and **verbs**.

english	turkish	translit	example	translit
by/using	*-la, -le*	·la, ·le	*trenle* (lit: train-by)	tren·le
with	*-lı, -li, -lu, -lü*	·luh, ·lee, ·loo, ·lew	*buzlu* (lit: ice-with)	booz·loo
without	*-sız, -siz, -suz, -süz*	·suhz, ·seez, ·sooz, ·sewz	*sütsüz* (lit: milk-without)	sewt·sewz

there is/are

To express 'there is' or 'there are', Turkish uses the word *var* var. To say 'there isn't' or 'there aren't', use the word *yok* yok. These are also the words used to show ownership (see **possession**).

There's a telephone in my room.
Odamda telefon var.   o·dam·*da* te·le·*fon* var
(lit: room-loc-my-in telephone-nom there-is)

There isn't a telephone in my room.
Odamda telefon yok.   o·dam·*da* te·le·*fon* yok
(lit: room-loc-my-in telephone-nom there-isn't)

verbs

Turkish verbs have a regular structure. The infinitives of Turkish verbs (the dictionary form) end with *-mak* mak or *-mek* mek, such as *konuşmak* ko·noosh·*mak* (speak) or *gelmek* gel·*mek* (come). Suffixes replace this ending to form different tenses.

She wants to speak.
O konuşmak istiyor.   o ko·noosh·*mak* ees·*tee*·yor
(lit: she to-speak wanting)

She is speaking.
O konuşuyor.   o ko·noo·*shoo*·yor
(lit: she speaking)

She will speak.
O konuşacak.   o ko·noo·sha·*jak*
(lit: she speak-will)

The following table shows the suffixes used to form regular present tense verbs. In cases where the verb stem ends in a vowel, such as *yaşa* in *yaşamak* ya·sha·*mak* (live), drop the first vowel from the ending (marked in brackets in the table below). For example, 'I live' would be *yaşarım* ya·sha·*ruhm*.

present tense verb forms				
	if the final vowel in the stem is …			
	a or *ı* (eg *almak* get/buy)	*e* or *i* (eg *bilmek* know)	*o* or *u* (eg *oturmak* reside)	*ö* or *ü* (eg *yüzmek* swim)
I	-(ı)rım/ -(a)rım *alırım* a·*luh*·ruhm	-(i)rim/ -(e)rim *bilirim* bee·*lee*·reem	-(u)rum/ -(a)rım *otururum* o·too·roo·room	-(ü)rüm/ -(e)rim *yüzerim* yew·ze·reem
you sg inf	-(ı)rsın/ -(a)rsın *alırsın* a·*luhr*·suhn	-(i)rsin/ -(e)rsin *bilirsin* bee·*leer*·seen	-(u)rsun/ -(a)rsın *oturursun* o·too·*roor*·soon	-(ü)rsün/ -(e)rsin *yüzersin* yew·*zer*·seen
he/ she/it	-(ı)r/-(a)r *alır* a·*luhr*	-(i)r/-(e)r *bilir* bee·*leer*	-(u)r/-(a)r *oturur* o·too·*roor*	-(ü)r/-(e)r *yüzer* yew·*zer*
we	-(ı)rız/-(a)rız *alırız* a·*luh*·ruhz	-(i)riz/-(e)riz *biliriz* bee·*lee*·reez	-(u)ruz/-(a)rız *otururuz* o·too·roo·rooz	-(ü)rüz/-(e)riz *yüzeriz* yew·ze·reez
you sg pol & pl inf/pol	-(ı)rsınız/ -(a)rsınız *alırsınız* a·*luhr*·suh·nuhz	-(i)rsiniz/ -(e)rsiniz *bilirsiniz* bee·*leer*· see·neez	-(u)rsunuz/ -(a)rsınız *oturursunuz* o·too·*roor*· soo·nooz	-(ü)rsünüz/ -(e)rsiniz *yüzersiniz* yew·*zer*· see·neez
they	-(ı)rlar/ -(a)rlar *alırlar* a·*luhr*·lar	-(e)rler/ -(e)rler *bilirler* bee·*leer*·ler	-(u)rlar/ -(a)rlar *otururlar* o·too·*roor*·lar	-(ü)rler/ -(e)rler *yüzerler* yew·*zer*·ler

See also **be**, **suffixes**, and the box on **vowel harmony**, page 13.

word order

Word order in Turkish is very flexible – the case endings and suffixes mean that you can change the order of words in a sentence and still know how they relate to each other. In speech it's often changed for emphasis or rhythm so you might hear words in a different order to the way we have them in this book. The most important element in a sentence is mentioned first – the place you're going, the person you're talking to, or the topic you're talking about. The main verb comes at the end, adjectives come before nouns and adverbs before verbs. See also **adjectives & adverbs**, **case**, **questions** and **suffixes**.

formal is as formal does

When speaking in Turkish you need either polite or informal language. The informal *sen* sen form (meaning 'you' sg inf) can be used with individual friends or relatives, while the *siz* seez form (meaning 'you' sg pol & pl inf/pol) must be used for strangers, important people, or more than one friend or relative. As a traveller, it's best to use the *siz* form with new people you meet. Nouns, verbs and personal pronouns ('you', 'she', 'we' and so on) will change depending on whether you're being polite or informal.

In this book we've chosen the appropriate form for the situation that the phrase is used in. For phrases where either form might be appropriate we have given both. Look for the symbols pol (polite) and inf (informal) to find out what form the phrase is in.

glossary

ablative	type of *case marking* which shows where/when the *subject* is from – 'the man **from the CIA**'
accusative	type of *case marking*, usually used for the *object* of the sentence – 'she searched **the files**'
adjective	a word that describes something – 'the **hidden** agenda'
adverb	a word that explains how an action was done – 'he answered **carefully**'
article	the words 'a', 'an' and 'the'
case (marking)	word ending (suffix) which tells us the role of a thing or person in the sentence
dative	type of *case marking* which shows the indirect *object* – 'I gave the file **to the agent**'
genitive	type of *case marking* which shows ownership or possession – 'the **spy's** notebook'
locative	type of *case marking* which shows where the *subject* is – 'the camera is **in the room**'
nominative	type of *case marking* used for the *subject* of the sentence – 'the **investigation** ended'
noun	a thing, person or idea – 'the **briefcase**'
object	the thing or person in the sentence that has the action directed to it – 'I found the **evidence**'
possessive pronoun	a word that means 'mine', 'yours', etc

postposition	a word like 'for' or 'before' in English; in Turkish these come after the noun or pronoun
present simple tense	the verb tense which tells what is happening now – 'the government **works** to protect the country'
pronoun	a word that means 'I', 'you', etc
subject	the thing or person in the sentence that does the action – 'the **police** entered the building'
suffix	extra syllable(s) added to the end of a word, eg ly is added to 'secret' to make 'secret**ly**'
transliteration	pronunciation guide for words and phrases
verb	the word that tells you what action happened – 'I **broke** the code'
verb stem	the part of a verb which does not change – 'search' in '**search**ing' and '**search**ed'

language difficulties

Do you speak (English)?
(İngilizce) konuşuyor musunuz?
(een·gee·*leez*·je) ko·noo·*shoo*·yor moo·soo·*nooz*

Does anyone speak (English)?
(İngilizce) bilen var mı?
(een·gee·*leez*·je) bee·*len* var muh

Do you understand?
Anlıyor musun?
an·*luh*·yor moo·*soon*

Yes, I understand.
Evet, anlıyorum.
e·*vet* an·*luh*·yo·room

No, I don't understand.
Hayır, anlamıyorum.
ha·yuhr an·*la*·muh·yo·room

I understand.
Anlıyorum.
an·*luh*·yo·room

I don't understand.
Anlamıyorum.
an·*la*·muh·yo·room

I speak (English).
(İngilizce) konuşuyorum.
(een·gee·*leez*·je) ko·noo·*shoo*·yo·room

I don't speak (Turkish).
(Türkçe) bilmiyorum.
(tewrk·che) *beel*·mee·yo·room

I speak a little.
Biraz konuşuyorum.
bee·raz ko·noo·*shoo*·yo·room

What does 'kitap' mean?
'Kitap' ne demektir?
kee·*tap* ne de·*mek*·teer

I would like to practise (Turkish).
(Türkçe) pratik yapmak istiyorum.
(tewrk·che) pra·*teek* yap·*mak* ees·*tee*·yo·room

Let's speak (Turkish).
(Türkçe) konuşalım.
(tewrk·che) ko·noo·*sha*·luhm

Pardon?
Anlamadım?
an·*la*·ma·duhm

How do you write 'yabancı'?
'Yabancı' kelimesini nasıl yazarsınız?
ya·ban·*juh* ke·lee·me·see·*nee* na·suhl ya·*zar*·suh·nuhz

How do you pronounce this?
Bunu nasıl telaffuz edersiniz?
boo·*noo* na·suhl te·laf·*fooz* e·*der*·see·neez

Could you please ...? | *Lütfen ...?* | *lewt*·fen ...
repeat that	*tekrarlar mısınız*	tek·*rar*·lar muh·suh·*nuhz*
speak more slowly	*daha yavaş konuşur musunuz*	da·*ha* ya·*vash* ko·noo·*shoor* moo·soo·*nooz*
write it down	*yazar mısınız*	ya·*zar* muh·suh·*nuhz*

signs

Açık	a·*chuhk*	Open
Çıkış	chuh·*kuhsh*	Exit
Danışma	da·nuhsh·*ma*	Information
Erkek	er·*kek*	Men
Fotoğraf Çekmek Yasaktır	fo·to·*raf* chek·mek ya·sak·*tuhr*	No Photography
Giriş	gee·*reesh*	Entrance
Kadın	ka·*duhn*	Women
Kapalı	ka·pa·*luh*	Closed
Sigara İçilmez	see·*ga*·ra ee·*cheel*·mez	No Smoking
Tuvaletler	too·va·let·*ler*	Toilets/WC
Yasak	ya·*sak*	Prohibited

cardinal numbers

You say Turkish numbers in the same order as English ones but you don't need a word for 'and'. The words for the individual numbers are normally joined together when you write them, so 517 is written as *beşyüzonyedi* besh·yewz·on·ye·dee (lit: five-hundred-ten-seven).

When you're counting nouns, the noun always takes the singular form – 'two books' is *iki kitap* ee·kee kee·tap (lit: two book).

0	*sıfır*	suh·*fuhr*
1	*bir*	beer
2	*iki*	ee·*kee*
3	*üç*	ewch
4	*dört*	dert
5	*beş*	besh
6	*altı*	al·*tuh*
7	*yedi*	ye·*dee*
8	*sekiz*	se·*keez*
9	*dokuz*	do·*kooz*
10	*on*	on
11	*onbir*	on·beer
12	*oniki*	on·ee·kee
13	*onüç*	on·ewch
14	*ondört*	on·dert
15	*onbeş*	on·besh
16	*onaltı*	on·al·*tuh*
17	*onyedi*	on·ye·*dee*
18	*onsekiz*	on·se·*keez*
19	*ondokuz*	on·do·*kooz*
20	*yirmi*	yeer·*mee*
21	*yirmibir*	yeer·*mee*·beer
22	*yirmiiki*	yeer·*mee*·ee·*kee*

30	otuz	o·tooz
40	kırk	kuhrk
50	elli	el·lee
60	altmış	alt·muhsh
70	yetmiş	yet·meesh
80	seksen	sek·sen
90	doksan	dok·san
100	yüz	yewz
200	ikiyüz	ee·kee·yewz
1,000	bin	been
1,000,000	bir milyon	beer meel·yon
1,000,000,000	bir milyar	beer meel·yar

hand gestures

To beckon or say 'follow me', Turks scoop one of their hands downward and toward themselves. Some people, particularly women, hold their hand the same way but flutter their fingers instead of scooping.

ordinal numbers

sıra sayılar

Ordinal numbers are formed by adding the suffix -ıncı ·uhn·juh to the number. This suffix can also be -inci ·een·jee, -uncu ·oon·joo or -üncü ·ewn·jew, depending on the last vowel in the number (see **vowel harmony**, page 13).

In writing, a full stop is put after a number to show that it's an ordinal. So '1st chapter' is written as 1. bölüm bee·reen·jee ber·lewm and '7th month' is 7. ay ye·deen·jee ai.

1st	birinci	bee·reen·jee
2nd	ikinci	ee·keen·jee
3rd	üçüncü	ew·chewn·jew
4th	dördüncü	der·dewn·jew
5th	beşinci	be·sheen·jee

fractions

a quarter	çeyrek	chay·*rek*
a third	*üçte bir*	ewch·*te* beer
a half	*yarım*	ya·*ruhm*
three-quarters	*üç çeyrek*	ewch chay·*rek*
all	*hepsi*	*hep*·see
none	*hiç*	heech

decimals

Turkish decimals are easy – use the same word order as in English and say *nokta* nok·*ta* (dot) instead of 'point'.

3.14	*üç nokta ondört*	ewch nok·*ta* on·dert
4.2	*dört nokta iki*	dert nok·*ta* ee·*kee*
5.1	*beş nokta bir*	besh nok·*ta* beer

yes & no

When you look in the English-Turkish dictionary, you'll find that *evet* e·*vet* means 'yes' and *hayır* ha·yuhr means 'no'. But it's not always that straightforward …

When answering questions, Turks sometimes say *var* var (lit: it-exists) instead of *evet* for 'yes'. They show this with body language by nodding their heads once, forward and down.

Wagging your head from side to side doesn't mean 'no' in Turkish, it means 'I don't understand'. To show 'no' Turks nod their heads up and back, lifting their eyebrows at the same time – simply raising the eyebrows means the same thing. They may also say tsk.

useful amounts

| How much? | Ne kadar? | ne ka·dar |
| How many? | Kaç tane? | kach ta·ne |

Please give me ...	Lütfen bana ... verin.	lewt·fen ba·na ... ve·reen
(100) grams	(yüz) gram	(yewz) gram
half a dozen	yarım düzine	ya·ruhm dew·zee·ne
half a kilo	yarım kilo	ya·ruhm kee·lo
a kilo	bir kilo	beer kee·lo
a bottle	bir şişe	beer shee·she
a jar	bir kavanoz	beer ka·va·noz
a packet	bir paket	beer pa·ket
a slice	bir dilim	beer dee·leem
a tin	bir kutu	beer koo·too
a few	birkaç tane	beer·kach ta·ne
less	daha az	da·ha az
(just) a little	(sadece) biraz	(sa·de·je) bee·raz
a lot/many	çok	chok
more	daha fazla	da·ha faz·la
some	biraz	bee·raz

ums & ahs

In those dreaded moments when your Turkish won't flow freely, try not to say 'um' to fill the gap. In Turkish you're actually saying *am* am (a vulgar term for 'vagina') – if your audience has a good sense of humour, they could be hiding a smirk, but you could also be causing serious offence. Use the more neutral 'ah' instead.

telling the time

Telling the time in Turkish is quite straightforward. For the hour, say *saat* sa·*at* and the number (eg *saat yedi* sa·*at* ye·*dee* is 'it's seven o'clock'), and for half-hours say *saat* plus the hour and the word *buçuk* boo·*chook* (eg *saat yedi buçuk* sa·*at* ye·*dee* boo·*chook* is 'it's half-past seven').

For times 'to' or 'past' the hour, say the hour first, then the minutes plus *geçiyor* ge·*chee*·yor for 'past' or *var* var for 'to'. Use *çeyrek* chay·*rek* for a quarter of an hour. For example, 'it's twenty past six' is *saat yediyi yirmi geçiyor* sa·*at* ye·*dee*·yee yeer·*mee* ge·*chee*·yor, and 'it's a quarter to two' is *saat ikiye çeyrek var* sa·*at* ee·*kee*·ye chay·*rek* var.

What time is it?	*Saat kaç?*	sa·*at* kach
It's (ten) o'clock.	*Saat (on).*	sa·*at* (on)
Five past (ten).	*(Onu) beş geçiyor.*	(o·*noo*) besh ge·*chee*·yor
Quarter past (ten).	*(Onu) çeyrek geçiyor.*	(o·*noo*) chay·*rek* ge·*chee*·yor
Half past (ten).	*(On) buçuk.*	(on) boo·*chook*
Twenty to (eleven).	*(Onbire) yirmi var.*	(on·bee·*re*) yeer·*mee* var
Quarter to (eleven).	*(Onbire) çeyrek var.*	(on·bee·*re*) chay·*rek* var
At what time …?	*Saat kaçta …?*	sa·*at* kach·*ta* …
At (ten).	*Saat (onda).*	sa·*at* (on·*da*)
At 7.57pm.	*Akşam saat yedi elliyedide.*	ak·*sham* sa·*at* ye·*dee* el·*lee*·ye·dee·*de*

(lit: evening hour seven fifty-seven-at)

Saat sa·*at* means 'hour', 'watch', 'clock' or 'o'clock', depending on context. When *saat* comes before a number it means 'o'clock', but when it follows it means 'hour' – *saat beş* sa·*at* besh means 'it's five o'clock', while *beş saat* besh sa·*at* means 'five hours'. *Beş saat* would also be 'five clocks' or 'five watches'.

the calendar

takvim

days

Monday	Pazartesi	pa·zar·te·see
Tuesday	Salı	sa·luh
Wednesday	Çarşamba	char·sham·ba
Thursday	Perşembe	per·shem·be
Friday	Cuma	joo·ma
Saturday	Cumartesi	joo·mar·te·see
Sunday	Pazar	pa·zar

months

January	Ocak	o·jak
February	Şubat	shoo·bat
March	Mart	mart
April	Nisan	nee·san
May	Mayıs	ma·yuhs
June	Haziran	ha·zee·ran
July	Temmuz	tem·mooz
August	Ağustos	a·oos·tos
September	Eylül	ay·lewl
October	Ekim	e·keem
November	Kasım	ka·suhm
December	Aralık	a·ra·luhk

dates

What date is it today?
Bugün ayın kaçı? · *boo·gewn a·yuhn ka·chuh*

It's (18 October).
(Onsekiz Ekim). · *(on·se·keez e·keem)*
(lit: eighteen October)

seasons

spring	*ilkbahar*	*eelk·ba·har*
summer	*yaz*	*yaz*
autumn/fall	*sonbahar*	*son·ba·har*
winter	*kış*	*kuhsh*

present

şimdiki zaman

now	*şimdi*	*sheem·dee*
today	*bugün*	*boo·gewn*
tonight	*bu gece*	*boo ge·je*
this ...	*bu ...*	*boo ...*
morning	*sabah*	*sa·bah*
afternoon	*öğleden sonra*	*er·le·den son·ra*
week	*hafta*	*haf·ta*
month	*ay*	*ai*
year	*yıl*	*yuhl*

past

day before yesterday	bir önceki gün	beer ern·je·kee gewn
(three days) ago	(üç gün) önce	(ewch gewn) ern·je
since (May)	(Mayıs'tan) beri	(ma·yuhs·tan) be·ree

last ...	geçen ...	ge·chen ...
night	gece	ge·je
week	hafta	haf·ta
month	ay	ai
year	yıl	yuhl

yesterday ...	dün ...	dewn ...
morning	sabah	sa·bah
afternoon	öğleden sonra	er·le·den son·ra
evening	akşam	ak·sham

12 or 24?

In speech, the Turkish use the 12-hour clock, but you'll see the 24-hour clock written in schedules and timetables.

future

geleçek zaman

day after tomorrow	öbür gün	er·bewr gewn
in (six days)	(altı gün) içinde	(al·tuh gewn) ee·cheen·de
until (June)	(Haziran'a) kadar	(ha·zee·ra·na) ka·dar

next ...	gelecek ...	ge·le·jek ...
week	hafta	haf·ta
month	ay	ai
year	yıl	yuhl

TOOLS

42

tomorrow ...	*yarın ...*	*ya·ruhn ...*
morning	*sabah*	*sa·bah*
afternoon	*öğleden sonra*	*er·le·den son·ra*
evening	*akşam*	*ak·sham*

during the day

gün içinde

afternoon	*öğleden sonra*	*er·le·den son·ra*
dawn	*şafak*	*sha·fak*
day	*gün*	*gewn*
evening	*akşam*	*ak·sham*
midday	*gün ortası*	*gewn or·ta·suh*
midnight	*gece yarısı*	*ge·je ya·ruh·suh*
morning	*sabah*	*sa·bah*
night	*gece*	*ge·je*
sunrise	*gün doğumu*	*gewn do·oo·moo*
sunset	*gün batımı*	*gewn ba·tuh·muh*

when is it again?

You can say 'morning' or 'am' in two ways in Turkish. To refer to any time between midnight and noon, say *sabah* sa·*bah*. For times between breakfast and lunch, you can also use *öğleden evvel* er·le·*den* ev·*vel* (lit: noon before). After lunch, use *öğleden sonra* er·le·*den* son·ra (lit: noon after) for 'pm'. Between 6pm and 8pm say *akşam* ak·*sham* (evening) and from 8pm onwards say *gece* ge·*je* (night).

Bayram bai·*ram* means 'religious or national festival'. There are two religious *bayrams* in Turkey, and during both it's customary for young people to visit older family members and friends and kiss their hands.

One is called *Şeker Bayramı* she·*ker* bai·ra·*muh* (the feast of the sweets) or *Ramazan Bayramı* ra·ma·*zan* bai·ra·*muh* (the feast of Ramadan). During the lunar month of Ramadan that precedes *Ramazan Bayramı*, Muslims fast during the day and feast at night for one month. At the end of the month they celebrate this three-day *bayram* and public holiday, making sweets and visiting each other. Children also go from house to house wishing people *Mutlu bayramlar!* moot·*loo* bai·ram·*lar* (Happy *Bayrams!*) and receiving sweets, chocolate or money.

During *Kurban Bayramı* koor·*ban* bai·ra·*muh* (the feast of the sacrifice), the second *bayram*, people make animal sacrifices and give the meat to the poor and needy. This festival lasts for four days and is also a public holiday.

Below are some other *bayrams* held in Turkey.

National Sovereignty and Children's Festival (23 April)
23 Nisan Ulusal Egemenlik ve Çocuk Bayramı
yeer·mee·ewch nee·*san* oo·loo·*sal* e·ge·men·*leek* ve cho·*jook* bai·ra·*muh*

Commemoration of Atatürk and Youth & Sports Festival (19 May)
19 Mayıs Atatürk'ü Anma ve Gençlik ve Spor Bayramı
on·do·*kooz* ma·*yuhs* a·ta·tewr·*kew* an·*ma* ve gench·*leek* ve spor bai·ra·*muh*

Victory Festival (30 August)
30 Ağustos Zafer Bayramı
o·*tooz* a·oos·*tos* za·*fer* bai·ra·*muh*

Republic Festival (29 October)
29 Ekim Cumhuriyet Bayramı
yeer·mee·do·*kooz* e·*keem* joom·hoo·ree·*yet* bai·ra·*muh*

How much is it?
Bu ne kadar? — boo ne ka·dar

Can you write down the price?
Fiyatı yazabilir misiniz? — fee·ya·tuh ya·za·bee·leer mee·see·neez

Do you accept ...? — ... kabul ediyor musunuz? — ... ka·bool e·dee·yor moo·soo·nooz

credit cards	Kredi kartı	kre·dee kar·tuh
debit cards	Banka kartı	ban·ka kar·tuh
foreign currency	Döviz	der·veez
travellers cheques	Seyahat çeki	se·ya·hat che·kee

I'd like to ... — ... istiyorum. — ... ees·tee·yo·room

cash a cheque	Çek bozdurmak	chek boz·door·mak
change money	Para bozdurmak	pa·ra boz·door·mak
change a travellers cheque	Seyahat çeki bozdurmak	se·ya·hat che·kee boz·door·mak
get a cash advance	Avans çekmek	a·vans chek·mek
withdraw money	Para çekmek	pa·ra chek·mek

What's the ...? — ... nedir? — ... ne·deer

charge	Ücreti	ewj·re·tee
exchange rate	Döviz kuru	der·veez koo·roo

I'd like ... please. — ... istiyorum lütfen. — ... ees·tee·yo·room lewt·fen

my change	Paramın üstünü	pa·ra·muhn ews·tew·new
a receipt	Makbuz	mak·booz
a refund	Para iadesi	pa·ra ee·a·de·see
to return this	Bunu iade etmek	boo·noo ee·a·de et·mek

money

45

Where's (a/an) ...?	... nerede var?	... ne·re·de var
automated teller machine	*Bankamatik*	ban·ka·ma·*teek*
foreign exchange office	*Döviz bürosu*	der·*veez* bew·ro·*soo*

How much is it per ...?	... ne kadar?	... ne ka·dar
day	*Günlüğü*	gewn·lew·*ew*
game	*Oyun ücreti*	o·*yoon* ewj·re·*tee*
hour	*Saati*	sa·a·*tee*
(five) minutes	*(Beş) dakikası*	(besh) da·kee·ka·*suh*
night	*Geceliği*	ge·je·lee·*ee*
page	*Sayfası*	sai·fa·*suh*
person	*Kişi başına ücreti*	kee·*shee* ba·shuh·*na* ewj·re·*tee*
tent	*Çadır başına ücreti*	cha·*duhr* ba·shuh·*na* ewj·re·*tee*
week	*Haftalığı*	haf·ta·luh·*uh*
vehicle	*Araç başına ücreti*	a·*rach* ba·shuh·*na* ewj·re·*tee*
visit	*Giriş*	gee·*reesh*

It's ...		
free	*Ücretsiz.*	ewj·ret·*seez*
(12) euros	*(Oniki) euro.*	(on·ee·kee) yoo·*ro*
(25) lira	*(Yirmibeş) lira.*	(yeer·*mee*·besh) lee·*ra*

on the money

Denizde kum onda para.
   de·neez·*de* koom on·*da* pa·ra — **He/She has money to burn.**
   (lit: sea has sand, he/she has money)

para içinde yüzmek
   pa·ra ee·cheen·*de* yewz·*mek* — **to be rich**
   (lit: to float in money)

parayı denize atmak
   pa·ra·*yuh* de·nee·ze at·*mak* — **to spend money foolishly**
   (lit: to throw money into the sea)

getting around

gezerken

You'll often use a *dolmuş* dol·*moosh* or *midibüs* mee·dee·*bews* while travelling in the cities and busier regions of Turkey. The *dolmuş* was originally a shared taxi (nowadays often minibuses), and a *midibüs* is a small bus which operates on routes that aren't busy enough for a bus or coach. To let the driver know you want to get off, say *inecek var* ee·ne·*jek* var (someone wants to get off) or *sağda* sa·*da* ('on the right', meaning 'pull over here').

Which ... goes	*Hangi ...*	han·gee ...
to (Sirkeci)?	*(Sirkeci'ye) gider?*	(seer·ke·jee·ye) gee·*der*
Is this the ...	*(Sirkeci'ye) giden*	(seer·ke·jee·ye) gee·*den*
to (Sirkeci)?	*... bu mu?*	... boo moo
boat	*vapur*	va·*poor*
bus	*otobüs*	o·to·*bews*
dolmuş	*dolmuş*	dol·*moosh*
midibus	*midibüs*	mee·dee·*bews*
minibus	*minibüs*	mee·nee·*bews*
shuttle bus	*servis otobüsü*	ser·*vees* o·to·bew·*sew*
train	*tren*	tren

When's the	*... (otobüs)*	... (o·to·*bews*)
... (bus)?	*ne zaman?*	ne za·*man*
first	*İlk*	eelk
last	*Son*	son
next	*Sonraki*	son·ra·*kee*

Where's the bus terminal?
Otobüs terminali nerede?   o·to·*bews* ter·mee·na·*lee* ne·re·de

How do I get to the bus terminal?
Otobüs terminaline   o·to·*bews* ter·mee·na·lee·*ne*
nasıl gidebilirim?   na·suhl gee·*de*·bee·lee·reem

What time does it leave?
Ne zaman kalkacak?   ne za·*man* kal·ka·*jak*

What time does it get to (Beşiktaş)?
(Beşiktaş'a) ne zaman varır? (be·*sheek*·ta·sha) ne za·*man* va·*ruhr*

How long will it be delayed?
Ne kadar gecikecek?   ne ka·*dar* ge·jee·ke·*jek*

Please tell me when we get to (Beşiktaş).
(Beşiktaş'a)   (be·*sheek*·ta·sha)
vardığımızda   var·duh·uh·muhz·*da*
lütfen bana söyleyin.   *lewt*·fen ba·*na* say·*le*·yeen

Please stop here.
Lütfen burada durun.   *lewt*·fen boo·ra·*da* doo·roon

How long do we stop here?
Burada ne kadar   boo·ra·*da* ne ka·*dar*
duracağız?   doo·ra·ja·uhz

Are you waiting for more people?
Daha fazla yolcu   da·*ha* faz·*la* yol·*joo*
mu bekliyorsunuz?   moo bek·*lee*·yor·soo·nooz

How many people can ride on this?
Buna kaç kişi   boo·*na* kach kee·*shee*
binebilir?   bee·*ne*·bee·leer

Can you take us around the city, please?
Bizi şehirde   bee·*zee* she·heer·*de*
dolaştırabilir   do·lash·tuh·*ra*·bee·leer
misiniz?   mee·see·*neez*

Is this seat available?
Bu koltuk boş mu?   boo kol·*took* bosh moo

That's my seat.
Burası benim yerim.   boo·ra·*suh* be·*neem* ye·*reem*

tickets

Where do I buy a ticket?
Nereden bilet   ne·*re*·den bee·*let*
alabilirim?   a·*la*·bee·lee·reem

Where's a ticket kiosk?
Bilet gişesi nerede var?   bee·*let* gee·she·*see* ne·re·de var

Do I need to book (well in advance)?
(Çok önceden) Yer   (chok ern·je·*den*) yer
ayırtmam gerekli mi?   a·*yuhrt*·mam ge·rek·*lee* mee

A ... ticket	*(Bostancı'ya) ...*	(bos·*tan*·juh·ya) ...
to (Bostancı).	*bir bilet lütfen.*	beer bee·*let* lewt·fen
1st-class	*birinci mevki*	bee·reen·*jee* mev·*kee*
2nd-class	*ikinci mevki*	ee·keen·*jee* mev·*kee*
child's	*çocuk için*	cho·*jook* ee·*cheen*
return	*gidiş-dönüş*	gee·deesh·der·*newsh*

A one-way ticket to (Bostancı).
(Bostancı'ya) bir   (bos·*tan*·juh·ya) beer
gidiş bileti lütfen.   gee·*deesh* bee·le·*tee* lewt·fen

A student ticket to (Trabzon).
(Trabzon'a) bir   (*trab*·zo·na) beer
öğrenci bileti.   er·ren·*jee* bee·le·*tee*

I'd like	… bir yer	… beer yer
a/an … seat.	istiyorum.	ees·tee·yo·room
aisle	Koridor	ko·ree·dor
	tarafında	ta·ra·fuhn·da
nonsmoking	Sigara	see·ga·ra
	içilmeyen	ee·cheel·me·yen
	kısımda	kuh·suhm·da
smoking	Sigara	see·ga·ra
	içilen kısımda	ee·chee·len kuh·suhm·da
window	Cam kenarı	jam ke·na·ruh

Is there (a) …?	… var mı?	… var muh
air conditioning	Klima	klee·ma
blanket	Battaniye	bat·ta·nee·ye
sick bag	Kusma torbası	koos·ma tor·ba·suh
toilet	Tuvalet	too·va·let

How much is it?
Şu ne kadar? — shoo ne ka·dar

That's too expensive.
Çok pahalı. — chok pa·ha·luh

How long does the trip take?
Yolculuk ne kadar sürer? — yol·joo·look ne ka·dar sew·rer

Is it a direct route?
Direk güzergah mı? — dee·rek gew·zer·gah muh

Can I get a stand-by ticket?
Açık bilet alabilir miyim? — a·chuhk bee·let a·la·bee·leer mee·yeem

Can I get a sleeping berth?
Yataklı bir yer istiyorum. — ya·tak·luh beer yer ees·tee·yo·room

What time should I check in?
Ne zaman giriş yapmalıyım? — ne za·man gee·reesh yap·ma·luh·yuhm

I'd like to … my	Biletimi …	bee·le·tee·mee …
ticket, please.	istiyorum.	ees·tee·yo·room
cancel	iptal ettirmek	eep·tal et·teer·mek
change	değiştirmek	de·eesh·teer·mek
confirm	onaylatmak	o·nai·lat·mak

bilet gişesi	bee·*let* gee·she·*see*	**ticket window**
bunu	boo·*noo*	**this one**
dolu	do·*loo*	**full**
ertelendi	er·te·len·*dee*	**delayed**
grev	grev	**strike** n
iptal edildi	eep·*tal* e·deel·*dee*	**cancelled**
peron	pe·*ron*	**platform**
seyahat acentesi	se·ya·*hat* a·jen·te·*see*	**travel agent**
şunu	shoo·*noo*	**that one**
tarife	ta·ree·*fe*	**timetable**

luggage

bagaj

Where can I find a trolley?
*Nereden trolli
bulabilirim?*
ne·re·den *trol*·lee
boo·*la*·bee·lee·reem

Where's (a/the)...?	... *nerede?*	... *ne*·re·de
baggage claim	*Bagaj konveyörü*	ba·*gazh* kon·ve·yer·*rew*
left-luggage office	*Emanet bürosu*	e·ma·*net* bew·ro·*soo*
luggage locker	*Emanet dolabı*	e·ma·*net* do·la·*buh*

My luggage has been ...	*Bagajım ...*	ba·ga·*zhuhm* ...
damaged	*zarar gördü*	za·*rar* ger·*dew*
lost	*kayboldu*	kai·bol·*doo*
stolen	*çalındı*	cha·luhn·*duh*

el bagajı	el ba·ga·*zhuh*	**carry-on luggage**
fazla yük	faz·*la* yewk	**excess luggage**
jeton	zhe·*ton*	**token**

That's (not) mine.
  Bu benim (değil).
  boo be·*neem* (de·*eel*)

Can I have some tokens?
  Jeton alabilir miyim?
  zhe·*ton* a·*la*·bee·leer mee·*yeem*

plane

Where does	(TK0060)	(te·ka suh·*fuhr*
flight	*sefer sayılı*	suh·*fuhr* alt·*muhsh*)
(TK0060) ...?	*uçak ...*	se·*fer* sa·yuh·luh oo·*chak* ...
arrive	*nereye iniyor*	ne·re·ye ee·*nee*·yor
depart	*nereden*	ne·re·den
	kalkıyor	kal·*kuh*·yor
Where's (the) ...?	... *nerede?*	... ne·re·de
airport shuttle	*Servis otobüsü*	ser·*vees* o·to·bew·*sew*
arrivals hall	*Gelen yolcu*	ge·*len* yol·*joo*
	bölümü	ber·*lew*·mew
departures hall	*Giden yolcu*	gee·*den* yol·*joo*
	bölümü	ber·*lew*·mew
duty-free shop	*Gümrüksüz*	gewm·rewk·*sewz*
	satış mağazası	sa·*tuhsh* ma·a·za·*suh*
gate (7)	*(Yedi)*	(ye·*dee*)
	numaralı kapı	noo·ma·ra·*luh* ka·*puh*

listen for ...		
aktarma	ak·tar·*ma*	**transfer**
biniş kartı	bee·*neesh* kar·*tuh*	**boarding pass**
pasaport	pa·sa·*port*	**passport**
transit	tran·*seet*	**transit**

bus & coach

How often do buses come?
*Otobüs ne kadar zamanda
bir geliyor?*

o·to·*bews* ne ka·*dar* za·man·*da*
beer ge·*lee*·yor

What's the next stop?
Sonraki durak hangisi?

son·ra·*kee* doo·*rak* han·gee·see

Does it stop at (Kadıköy)?
(Kadıköy'de) durur mu?

(ka·*duh*·kay·de) doo·*roor* moo

I'd like to get off at (Kadıköy).
*(Kadıköy'de) inmek
istiyorum.*

(ka·*duh*·kay·de) een·*mek*
ees·*tee*·yo·room

city n	şehir	she·*heer*
dolmuş	dolmuş	dol·*moosh*
intercity a	şehirlerarası	she·heer·*ler*·a·ra·suh
local a	yerel	ye·*rel*
midibus	midibüs	mee·dee·*bews*
minibus	minibüs	mee·nee·*bews*
municipal bus	belediye otobüsü	be·le·dee·*ye* o·to·bew·*sew*
private bus	özel otobüs	er·*zel* o·to·*bews*
shuttle bus	servis otobüsü	ser·*vees* o·to·bew·*sew*

For bus numbers, see **numbers & amounts**, page 35.

train

What station is this?
Bu hangi istasyon?

boo *han*·gee ees·tas·*yon*

What's the next station?
*Sonraki istasyon
hangisi?*

son·ra·*kee* ees·tas·*yon*
han·gee·see

Does it stop at (Maltepe)?
(Maltepe'de) durur mu?

(*mal*·te·pe·de) doo·*roor* moo

Do I need to change?	Aktarma yapmam gerekli mi?	ak·tar·ma yap·mam ge·rek·lee mee
Is it …?	… mi?	… mee
direct	Aktarmasız gider	ak·tar·ma·suhz gee·der
express	Ekspres	eks·pres
Which carriage is (for) …?	Hangisi … vagon?	han·gee·see … va·gon
1st class	birinci mevki	bee·reen·jee mev·kee
dining	yemekli	ye·mek·lee
Pullman (reclining seats)	pulman	pool·man
I'd like a … compartment.	… kuşet istiyorum.	… koo·shet ees·tee·yo·room
European-style sleeping	Örtülü	er·tew·lew
four-bed couchette	Dört yataklı bir	dert ya·tak·luh beer
six-bed couchette	Altı kişilik bir	al·tuh kee·shee·leek beer

boat

vapur

What's the sea like today?
Bugün deniz nasıl? boo·gewn de·neez na·suhl

Are there life jackets?
Can yeleği var mı? jan ye·le·ee var muh

What island/beach is this?
Bu hangi ada/sahil? boo han·gee a·da/sa·heel

I feel seasick.
Deniz tutuyor. de·neez too·too·yor

cabin	kamara	ka·ma·ra
captain	kaptan	kap·tan
car deck	araba güvertesi	a·ra·ba gew·ver·te·see
car ferry	araba vapuru	a·ra·ba va·poo·roo
cruise n	gemi gezisi	ge·mee ge·zee·see
deck	güverte	gew·ver·te
ferry	feribot	fe·ree·bot
hammock	hamak	ha·mak
lifeboat	filika	fee·lee·ka
life jacket	can yeleği	jan ye·le·ee
yacht	yat	yat

taxi

I'd like a taxi …	… bir taksi istiyorum.	… beer tak·see ees·tee·yo·room
at 9am	Sabah dokuzda	sa·bah do·kooz·da
now	Hemen	he·men
tomorrow	Yarın	ya·ruhn

Where's the taxi rank?
Taksi durağı nerede? — tak·see doo·ra·uh ne·re·de

Is this taxi available?
Bu taksi boş mu? — boo tak·see bosh moo

Please put the meter on.
Lütfen taksimetreyi çalıştırın. — lewt·fen tak·see·met·re·yee cha·luhsh·tuh·ruhn

How much is it (to Şişli)?
(Şişli'ye) Ne kadar? — (sheesh·lee·ye) ne ka·dar

I agree to pay that amount.
Bu fiyatı ödemeyi kabul ediyorum. — boo fee·ya·tuh er·de·me·yee ka·bool e·dee·yo·room

I won't pay a flat fare.
Sabit ücret ödemeyi reddediyorum. — sa·beet ewj·ret er·de·me·yee red·de·dee·yo·room

I'm going to complain to the police.
Sizi polise şikayet
edeceğim.
see·zee po·lee·se shee·ka·yet
e·de·je·eem

Please take me to (this address).
Lütfen beni (bu adrese)
götürün.
lewt·fen be·nee (boo ad·re·se)
ger·tew·rewn

Please ...	Lütfen ...	lewt·fen ...
slow down	yavaşlayın	ya·vash·la·yuhn
stop here	burada durun	boo·ra·da doo·roon
wait here	burada	boo·ra·da
	bekleyin	bek·le·yeen

For other useful phrases, see **directions**, page 63.

car & motorbike

araba & motosiklet

car & motorbike hire

I'd like to	Bir ... kiralamak	beer ... kee·ra·la·mak
hire a/an ...	istiyorum.	ees·tee·yo·room
4WD	dört çeker	dert che·ker
automatic	otomatik	o·to·ma·teek
	vitesli araba	vee·tes·lee a·ra·ba
car	araba	a·ra·ba
driver	şoför	sho·fer
manual	vitesli araba	vee·tes·lee a·ra·ba
motorbike	motosiklet	mo·to·seek·let

How much	... kirası ne	... kee·ra·suh ne
for ... hire?	kadar?	ka·dar
daily	Günlük	gewn·lewk
weekly	Haftalık	haf·ta·luhk

Does that include insurance/mileage?
Buna sigorta/kilometre
dahil mi?
boo·na see·gor·ta/kee·lo·met·re
da·heel mee

Do you have a guide to the road rules (in English)?
  (İngilizce) Yol kuralları   (een·gee·*leez*·je) yol koo·ral·la·*ruh*
  kitabınız var mı?   kee·ta·buh·*nuhz* var muh

Do you have a road map?
  Yol haritanız var mı?   yol ha·ree·ta·*nuhz* var muh

on the road

What's the speed limit?
  Hız sınırı nedir?   huhz suh·nuh·*ruh* ne·deer

Is this the road to (Taksim)?
  (Taksim'e) giden   (tak·see·me) gee·*den*
  yol bu mu?   yol boo moo

Where's a petrol station?
  Benzin istasyonu nerede?   ben·*zeen* ees·tas·yo·*noo* ne·re·de

Please fill it up.
  Lütfen depoyu doldurun.   *lewt*·fen de·po·yoo dol·*doo*·roon

I'd like (20) litres.
  (Yirmi) litre istiyorum.   (yeer·*mee*) *leet*·re ees·*tee*·yo·room

diesel	*dizel*	dee·*zel*
leaded	*kurşunlu*	koor·shoon·*loo*
LPG	*LPG*	le·pe·*ge*
regular	*normal*	nor·*mal*
premium	*birinci kalite*	bee·reen·*jee* ka·lee·*te*
unleaded	*kurşunsuz*	koor·shoon·*sooz*
unleaded	*kurşunsuz*	koor·shoon·*sooz*
Can you	*Lütfen ... kontrol*	*lewt*·fen ... kon·*trol*
check the ...?	*eder misiniz?*	e·*der* mee·see·*neez*
oil	*yağını*	ya·uh·*nuh*
tyre pressure	*lastikleri*	las·teek·le·*ree*
water	*suyunu*	soo·yoo·*noo*

How long can I park here?
Buraya ne kadar süre
park edebilirim?

boo·ra·*ya* ne ka·*dar* sew·*re*
park e·*de*·bee·lee·reem

Do I have to pay?
Park ücreti ödemem
gerekli mi?

park ewj·re·*tee* er·de·*mem*
ge·rek·*lee* mee

problems

I need a mechanic.
Tamirciye ihtiyacım var.

ta·meer·jee·*ye* eeh·tee·ya·*juhm* var

I've had an accident.
Kaza yaptım.

ka·*za* yap·*tuhm*

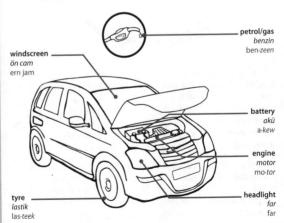

petrol/gas
benzin
ben·zeen

windscreen
ön cam
ern jam

battery
akü
a·kew

engine
motor
mo·tor

tyre
lastik
las·teek

headlight
far
far

The car/motorbike has broken down (at Osmanbey).
Arabam/motosikletim   a·ra·*bam*/mo·to·seek·le·*teem*
(Osmanbey'de) bozuldu.   (os·*man*·bay·de) bo·zool·*doo*

The car/motorbike won't start.
Arabam/motosikletim   a·ra·*bam*/mo·to·seek·le·*teem*
çalışmıyor.   cha·*luhsh*·muh·yor

I have a flat tyre.
Lastiğim patladı.   las·tee·*eem* pat·la·*duh*

I've lost my car keys.
Anahtarlarımı kaybettim.   a·nah·tar·la·ruh·*muh* kai·bet·*teem*

I've locked the keys inside.
Anahtarlarımı   a·nah·tar·la·ruh·*muh*
içeride unuttum.   ee·che·ree·*de* oo·noot·*toom*

I've run out of petrol.
Benzinim bitti.   ben·zee·*neem* beet·*tee*

Can you fix it (today)?
(Bugün) Tamir   (boo·gewn) ta·*meer*
edebilir misiniz?   e·*de*·bee·leer mee·see·*neez*

How long will it take?
Ne kadar sürer?   ne ka·*dar* sew·*rer*

signs

Dur	door	**Stop**
Girilmez	gee·*reel*·mez	**No Entry**
Giriş	gee·*reesh*	**Entrance**
Otoban	o·to·*ban*	**Motorway**
Otoban Çıkışı	o·to·*ban* chuh·kuh·*shuh*	**Exit Freeway**
Otoyol	o·*to*·yol	**Expressway**
Otoyol Gişeleri	o·*to*·yol gee·she·le·*ree*	**Toll Booths**
Paralı Yol	pa·ra·*luh* yol	**Toll Highway**
Park Yeri	park ye·*ree*	**Parking Garage**
Şehir Merkezi	she·*heer* mer·ke·*zee*	**City Centre**
Tek Yön	tek yern	**One Way**
Ücret Ödenir	ewj·*ret* er·de·*neer*	**Toll Collection**
Yavaş	ya·*vash*	**Slow Down**
Yol Ver	yol ver	**Give Way**

bicycle

bisiklet

I'd like ...	... istiyorum.	... ees·tee·yo·room
my bicycle	Bisikletimin	bee·seek·le·tee·meen
repaired	tamir edilmesini	ta·meer e·deel·me·see·nee
to buy a bicycle	Bisiklet almak	bee·seek·let al·mak
to hire a bicycle	Bisiklet kiralamak	bee·seek·let kee·ra·la·mak

I'd like a ... bike.	Bir ... istiyorum.	beer ... ees·tee·yo·room
mountain	dağ bisikleti	da bee·seek·le·tee
racing	yarış bisikleti	ya·ruhsh bee·seek·le·tee
second-hand	ikinci-el bisiklet	ee·keen·je·el bee·seek·let

How much is it per ...?	... ne kadar?	... ne ka·dar
day	Günlüğü	gewn·lew·ew
hour	Saati	sa·a·tee

Do I need a helmet?
Kask takmam gerekli mi?   kask tak·mam ge·rek·lee mee

Are there bicycle paths?
Bisiklet yolu var mı?   bee·seek·let yo·loo var muh

Is there a bicycle-path map?
Bisiklet yolu haritası var mı?   bee·seek·let yo·loo ha·ree·ta·suh var muh

I have a puncture.
Lastiğim patladı.   las·tee·eem pat·la·duh

---

traffic monsters

Prominent road signs advise drivers *İçinizdeki trafik canavarını control edin!* ee·chee·neez·de·kee tra·feek ja·na·va·ruh·nuh kon·trol e·deen (Control the Traffic Monster Inside You!).

border crossing

sınırdan geçerken

I'm ...	Ben ...	ben ...
in transit	transit	tran·*seet*
	yolcuyum	yol·*joo*·yoom
on business	iş	eesh
	gezisindeyim	ge·zee·seen·*de*·yeem
on holiday	tatildeyim	ta·teel·*de*·yeem
I'm here for ...	Ben ... buradayım.	ben ... boo·ra·*da*·yuhm
(10) days	(on) günlüğüne	(on) gewn·lew·ew·*ne*
(three) weeks	(üç) haftalığına	(ewch) haf·ta·luh·uh·*na*
(two) months	(iki) aylığına	(ee·*kee*) ai·luh·uh·*na*

I'm going to (Sarıyer).
(Sarıyer'e) gidiyorum.   (sa·*ruh*·ye·re) gee·dee·*yo*·room

I'm staying at (the Divan).
(Divan'da) kalıyorum.   (*dee*·van·da) ka·luh·*yo*·room

The children are on this passport.
Çocuklar bu   cho·jook·*lar* boo
pasaportta yazılı.   pa·sa·port·*ta* ya·zuh·*luh*

---

listen for ...

aile	a·ee·*le*	family
gurup	goo·*roop*	group
pasaport	pa·sa·*port*	passport
vize	*vee*·ze	visa
yalnız	yal·*nuhz*	alone

at customs

I have nothing to declare.
Beyan edecek   be·*yan* e·de·*jek*
hiçbir şeyim yok.   *heech*·beer she·*yeem* yok

I have something to declare.
Beyan edecek bir şeyim var.   be·*yan* e·de·*jek* beer she·*yeem* var

Do I have to declare this?
Bunu beyan   boo·*noo* be·*yan*
etmem gerekli mi?   et·*mem* ge·rek·*lee* mee

That's (not) mine.
Bu benim (değil).   boo be·*neem* (de·*eel*)

I didn't know I had to declare it.
Bunu beyan etmem   boo·*noo* be·*yan* et·*mem*
gerektiğini   ge·rek·tee·ee·*nee*
bilmiyordum.   beel·mee·yor·doom

I didn't realise I couldn't take this out of the country.
Bunu ülkeden   boo·*noo* ewl·ke·*den*
çıkaramıyacağımı   chuh·ka·*ra*·muh·ya·ja·uh·muh
bilmiyordum.   beel·mee·yor·doom

I have permission to take this out of the country.
Bunu ülkeden   boo·*noo* ewl·ke·*den*
çıkarma iznim var.   chuh·kar·*ma* eez·*neem* var

For phrases on payments and receipts, see **money**, page 45.

signs

Göçmen Bürosu	gerch·men bew·ro·soo	Immigration
Gümrük	gewm·rewk	Customs
Gümrüksüz	gewm·rewk·sewz	Duty-Free
Satış	sa·tuhsh	
Karantina	ka·ran·tee·na	Quarantine
Pasaport	pa·sa·port	Passport Control
Kontrolü	kon·tro·lew	

Where's (the tourist office)?
(Turizm bürosu) nerede? (too·reezm bew·ro·*soo*) ne·re·de

What's the address?
Adresi nedir? ad·re·*see* ne·deer

How do I get there?
Oraya nasıl o·ra·*ya* na·suhl
gidebilirim? gee·*de*·bee·lee·reem

How far is it?
Ne kadar uzakta? ne ka·*dar* oo·zak·*ta*

Can you show me (on the map)?
Bana (haritada) ba·*na* (ha·ree·ta·*da*)
gösterebilir misiniz? gers·te·*re*·bee·leer mee·seen·*neez*

It's ...

close	*Yakın.*	ya·*kuhn*
here	*Burada.*	boo·ra·*da*
on the corner	*Köşede.*	ker·she·*de*
straight ahead	*Tam karşıda.*	tam kar·shuh·*da*
there	*Şurada.*	shoo·ra·*da*

It's ...

behind ...	*... arkasında.*	... ar·ka·suhn·*da*
in front of ...	*... önünde.*	... er·newn·*de*
near ...	*... yakınında.*	... ya·kuh·nuhn·*da*
next to ...	*... yanında.*	... ya·nuhn·*da*
opposite ...	*... karşısında.*	... kar·shuh·suhn·*da*

listen for ...

dakika	da·kee·*ka*	minutes
kilometre	kee·*lo*·met·re	kilometres
metre	*met*·re	metres

north	kuzey	koo·zay
south	güney	gew·nay
east	doğu	do·oo
west	batı	ba·tuh
Turn ...	... dön.	... dern
at the corner	Köşeden	ker·she·den
at the	Trafik	tra·feek
traffic lights	ışıklarından	uh·shuhk·la·ruhn·dan
left	Sola	so·la
right	Sağa	sa·a
What ... is this?	Bu hangi ...?	boo han·gee ...
avenue	cadde	jad·de
boulevard	bulvar	bool·var
lane	ara sokak	a·ra so·kak
square	meydan	may·dan
street	sokak	so·kak
village	köy	kay

For information on Turkish addresses, see the box on page 72.

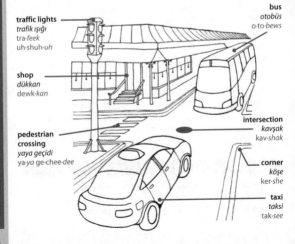

traffic lights
trafik ışığı
tra·feek
uh·shuh·uh

shop
dükkan
dewk·kan

**pedestrian
crossing**
yaya geçidi
ya·ya ge·chee·dee

bus
otobüs
o·to·bews

intersection
kavşak
kav·shak

corner
köşe
ker·she

taxi
taksi
tak·see

accommodation

finding accommodation

Where's a ...?	Buralarda nerede ... var?	boo·ra·lar·da ne·re·de ... var
bed and breakfast	yatacak yer ve kahvaltı veren bir yer	ya·ta·jak yer ve kah·val·tuh ve·ren beer yer
camping ground	kamp yeri	kamp ye·ree
guesthouse	misafirhane	mee·sa·feer·ha·ne
hotel	otel	o·tel
(one)-star hotel	(bir) yıldızlı otel	(beer) yuhl·duhz·luh o·tel
pension	pansiyon	pan·see·yon
room in a private home	kiralık oda	kee·ra·luhk o·da
tree house	ağaç ev	a·ach ev
youth hostel	gençlik hosteli	gench·leek hos·te·lee
Can you recommend somewhere ...?	... bir yer tavsiye edebilir misiniz?	... beer yer tav·see·ye e·de·bee·leer mee·see·neez
cheap	Ucuz	oo·jooz
good	İyi	ee·yee
luxurious	Lüks	lewks
nearby	Yakın	ya·kuhn
romantic	Romantik	ro·man·teek
safe for women travellers	Bayanlar için emniyetli	ba·yan·lar ee·cheen em·nee·yet·lee
What's the address?	Adresi nedir?	ad·re·see ne·deer

For responses, see **directions**, page 63, and also page 72 of this chapter.

booking ahead & checking in

I'd like to book a room, please.
*Bir oda ayırtmak
istiyorum lütfen.*
beer o·*da* a·yuhrt·*mak*
ees·*tee*·yo·room *lewt*·fen

I have a reservation.
Rezervasyonum var.
re·zer·vas·yo·*noom* var

My name's …
Benim ismim …
be·*neem* ees·*meem* …

For (three) nights/weeks.
*(Üç) geceliğine/
haftalığına.*
(ewch) ge·je·lee·ee·*ne*/
haf·ta·luh·uh·*na*

From (2 July) to (6 July).
*(2 Temmuz'dan)
(6 Temmuz'a) kadar.*
(ee·*kee* tem·mooz·*dan*)
(al·*tuh* tem·moo·za) ka·*dar*

Do I need to pay upfront?
*Ön ödeme yapmam
gerekli mi?*
ern er·de·*me* yap·*mam*
ge·rek·*lee* mee

Do you have a … room?	… *odanız var mı?*	… o·da·*nuhz* var muh
single	*Tek kişilik*	tek kee·shee·*leek*
double	*İki kişilik*	ee·*kee* kee·shee·*leek*
twin	*Çift yataklı*	cheeft ya·tak·*luh*

How much is it per …?	… *ne kadar?*	… ne ka·*dar*
night	*Geceliği*	ge·je·lee·*ee*
person	*Kişi başına*	kee·*shee* ba·shuh·*na*
week	*Haftalığı*	haf·ta·luh·*uh*

signs

banyo	ban·yo	**bathroom**
boş oda	bosh o·*da*	**vacancy**
boş yer yok	bosh yer yok	**no vacancy**

PRACTICAL

66

Can I see it?	Görebilir miyim.	ger·re·bee·leer mee·yeem
I'll take it.	Tutuyorum.	too·too·yo·room
Can I pay by ...?	... ile ödeyebilir miyim?	... ee·le er·de·ye·bee·leer mee·yeem
credit card	Kredi kartı	kre·dee kar·tuh
travellers cheque	Seyahat çeki	se·ya·hat che·kee

For other methods of payment, see **money**, page 45, and **banking**, page 89.

For other methods of payment, see **money**, page 45, and **banking**, page 89.

listen for ...

Kaç gece için?	kach ge·je ee·cheen	How many nights?
anahtar	a·nah·tar	key
dolu	do·loo	full
pasaport	pa·sa·port	passport
resepsiyon	re·sep·see·yon	reception

requests & queries

ricalar & sorular

When/Where is breakfast served?
Kahvaltı ne zaman/
nerede veriliyor?
kah·val·tuh ne za·man/
ne·re·de ve·ree·lee·yor

Is breakfast included?
Kahvaltı dahil mi?
kah·val·tuh da·heel mee

Please wake me at (seven).
Lütfen beni
(yedide) kaldırın.
lewt·fen be·nee
(ye·dee·de) kal·duh·ruhn

Can I use the ...?	... kullanabilir miyim?	... kool·la·na·bee·leer mee·yeem
kitchen	Mutfağı	moot·fa·uh
laundry	Çamaşırlığı	cha·ma·shuhr·luh·uh
telephone	Telefonu	te·le·fo·noo

accommodation

67

Who is it?	*Kim o?*	keem o
Just a moment.	*Bir dakika.*	beer da·kee·*ka*
Come in.	*Girin.*	gee·reen
Come back later, please.	*Lütfen sonra gelin.*	*lewt*·fen son·ra ge·leen

Do you have a/an …?	*… var mı?*	… var muh
elevator	*Asansör*	a·san·*ser*
laundry service	*Çamaşır yıkama hizmetiniz*	cha·ma·*shuhr* yuh·ka·*ma* heez·me·tee·*neez*
message board	*İlan panonuz*	ee·*lan* pa·no·*nooz*
safe	*Kasanız*	ka·sa·*nuhz*
swimming pool	*Yüzme havuzu*	yewz·me ha·voo·*zoo*
Do you … here?	*Burada … musunuz?*	boo·ra·*da* … moo·soo·*nooz*
arrange tours	*tur düzenliyor*	toor dew·zen·lee·yor
change money	*döviz bozuyor*	der·*veez* bo·*zoo*·yor
Could I have (a) …, please?	*… alabilir miyim?*	… a·*la*·bee·leer mee·*yeem*
my key	*Anahtarımı*	a·nah·ta·ruh·*muh*
mosquito net	*Cibinlik*	jee·been·*leek*
receipt	*Makbuz*	mak·*booz*

Is there a message for me?
Bana mesaj var mı?   ba·*na* me·*sazh* var muh

Can I leave a message for someone?
Birisi için mesaj   bee·ree·*see* ee·*cheen* me·*sazh*
bırakabilir miyim?   buh·ra·*ka*·bee·leer mee·*yeem*

I'm locked out of my room.
Dışarıda kaldım.   duh·sha·ruh·*da* kal·*duhm*

complaints

It's too ...	Çok ...	chok ...
bright	aydınlık	ai·duhn·luhk
cold	soğuk	so·ook
dark	karanlık	ka·ran·luhk
expensive	pahalı	pa·ha·luh
noisy	gürültülü	gew·rewl·tew·lew
small	küçük	kew·chewk

The ... doesn't work.	... çalışmıyor.	... cha·luhsh·muh·yor
air conditioning	Klima	klee·ma
fan	Fan	fan
toilet	Tuvalet	too·va·let

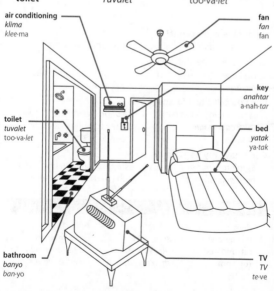

air conditioning
klima
klee·ma

fan
fan
fan

key
anahtar
a·nah·tar

toilet
tuvalet
too·va·let

bed
yatak
ya·tak

bathroom
banyo
ban·yo

TV
TV
te·ve

accommodation

69

Can I get another (blanket)?
  Başka bir (battaniye)
  alabilir miyim?

bash·*ka* beer (bat·*ta*·nee·ye)
a·*la*·bee·leer mee·*yeem*

This (pillow) isn't clean.
  Bu (yastık) temiz değil.

boo (yas·*tuhk*) te·*meez* de·*eel*

There's no hot water.
  Sıcak su yok.

suh·*jak* soo yok

checking out

ayrılırken

What time is checkout?
  Çıkış ne zaman?

chuh·*kuhsh* ne za·*man*

Can I have a late checkout?
  Daha geç ayrılabilir
  miyim?

da·*ha* gech ay·ruh·*la*·bee·leer
mee·*yeem*

Can you call a taxi for me (for 11 o'clock)?
  (Saat onbire) bana bir
  taksi çağırabilir
  misiniz?

(sa·*at* on·bee·*re*) ba·*na* beer
tak·*see* cha·uh·*ra*·bee·leer
mee·seen·*neez*

Can I leave my bags here?
  Eşyalarımı burada
  bırakabilir miyim?

esh·ya·la·ruh·*muh* boo·ra·*da*
buh·ra·*ka*·bee·leer mee·*yeem*

local talk		
dive n	*vasat*	va·*sat*
like a palace	*saray gibi*	sa·*rai* gee·bee
rat-infested	*fare yuvası*	fa·*re* yoo·va·*suh*
top spot	*merkezi yer*	mer·ke·*zee* yer

I'm leaving now.
Şimdi ayrılıyorum.   sheem·dee ai·ruh·*luh*·yo·room

There's a mistake in the bill.
Hesapta bir yanlışlık var.   he·sap·*ta* beer yan·luhsh·*luhk* var

I had a great stay, thank you.
Çok rahat ettim,   chok ra·*hat* et·*teem*
teşekkürler.   te·shek·kewr·*ler*

I'll recommend it to my friends.
Arkadaşlarıma burayı   ar·ka·dash·la·ruh·*ma* boo·ra·*yuh*
tavsiye edeceğim.   tav·see·*ye* e·de·je·eem

Could I have	... *alabilir*	... a·*la*·bee·leer
my ... please?	*miyim lütfen?*	mee·*yeem* lewt·fen
deposit	*Depozitomu*	de·po·zee·to·*moo*
passport	*Pasaportumu*	pa·sa·por·too·*moo*
valuables	*Değerli*	de·er·*lee*
	eşyalarımı	esh·ya·la·ruh·*muh*

I'll be back ...	... *geri döneceğim.*	... ge·*ree* der·ne·je·eem
in (three) days	*(Üç) gün*	(ewch) gewn
	içinde	ee·cheen·*de*
on (Tuesday)	*(Salı) günü*	(sa·*luh*) gew·*new*

camping

Do you have	... *var mı?*	... var muh
(a) ...?		
electricity	*Elektrik*	e·lek·*treek*
laundry	*Çamaşırhane*	cha·ma·shuhr·*ha*·ne
shower facilities	*Duş imkanı*	doosh eem·ka·*nuh*
site	*Yer*	yer
tents for hire	*Kiralık çadır*	kee·ra·*luhk* cha·*duhr*

the correct form of address

In Turkish addresses, the street name comes first and is followed by the house or street number. The street and floor numbers are separated by a *taksim* tak·*seem* (slash), then comes the apartment number, suburb, city and country. *Kat* kat means 'floor' and *daire* da·ee·*re* (written as *D:* as in the example below) means 'apartment'. A building's *zemin kat* ze·*meen* kat (ground floor) is always marked 'Z'. So apartment 21 on the 5th floor of 1137 Mithatpaşa Avenue in the suburb of Güzelyalı in İzmir is written as:

Mithatpaşa Cad. No:1137/5 D:21
Güzelyalı 35290
İzmir–Türkiye

How much is it per ...?	... başına ücreti ne kadar?	... ba·shuh·na ewj·re·tee ne ka·dar
caravan	Karavan	ka·ra·van
person	Kişi	kee·shee
tent	Çadır	cha·duhr
vehicle	Araç	a·rach
Can I ...?	... miyim?	... mee·yeem
camp here	Burada kamp yapabilir	boo·ra·da kamp ya·pa·bee·leer
park next to my tent	Çadırımın yanına park edebilir	cha·duh·ruh·muhn ya·nuh·na park e·de·bee·leer

Who do I ask to stay here?
Burada kalmak için kimden izin alabilirim? boo·ra·da kal·mak ee·cheen keem·den ee·zeen a·la·bee·lee·reem

Is it coin-operated?
Madeni parayla mı çalışıyor? ma·de·nee pa·rai·la muh cha·luh·shuh·yor

Is the water drinkable?
Su içilebilir mi? soo ee·chee·le·bee·leer mee

renting

I'm here about the ... for rent.	Kiralık ... için buradayım.	kee·ra·luhk ... ee·cheen boo·ra·da·yuhm
Do you have a/an ... for rent?	Kiralık ... var mı?	kee·ra·luhk ... var muh
apartment	daireniz	da·ee·re·neez
cabin	kabininiz	ka·bee·nee·neez
house	eviniz	e·vee·neez
room	odanız	o·da·nuhz
villa	villanız	veel·la·nuhz
(partly) furnished	(yarı) mobilyalı	(ya·ruh) mo·beel·ya·luh
unfurnished	mobilyasız	mo·beel·ya·suhz

staying with locals

Can I stay at your place?
Sizde kalabilir miyim?   seez·de ka·la·bee·leer mee·yeem

Is there anything I can do to help?
Benim yapabileceğim   be·neem ya·pa·bee·le·je·eem
birşey var mı?   beer·shay var muh

I have my own ...	Kendi ... var.	ken·dee ... var
mattress	şiltem	sheel·tem
sleeping bag	uyku tulumum	ooy·koo too·loo·moom

visiting etiquette

When visiting someone, it's polite to offer gifts of fine whisky or liqueurs to your host (if you're sure they drink alcohol), chocolates, a scarf or flowers to your hostess and chocolates or small toys to any children. In business situations items for the office, such as good quality pens with your company's logo, will be appreciated.

accommodation

73

Turks eat three sit-down meals a day, and all family members generally attend. If you're staying with a family they'll expect you to eat with them unless you've told them otherwise.

When you sit down to share a meal, say *Kesenize bereket!* ke·se·nee·ze be·re·ket (May it contribute to your wealth!) or *Elinize sağlık!* e·lee·nee·ze sa·luhk (Health to your hand!) to thank your host or hostess for their generosity.

Can I …?	… miyim?	… mee·yeem
bring anything for the meal	Yemek için birşeyler getirebilir	ye·mek ee·cheen beer·shay·ler ge·tee·re·bee·leer
do the dishes	Bulaşığı yıkayabilir	boo·la·shuh·uh yuh·ka·ya·bee·leer
set/clear the table	Sofrayı kurabilir/ kaldırabilir	sof·ra·yuh koo·ra·bee·leer/ kal·duh·ra·bee·leer
take out the rubbish	Çöpleri çıkarabilir	cherp·le·ree chuh·ka·ra·bee·leer

Thanks for your hospitality.
   *Misafirperverliğiniz   *mee·sa·feer·per·ver·lee·ee·neez
   için çok teşekkürler.   ee·cheen chok te·shek·kewr·ler

The food was delicious.
   Yiyecekler nefisti.   yee·ye·jek·ler ne·fees·tee

To compliment your hosts' cooking, see **eating out**, page 155.

looking for ...

Where's a (carpet shop)?
Buralarda (halıcı)
nerede var?
    boo·ra·lar·*da* (ha·luh·*juh*)
    ne·re·de var

Where's the (bazaar)?
(Pazar yeri) nerede?
    (pa·*zar* ye·*ree*) ne·re·de

Where can I buy (a padlock)?
Nereden (asma kilit)
alabilirim?
    ne·re·den (as·ma kee·*leet*)
    a·*la*·bee·lee·reem

For more items and shopping locations, see the **dictionary**. For **directions**, see page 63, and address information on page 72.

making a purchase

I'm just looking.
Sadece bakıyorum.
    sa·de·*je* ba·*kuh*·yo·room

I'd like to buy (an adaptor plug).
(Adaptör priz) almak
istiyorum.
    (a·dap·*ter* preez) al·*mak*
    ees·*tee*·yo·room

How much is it?
Ne kadar?
    ne ka·*dar*

Can you write down the price?
Fiyatı yazabilir
misiniz?
    fee·ya·*tuh* ya·*za*·bee·leer
    mee·see·*neez*

Do you have any others?
Başka var mı?
    bash·*ka* var muh

Can I look at it?
Bakabilir miyim?
    ba·*ka*·bee·leer mee·*yeem*

bargain n	*pazarlık*	pa·zar·*luhk*
rip off	*kazıklamak*	ka·zuhk·la·*mak*
sale	*indirimli satış*	een·dee·reem·*lee* sa·*tuhsh*
specials	*özel indirim*	er·*zel* een·dee·*reem*

Do you accept …?	… *kabul ediyor*	… ka·*bool* e·*dee*·yor
	musunuz?	moo·soo·*nooz*
credit cards	*Kredi kartı*	kre·dee kar·*tuh*
debit cards	*Banka kartı*	ban·ka kar·*tuh*
travellers cheques	*Seyahat çeki*	se·ya·*hat* che·*kee*

Could I have a …, please?	… *alabilir miyim lütfen?*	… a·*la*·bee·leer mee·*yeem* lewt·fen
bag	*Poşet*	po·*shet*
receipt	*Makbuz*	mak·*booz*

I don't need a bag, thanks.
Teşekkür ederim,   tesh·shek·*kewr* e·*de*·reem
poşet istemiyorum.   po·*shet* ees·te·*mee*·yo·room

Could I have it wrapped?
Sarabilir misiniz?   sa·*ra*·bee·leer mee·see·*neez*

Does it have a guarantee?
Garantisi var mı?   ga·ran·tee·*see* var muh

Can I have it sent abroad?
Yurt dışına   yoort duh·shuh·*na*
gönderebilir misiniz?   gern·de·*re*·bee·leer mee·see·*neez*

Can you order it for me?
Benim için sipariş   be·*neem* ee·*cheen* see·pa·*reesh*
eder misiniz?   e·*der* mee·see·*neez*

Can I pick it up later?
Daha sonra alabilir miyim?   da·ha son·ra a·*la*·bee·leer mee·*yeem*

It's faulty. (for clothes)
Defolu.   de·fo·*loo*

It doesn't work. (for electrical/mechanical goods)
Arızalı.   a·ruh·za·*luh*

The quality isn't good.		
Kalitesi iyi değil.		ka·lee·te·*see* ee·*yee* de·*eel*

I'd like …,	*… istiyorum*	*… ees·tee·*yo·room
please.	*lütfen.*	*lewt·*fen
my change	*Paramın*	pa·ra·*muhn*
	üstünü	ews·tew·*new*
a refund	*Para iadesi*	pa·*ra* ee·a·de·*see*
to return this	*Bunu iade*	boo·*noo* ee·a·*de*
	etmek	et·*mek*

bargaining

That's too expensive.		
Bu çok pahalı.		boo chok pa·ha·*luh*
Is that your lowest price?		
Son fiyatınız bu mu?		son fee·ya·tuh·*nuhz* boo moo
Do you have something cheaper?		
Daha ucuz birşey var mı?		da·ha oo·jooz beer·*shay* var muh
I'll give you (30 lira).		
(Otuz lira) veririm.		(o·*tooz* lee·*ra*) ve·*ree*·reem

books & reading

Do you have …?	*… var mı?*	… var muh
a book by	*(Yaşar Kemal'in)*	(ya·shar ke·mal·*een*)
(Yaşar Kemal)	*kitabı*	kee·ta·*buh*
an entertainment guide	*Eğlence rehberi*	e·len·je reh·be·*ree*

Is there an (English)-	*(İngilizce)*	(een·gee·*leez*·je)
language …?	*… var mı?*	… var muh
bookshop	*yayın satan*	ya·*yuhn* sa·tan
	bir dükkan	beer dewk·kan
section	*bölümü*	ber·lew·*mew*

I'd like a …	… istiyorum.	… ees·tee·yo·room
dictionary	Sözlük	serz·lewk
newspaper	(İngilizce)	(een·gee·leez·je)
(in English)	bir gazete	beer ga·ze·te
notepad	Not defteri	not def·te·ree

Can you recommend a book for me?
Tavsiye ettiğiniz   tav·see·ye et·tee·ee·neez
bir kitap var mı?   beer kee·tap var muh

Do you have Lonely Planet guidebooks?
Lonely Planet'in rehber   lon·lee pla·ne·teen reh·ber
kitapları var mı?   kee·tap·la·ruh var muh

carpets

halı

Is it 100% wool?
Yüzde yüz yün mü?   yewz·de yewz yewn mew

Is it a silk-wool blend?
İpek ve yün   ee·pek ve yewn
karışımı mı?   ka·ruh·shuh·muh muh

I don't believe this is pure wool.
Bunun has yün   boo·noon has yewn
olduğuna   ol·doo·oo·na
inanmıyorum.   ee·nan·muh·yo·room

I'd like something with a tighter weave.
Daha sık dokunmuş   da·ha suhk do·koon·moosh
birşey istiyorum.   beer·shay ees·tee·yo·room

Are they natural dyes?
Bunlar doğal boya mı?   boon·lar do·al bo·ya muh

How old is this carpet?
Bu halı kaç yaşında?   boo ha·luh kach ya·shuhn·da

This carpet has been patched/repainted.
Bu halı yamalanmış/   boo ha·luh ya·ma·lan·muhsh/
boyanmış.   bo·yan·muhsh

clothes

My size is …	… beden	… be·den
	giyiyorum.	gee·yee·yo·room
(40)	(Kırk)	(kuhrk)
small	Küçük	kew·chewk
medium	Orta	or·ta
large	Büyük	bew·yewk

Can I try it on?
Deneyebilir miyim?   de·ne·ye·bee·leer mee·yeem

It doesn't fit.
Olmuyor.   ol·moo·yor

It's not well made.
Kesimi iyi değil.   ke·see·mee ee·yee de·eel

For different types of clothing, see the **dictionary**, and for sizes, see **numbers & amounts**, page 35.

electronic goods

Will this work on any DVD player?
Her DVD'de   her dee·vee·dee·de
çalışır mı?   cha·luh·shuhr muh

Is this a (PAL/NTSC) system?
Bu (PAL/NTSC) sistem mi?   boo (pal/ne·te·se·je) sees·tem mee

Is this the latest model?
Bu en son model mi?   boo en son mo·del mee

Is this (240) volts?
Bu (ikiyüzkırk) volt mu?   boo (ee·kee·yewz·kuhrk) volt moo

Where can I buy duty-free electronic goods?
Gümrüksüz elektronik   gewm·rewk·sewz e·lek·tro·neek
eşya nereden alabilirim?   esh·ya ne·re·den a·la·bee·lee·reem

listen for ...

Başka birşey var mı?
  bash·ka beer·shay var muh — **Anything else?**

Hayır, hiç kalmadı.
  ha·yuhr heech kal·ma·duh — **No, we don't have any.**

Yardımcı olabilir miyim?
  yar·duhm·juh o·la·bee·leer
  mee·yeem — **Can I help you?**

hairdressing

saç bakımı

I'd like (a) ...	... istiyorum.	... ees·tee·yo·room
colour	Saçımı	sa·chuh·muh
	boyatmak	bo·yat·mak
haircut	Saçımı	sa·chuh·muh
	kestirmek	kes·teer·mek
my beard	Sakalımı	sa·ka·luh·muh
trimmed	düzelttirmek	dew·zelt·teer·mek
shave	Tıraş olmak	tuh·rash ol·mak
trim	Saçımı biraz	sa·chuh·muh bee·raz
	kestirmek	kes·teer·mek

Don't cut it too short.
  Çok kısa kesmeyin. — chok kuh·sa kes·me·yeen

Please use a new blade.
  Lütfen yeni jilet kullanın. — lewt·fen ye·nee jee·let kool·la·nuhn

Shave it all off!
  Hepsini kes. — hep·see·nee kes

clean cut

If your Turkish friend has just had a shave or a haircut, or just emerged from a bath or a shower, you can wish them *Sıhhatler olsun!* suh·hat·ler ol·soon (Good health to you!).

music

I'd like a ...   *... istiyorum.*   *... ees·tee·yo·room*
- **blank tape**   *Boş bir kaset*   bosh beer ka·*set*
- **CD**   *CD almak*   *see*·dee al·*mak*
- **DVD**   *DVD almak*   dee·vee·dee al·*mak*

I'm looking for something by (Tarkan).
(Tarkan'ın) albümlerine   (tar·ka·*nuhn*) al·bewm·le·ree·*ne*
bakmak istiyorum.   bak·*mak* ees·*tee*·yo·room

What's their best recording?
En iyi albümü hangisi?   en ee·*yee* al·bew·*mew* han·gee·see

Can I listen to this?
Bunu dinleyebilir   boo·*noo* deen·le·*ye*·bee·leer
miyim?   mee·*yeem*

photography

Can you ...?   *... misiniz?*   *... mee·see·neez*
- **develop digital**   *Dijital fotoğraf*   dee·zhee·*tal* fo·to·*raf*
  photos   *basabilir*   ba·*sa*·bee·leer
- **develop this**   *Bu filmi*   boo feel·*mee*
  film   *basabilir*   ba·*sa*·bee·leer
- **load my film**   *Filmi makineye*   feel·*mee* ma·kee·ne·*ye*
    takabilir   ta·*ka*·bee·leer
- **recharge the**   *Dijital*   dee·zhee·*tal*
  battery for   *kameram için*   ka·me·*ram* ee·*cheen*
  my digital   *bu pilleri*   boo peel·le·*ree*
  camera   *şarj edebilir*   sharzh e·*de*·bee·leer
- **transfer photos**   *Kameramdaki*   ka·me·ram·da·*kee*
  from my   *fotoğrafları*   fo·to·raf·la·*ruh*
  camera to CD   *CD'ye*   *see*·dee·ye
    aktarabilir   ak·ta·*ra*·bee·leer

I need ... film for this camera.	Bu kamera için ... film istiyorum.	boo ka·me·ra ee·cheen ... feelm ees·tee·yo·room
APS	APS	a·pe·se
B&W	siyah-beyaz	see·yah·be·yaz
colour	renkli	renk·lee
slide	slayt	slayt
(200) speed	(200) hızlı	(ee·kee·yewz) huhz·luh

When will it be ready?
Ne zaman hazır olur?   ne za·man ha·zuhr o·loor

I need a passport photo taken.
Vesikalık fotoğraf   ve·see·ka·luhk fo·to·raf
çektirmek istiyorum.   chek·teer·mek ees·tee·yo·room

I'm not happy with these photos.
Bu fotoğrafları   boo fo·to·raf·la·ruh
beğenmedim.   be·en·me·deem

I don't want to pay the full price.
Fiyatın tamamını   fee·ya·tuhn ta·ma·muh·nuh
ödemek istemiyorum.   er·de·mek ees·te·mee·yo·room

repairs

Can I have my ... repaired here?	... burada tamir ettirebilir miyim?	... boo·ra·da ta·meer et·tee·re·bee·leer mee·yeem
When can I pick my ... up?	... ne zaman alabilirim?	... ne za·man a·la·bee·lee·reem
backpack	Çantamı	chan·ta·muh
camera	Kameramı	ka·me·ra·muh
glasses	Gözlüğümü	gerz·lew·ew·mew
shoes	Ayakkabımı	a·yak·ka·buh·muh
sunglasses	Güneş gözlüğümü	gew·nesh gerz·lew·ew·mew

the internet

Where's the local Internet café?
En yakın internet kafe nerede?
en ya·*kuhn* een·ter·*net* ka·*fe* ne·re·de

I'd like to ... ... *istiyorum.* ... ees·*tee*·yo·room
  check my email | *E-postama bakmak* | e·pos·ta·ma bak·*mak*
  get Internet access | *İnternete girmek* | een·ter·ne·*te* geer·*mek*
  use a printer/ scanner | *Yazıcıyı/ Tarayıcıyı kullanmak* | ya·zuh·juh·*yuh*/ ta·ra·yuh·juh·*yuh* kool·lan·*mak*

Do you have (a) ...? | ... *var mı?* | ... var muh
  PCs | *PC* | *pee*·see
  Macs | *Mac* | mak
  Zip drive | *Zip drive* | zeep draiv

How much per ...? | ... *ne kadar?* | ... ne ka·*dar*
  hour | *Saati* | sa·a·*tee*
  (five) minutes | *(Beş) dakikası* | (besh) da·kee·ka·*suh*
  page | *Sayfası* | sai·fa·*suh*

Please change it to the (English)-language setting.
Lütfen komutları (İngilizce'ye) çevirir misiniz?
lewt·fen ko·moot·la·*ruh* (een·gee·*leez*·je·ye) che·vee·*reer* mee·see·*neez*

Do you have (English) keyboards?
(İngilizce) klavyeniz var mı?
(een·gee·*leez*·je) klav·ye·*neez* var muh

How do I log on?
Nasıl bağlanabilirim?
na·suhl ba·la·na·bee·lee·reem

chat ups

Here are some abbreviations your Turkish friends might use to *sohbet etmek* soh·*bet* et·*mek* (chat) with you or in *SMS mesajları* es·em·*es* me·sazh·la·*ruh* (SMS messages):

ii	*iyi*	ee·*yee*	good
kib	*kendine*	ken·dee·*ne*	take care
	iyi bak	ee·*yee* bak	
mrb	*merhaba*	mer·ha·*ba*	hello
nbr	*naber?*	na·*ber*	how's it going?
opt	*öptüm*	erp·*tewm*	'I kiss' (a farewell)
slm	*selam*	se·*lam*	hi
scs	*seni çok*	se·*nee* chok	I love you
	seviyorum	se·*vee*·yo·room	
tsk	*teşekkür*	te·shek·*kewr*	thanks
	ederim	e·*de*·reem	

Damn Internet!	*Allah kahretsin*	al·*lah* kah·ret·*seen*
	şu İnterneti!	shoo een·ter·ne·*tee*
It's crashed.	*Kilitlendi.*	kee·leet·len·*dee*
I've finished.	*Bitirdim.*	bee·teer·*deem*

mobile/cell phone

cep telefonu

I'd like a ...	... *istiyorum.*	... ees·*tee*·yo·room
charger for my phone	*Cep telefonum için şarj aleti*	jep te·le·fo·*noom* ee·*cheen* sharzh a·le·*tee*
mobile/cell phone for hire	*Cep telefonu kiralamak*	jep te·le·fo·*noo* kee·ra·la·*mak*
prepaid mobile/cell phone	*Kontörlü cep telefonu*	kon·ter·*lew* jep te·le·fo·*noo*
SIM card for your network	*Buradaki şebeke için SİM kart*	boo·ra·da·*kee* she·be·*ke* ee·*cheen* seem kart

PRACTICAL

84

What are the rates?
Ücret tarifesi nedir?   ewj·*ret* ta·ree·fe·*see* ne·deer

(10) yeni kuruş per (1) minute.
(Bir) dakikası   (beer) da·kee·ka·*suh*
(on) yeni kuruş.   (on) ye·*nee* koo·*roosh*

phone

telefon

What's your phone number?
Telefon numaranız nedir?   te·le·*fon* noo·ma·ra·*nuhz* ne·deer

Where's the nearest public phone?
En yakın telefon   en ya·*kuhn* te·le·*fon*
kulübesi nerede?   koo·lew·be·*see* ne·re·de

Can I look at a phone book?
Telefon rehberine   te·le·*fon* reh·be·ree·*ne*
bakabilir miyim?   ba·*ka*·bee·leer mee·*yeem*

I want to ...	*... istiyorum.*	... ees·*tee*·yo·room
buy a (100 unit)	*(Yüz kontörlük)*	(yewz kon·ter·*lewk*)
phonecard	*telefon kartı*	te·le·*fon* kar·*tuh*
call (Singapore)	*(Singapur'u)*	(seen·ga·poo·roo)
	aramak	a·ra·*mak*
make a	*(Yerel) Bir*	(ye·*rel*) beer
(local) call	*görüşme*	ger·rewsh·*me*
	yapmak	yap·*mak*
reverse the	*Ödemeli*	er·de·me·*lee*
charges	*görüşme*	ger·rewsh·*me*
	yapmak	yap·*mak*
speak for	*(Üç) dakika*	(ewch) da·kee·*ka*
(three) minutes	*konuşmak*	ko·noosh·*mak*

How much	*... ne kadar eder?*	... ne ka·*dar* e·der
does ... cost?		
a (three)-	*(Üç) dakikalık*	(ewch) da·kee·ka·*luhk*
minute call	*konuşma*	ko·noosh·*ma*
each extra	*Her ekstra*	her eks·*tra*
minute	*dakika*	da·kee·*ka*

communications

85

The number is …
Telefon numarası …　　te·le·*fon* noo·ma·ra·*suh* …

What's the area/country code for (New Zealand)?
(Yeni Zelanda'nın)　　(ye·*nee* ze·*lan*·da·nuhn)
bölge/ülke kodu nedir?　　berl·*ge*/ewl·*ke* ko·doo ne·deer

It's engaged.
Hat meşgul.　　hat mesh·*gool*

I've been cut off.
Hat kesildi.　　hat ke·seel·*dee*

The connection's bad.
Bağlantı kötü.　　ba·lan·*tuh* ker·*tew*

Hello.　　*Alo.*　　a·*lo*
It's …　　*Ben …*　　ben …
Is (Ayşe) there?　　*(Ayşe) orada mı?*　　(ai·*she*) o·ra·*da* muh

---

listen for …

Bir dakika.	beer da·kee·*ka*	**One moment.**
Burada değil.	boo·ra·*da* de·*eel*	**He/She is not here.**
Kim arıyor?	keem a·*ruh*·yor	**Who's calling?**
Kiminle	kee·*meen*·le	**Who do you want**
görüşmek	ger·rewsh·*mek*	**to speak to?**
istiyorsunuz?	ees·tee·yor·soo·nooz	
Yanlış numara.	yan·*luhsh* noo·ma·*ra*	**Wrong number.**

Please tell him/her I called.
Lütfen aradığımı　　lewt·fen a·ra·duh·uh·*muh*
söyleyin.　　say·*le*·yeen

Can I leave a message?
Mesaj bırakabilir　　me·*sazh* buh·ra·*ka*·bee·leer
miyim?　　mee·*yeem*

I don't have a contact number.
Telefon numaram yok.　　te·le·*fon* noo·ma·*ram* yok

I'll call back later.
Daha sonra ararım.　　da·*ha* son·ra a·*ra*·ruhm

post office

I want to send a ...	Bir ... göndermek istiyorum.	beer ... gern·der·mek ees·tee·yo·room
fax	faks	faks
letter	mektup	mek·toop
parcel	paket	pa·ket
postcard	kartpostal	kart·pos·tal
I want to buy a/an ...	... satın almak istiyorum.	... sa·tuhn al·mak ees·tee·yo·room
aerogram	hava mektubu	ha·va mek·too·boo
envelope	zarf	zarf
stamp	pul	pool
customs declaration	gümrük beyanı	gewm·rewk be·ya·nuh
domestic	iç	eech
fragile	kırılabilir eşya	kuh·ruh·la·bee·leer esh·ya
international	uluslararası	oo·loos·lar·a·ra·suh
mail n	posta	pos·ta
mailbox	posta kutusu	pos·ta koo·too·soo
postcode	posta kodu	pos·ta ko·doo

Please send it by air/surface mail to (Australia).
Lütfen hava/deniz yoluyla lewt·fen ha·va/de·neez yo·looy·la
(Avustralya'ya) gönderin. (a·voos·tral·ya·ya) gern·de·reen

snail mail

air a	hava yoluyla	ha·va yo·looy·la
express a	ekspres	eks·pres
registered	taahhütlü	ta·ah·hewt·lew
sea a	deniz yoluyla	de·neez yo·looy·la
surface a	kara veya deniz yoluyla	ka·ra ve·ya de·neez yo·looy·la

communications

87

It contains (souvenirs).
İçinde (hediyelik ee·cheen·*de* (he·dee·ye·*leek*
eşya) var. esh·*ya*) var

Where's the poste restante section?
Güdümlü posta gew·dewm·*lew pos*·ta
bölümü nerede? ber·lew·*mew* ne·re·de

Is there any mail for me?
Bana posta var mı? ba·*na pos*·ta var muh

---

get with the idiom

I can't bring myself to say it.
Dilim varmıyor. dee·*leem* var·muh·yor
(lit: my tongue isn't arriving)

Well said!
Ağzına sağlık! a·zuh·*na* sa·*luhk*
(lit: health to your mouth)

Clean as a whistle.
Bal dök de yala. bal derk de ya·*la*
(lit: pour honey and lick)

Do I smell or something?
Benim başım kel mi? be·*neem* ba·*shuhm* kel mee
(lit: does my head have a bald spot)

He/She couldn't organise a piss-up in a brewery.
Denize girse kurutur. de·nee·*ze* geer·*se* koo·roo·*toor*
(lit: he/she makes the sea dry up if he/she enters it)

He/She can talk the hind legs off a donkey.
Şiir gibi konuşuyor. shee·*eer* gee·*bee* ko·noo·shoo·yor
(lit: he/she speaks like a poem)

He/She lies like a pig in mud.
Bir ayak üstünde bin beer a·*yak* ews·tewn·*de* been
yalan söyler. ya·*lan* say·*ler*
(lit: he/she tells thousands of lies on one foot)

Where can I ...?	Nerede ...	ne·re·de ...
	bozdurabilirim?	boz·doo·ra·bee·lee·reem
cash a cheque	çek	chek
change a travellers cheque	seyahat çeki	se·ya·hat che·kee
change money	döviz	der·veez

Where can I ...?	Nerede ...	ne·re·de ...
	çekebilirim?	che·ke·bee·lee·reem
get a cash advance	avans	a·vans
withdraw money	para	pa·ra

Where's (a/an) ...?	Buralarda ... nerede var?	boo·ra·lar·da ... ne·re·de var
automated teller machine	bankamatik	ban·ka·ma·teek
foreign exchange office	döviz bürosu	der·veez bew·ro·soo
post office	postane	pos·ta·ne

What time does the bank open?
Banka ne zaman açılıyor?　　ban·ka ne za·man a·chuh·luh·yor

---

turkish currency

The currency of Turkey is the *Yeni Türk Lirası* (YTL) ye·nee tewrk lee·ra·suh (New Turkish Lira), which replaced the *Türk Lirası* (TL) (Turkish Lira). Banknotes are available for 100, 50, 20, 10, 5 and 1 YTL, and coins for 1 YTL and 50, 25, 10, 5 and 1 *Yeni Kuruş* ye·nee koo·roosh (New *Kuruş*). 100 Yeni Kuruş equal 1 YTL.

Bir problem var.
beer prob·*lem* var — **There's a problem.**

Bunu yapamayız.
boo·*noo* ya·*pa*·ma·yuhz — **We can't do that.**

Burayı imzalayın.
boo·ra·*yuh* eem·za·*la*·yuhn — **Sign here, please.**

Hesabınızda para kalmadı.
he·sa·buh·nuhz·*da*
pa·*ra* kal·ma·duh — **You have no funds left.**

kimlik	keem·*leek*	**identification**
pasaport	pa·sa·*port*	**passport**

What's the ...?	... *nedir?*	... ne·*deer*
charge for that	*Ücreti*	ewj·re·*tee*
exchange rate	*Döviz kuru*	der·*veez* koo·*roo*

The automated teller machine took my card.
Bankamatik kartımı aldı. ban·ka·ma·*teek* kar·tuh·*muh* al·duh

I've forgotten my PIN.
Şifremi unuttum. sheef·re·mee oo·noot·*toom*

Can I use my credit card to withdraw money?
Kredi kartımla para kre·dee kar·tuhm·la pa·*ra*
çekebilir miyim? che·ke·bee·leer mee·*yeem*

Has my money arrived yet?
Param geldi mi? pa·*ram* gel·*dee* mee

How long will it take to arrive?
Gelmesi ne kadar sürer? gel·me·*see* ne ka·*dar* sew·*rer*

For other useful phrases, see **money**, page 45.

I'd like a/an ...	... istiyorum.	... ees·tee·yo·room
audio set	Kulaklık	koo·lak·luhk
catalogue	Katalog	ka·ta·log
guide	Rehber	reh·ber
guidebook	(İngilizce)	(een·gee·leez·je)
(in English)	Rehber kitap	reh·ber kee·tap
(local) map	(Yerel) Harita	(ye·rel) ha·ree·ta

Do you have	... yerler	... yer·ler
information on	hakkında	hak·kuhn·da
... sights?	bilgi var mı?	beel·gee var muh
cultural	Kültürel	kewl·tew·rel
Graeco-	Roma Yunan	ro·ma yoo·nan
Roman	tarihine ait	ta·ree·hee·ne a·eet
historical	Tarihi	ta·ree·hee
religious	Dini	dee·nee

I'd like to see ...
  ... *görmek istiyorum.* ... ger·mek ees·tee·yo·room

Who made it?
  Onu kim yaptı? o·noo keem yap·tuh

How old is it?
  Kaç yaşında? kach ya·shuhn·da

Could you take a photograph of me?
  Benim bir fotoğrafımı be·neem beer fo·to·ra·fuh·muh
  çeker misiniz? che·ker mee·see·neez

Can I take a photo (of you)?
  (Sizin) Bir fotoğrafınızı (see·zeen) beer fo·to·ra·fuh·nuh·zuh
  çekebilir miyim? che·ke·bee·leer mee·yeem

I'll send you the photograph.
  Size foroğrafı see·ze fo·to·ra·fuh
  göndereceğim. gern·de·re·je·eem

getting in

What time does it open/close?
Saat kaçta açılır/kapanır? sa·at kach·ta a·chuh·luhr/ka·pa·nuhr

What's the admission charge?
Giriş ücreti nedir? gee·reesh ewj·re·tee ne·deer

Is there a discount for …?	… indirimi var mı?	… een·dee·ree·mee var muh
children	Çocuk	cho·jook
families	Aile	a·ee·le
groups	Gurup	goo·roop
older people	Yaşlılara özel	yash·luh·la·ra er·zel
pensioners	Emekli	e·mek·lee
students	Öğrenci	er·ren·jee

tours

When's the next …?	Sonraki … ne zaman?	son·ra·kee … ne za·man
boat trip	vapur gezisi	va·poor ge·zee·see
day trip	gündüz turu	gewn·dewz too·roo
tour	tur	toor

Is … included?	… dahil mi?	… da·heel mee
accommodation	Kalacak yer	ka·la·jak yer
food	Yemek	ye·mek
transport	Ulaşım	oo·la·shuhm

The guide will pay.
Tur rehberi ödeyecek. toor reh·be·ree er·de·ye·jek

How long is the tour?
Tur ne kadar sürer? toor ne ka·dar sew·rer

What time should we be back?
Saat kaçta dönmeliyiz? sa·at kach·ta dern·me·lee·yeez

doing business

I'm attending a ...	Bir ...	beer ...
	katılıyorum.	ka·tuh·luh·yo·room
conference	konferansa	kon·fe·ran·sa
course	kursa	koor·sa
meeting	toplantıya	top·lan·tuh·ya
trade fair	ticaret fuarına	tee·ja·ret foo·a·ruh·na

I'm with ...	... birlikteyim.	... beer·leek·te·yeem
my	İş	eesh
colleague(s)	arkadaşlarımla	ar·ka·dash·la·ruhm·la
(two) others	Diğer (iki)	dee·er (ee·kee)
	kişiyle	kee·sheey·le

I'm with (Migros).
(Migros'ta) çalışıyorum. (meeg·ros·ta) cha·luh·shuh·yo·room

I'm alone.
Yalnızım. yal·nuh·zuhm

I have an appointment with (Derya).
(Derya Hanım) ile (der·ya ha·nuhm) ee·le
randevum var. ran·de·voom var

I'm staying at (the Ramada Hotel), room (19).
(Ramada'da), (ondokuz) (ra·ma·da·da) (on·do·kooz)
numaralı odada noo·ma·ra·luh o·da·da
kalıyorum. ka·luh·yo·room

I'm here for (two) days/weeks.
(İki) günlüğüne/ (ee·kee) gewn·lew·ew·ne/
haftalığına buradayım. haf·ta·luh·uh·na boo·ra·da·yuhm

Can I have your business card?
Bir kartvizitinizi beer kart·vee·zee·tee·nee·zee
alabilir miyim? a·la·bee·leer mee·yeem

Where's the ...?	... nerede?	... ne·re·de
business centre	İş merkezi	eesh mer·ke·zee
conference	Konferans	kon·fe·rans
meeting	Toplantı	top·lan·tuh

I need (a/an) ...	... ihtiyacım var.	... eeh·tee·ya·juhm var
computer	Bir bilgisayara	beer beel·gee·sa·ya·ra
Internet	İnternet	een·ter·net
connection	bağlantısına	ba·lan·tuh·suh·na
interpreter	Tercümana	ter·jew·ma·na
more	Daha fazla	da·ha faz·la
business cards	kartvizite	kart·vee·zee·te
some space	Hazırlık yapmak	ha·zuhr·luhk yap·mak
to set up	için daha	ee·cheen da·ha
	geniş yere	ge·neesh ye·re
to send a fax	Faks göndermeye	faks gern·der·me·ye

Here's my ...	Buyurun	boo·yoo·roon
	benim ...	be·neem ...
address	adresim	ad·re·seem
business card	kartvizitim	kart·vee·zee·teem
email address	e-posta adresim	e·pos·ta ad·re·seem
fax number	faks numaram	faks noo·ma·ram
mobile number	cep numaram	jep noo·ma·ram
pager number	çağrı numaram	cha·ruh noo·ma·ram
work number	iş numaram	eesh noo·ma·ram

What's your ...?	Sizin ... nedir?	see·zeen ... ne·deer
address	adresiniz	ad·re·see·neez
email	e-posta	e·pos·ta
address	adresiniz	ad·re·see·neez
fax number	faks numaranız	faks noo·ma·ra·nuhz
mobile number	cep numaranız	jep noo·ma·ra·nuhz
pager	çağrı	cha·ruh
number	numaranız	noo·ma·ra·nuhz
work number	iş numaranız	eesh noo·ma·ra·nuhz

Thank you for your time.

Zaman ayırdığınız	za·man a·yuhr·duh·uh·nuhz
için teşekkürler.	ee·cheen te·shek·kewr·ler

PRACTICAL

That went very well.
   Çok güzel geçti.   chok gew·*zel* gech·*tee*

Shall we go for a drink?
   Birşeyler içelim mi?   beer·shay·*ler* ee·che·*leem* mee

Shall we go for a meal?
   Birlikte yemeğe   beer·leek·*te* ye·me·*e*
   gidelim mi?   gee·de·*leem* mee

It's on me.
   Hesap benden.   he·*sap* ben·*den*

looking for a job

Where are jobs advertised?
   Münhal pozisyonlar   mewn·*hal* po·zees·yon·*lar*
   nerede ilan ediliyor?   ne·re·de ee·*lan* e·dee·*lee*·yor

I'm enquiring about the position advertised.
   İş ilanı ile ilgili   eesh ee·la·*nuh* ee·le eel·gee·*lee*
   görüşmek istiyorum.   ger·rewsh·*mek* ees·*tee*·yo·room

I'm looking for … work.   *… arıyorum.*   … a·*ruh*·yo·room

bar	*Bar işi*	bar ee·*shee*
casual	*Geçici iş*	ge·chee·*jee* eesh
English-teaching	*İngilizce öğretme işi*	een·gee·*leez*·je er·ret·*me* ee·*shee*
fruit-picking	*Meyve toplama işi*	may·*ve* top·la·*ma* ee·*shee*
full-time	*Tam mesai iş*	tam me·*sa*·ee eesh
labouring	*Vasıfsız iş*	va·suhf·*suhz* eesh
nannying	*Dadılık işi*	da·duh·*luhk* ee·*shee*
office	*Ofis işi*	o·*fees* ee·*shee*
part-time	*Yarım gün*	ya·*ruhm* gewn
volunteer	*Gönüllü çalışabileceğim bir iş*	ger·newl·*lew* cha·luh·sha·bee·le·*je*·eem beer eesh
waitering	*Garsonluk işi*	gar·son·*look* ee·*shee*

I've had experience.
  Deneyimim var. de·ne·yee·meem var

What's the wage?
  Maaş nedir? ma·ash ne·deer

Do I need (a/an) …?	… gerekli mi?	… ge·rek·lee mee
contract	Kontrat yapmam	kon·trat yap·mam
experience	Deneyim	de·ne·yeem
insurance	Sigorta	see·gor·ta
my own transport	Kendi arabam	ken·dee a·ra·bam
paperwork	Kağıt işlemleri	ka·uht eesh·lem·le·ree
uniform	Üniforma	ew·nee·for·ma
work permit	Çalışma izni	cha·luhsh·ma eez·nee

Here's my …	Buyurun benim …	boo·yoo·roon be·neem …
bank account	banka hesap bilgilerim	ban·ka he·sap beel·gee·le·reem
CV/résumé	özgeçmişim	erz·gech·mee·sheem
visa	vizem	vee·zem
work permit	çalışma iznim	cha·luhsh·ma eez·neem

I can start …	… başlayabilirim.	… bash·la·ya·bee·lee·reem
Can you start …?	… başlayabilir misin?	… bash·la·ya·bee·leer mee·seen
at (eight) o'clock	Saat (sekizde)	sa·at (se·keez·de)
next week	Gelecek hafta	ge·le·jek haf·ta
today	Bugün	boo·gewn
tomorrow	Yarın	ya·ruhn

What time do I …?	Saat kaçta …?	sa·at kach·ta …
start	işe başlarım	ee·she bash·la·ruhm
finish	bitiririm	bee·tee·ree·reem
have a break	mola verilir	mo·la ve·ree·leer

senior & disabled travellers
özürlü & yaşça büyük yolcular

I have a disability.
Özürlüyüm. — er·zewr·*lew*·yewm

I need assistance.
Yardıma ihtiyacım var. — yar·duh·*ma* eeh·tee·ya·*juhm* var

What services do you have for people with a disability?
Özürlü kişiler için hangi hizmetleriniz var? — er·zewr·*lew* kee·shee·*ler* ee·*cheen* han·gee heez·met·le·ree·*neez* var

Are there disabled toilets?
Özürlü tuvaleti var mı? — er·zewr·*lew* too·va·le·*tee* var muh

Are there disabled parking spaces?
Özürlüler için park yeri var mı? — er·zewr·lew·*ler* ee·*cheen* park ye·*ree* var muh

Is there wheelchair access?
Tekerlekli sandalye girişi var mı? — te·ker·lek·*lee* san·*dal*·ye gee·ree·*shee* var muh

How wide is the entrance?
Girişin genişliği nedir? — gee·ree·*sheen* ge·neesh·lee·*ee* ne·deer

I'm deaf.
Sağırım. — sa·*uh*·ruhm

I have a hearing aid.
İşitme cihazı kullanıyorum. — ee·sheet·*me* jee·ha·*zuh* kool·la·*nuh*·yo·room

I'm blind.
Ben körüm. — ben *ker*·rewm

I'm visually impaired.
Görme özürlüyüm. — ger·*me* er·zewr·*lew*·yewm

Are guide dogs permitted?
Rehber köpekler girebilir mi? — reh·*ber* ker·pek·*ler* gee·*re*·bee·leer mee

For extra politeness, add the word *acaba* a·ja·*ba* (I wonder) to the end of your questions. You could phrase your hunt for the post office as *Postane nerede, acaba?* pos·*ta*·ne ne·re·de a·ja·*ba* (lit: post-office where I-wonder).

How many steps are there?

Kaç basamak var?	kach ba·sa·*mak* var

Is there a lift/elevator?

Asansör var mı?	a·san·*ser* var muh

Are there rails in the bathroom?

Banyoda tutamak var mı?	ban·yo·*da* too·ta·*mak* var muh

Could you call me a disabled taxi?

Bana özürlülere özel	ba·*na* er·zewr·lew·le·*re* er·*zel*
bir taksi çağırabilir	beer tak·*see* cha·uh·*ra*·bee·leer
misiniz?	mee·see·*neez*

Could you help me cross the street safely?

Karşıya geçmeme	kar·shuh·*ya* gech·me·*me*
yardım eder misiniz?	yar·*duhm* e·*der* mee·see·*neez*

Is there somewhere I can sit down?

Oturabileceğim	o·too·ra·bee·le·*je*·eem
bir yer var mı?	beer yer var muh

guide dog	*rehber köpek*	reh·*ber* ker·*pek*
older person	*yaşlı kişi*	yash·*luh* kee·*shee*
person with a disability	*özürlü kişi*	er·zewr·*lew* kee·*shee*
ramp	*rampa*	*ram*·pa
walking frame	*yürüteç*	yew·rew·*tech*
walking stick	*baston*	bas·*ton*
wheelchair	*tekerlekli sandalye*	te·ker·lek·*lee* san·*dal*·ye

travelling with children

çocuklarla seyahat

Is there a ...?	... var mı?	... var muh
baby change room	Alt değiştirme odası	alt de·eesh·teer·me o·da·suh
child discount	Çocuk indirimi	cho·jook een·dee·ree·mee
child-minding service	Çocuk bakım hizmeti	cho·jook ba·kuhm heez·me·tee
child's portion	Çocuk porsiyonu	cho·jook por·see·yo·noo
children's menu	Çocuk menüsü	cho·jook me·new·sew
crèche	Kreş	kresh
family ticket	Aile bileti	a·ee·le bee·le·tee

I need a/an ...	... ihtiyacım var.	... eeh·tee·ya·juhm var
baby seat (English-speaking)	Bebek koltuğuna (İngilizce konuşan)	be·bek kol·too·oo·na (een·gee·leez·je ko·noo·shan)
babysitter	dadıya	da·duh·ya
booster seat	Yükseltici koltuğa	yewk·sel·tee·jee kol·too·a
cot	Çocuk yatağına	cho·jook ya·ta·uh·na
highchair	Mama sandalyesine	ma·ma san·dal·ye·see·ne
plastic sheet	Plastik yazgıya	plas·teek yaz·guh·ya
plastic bag	Naylon torbaya	nai·lon tor·ba·ya
potty	Oturağa	o·too·ra·a
pram	Çocuk arabasına	cho·jook a·ra·ba·suh·na
pushchair/ stroller	Pusete	poo·se·te
sick bag	Kusma torbasına	koos·ma tor·ba·suh·na

Where's the nearest ...?	En yakın ... nerede?	en ya·kuhn ... ne·re·de
drinking fountain	çeşme	chesh·me
park	park	park
playground	oyun alanı	o·yoon a·la·nuh
swimming pool	yüzme havuzu	yewz·me ha·voo·zoo
tap	musluk	moos·look
theme park	eğlence parkı	e·len·je par·kuh
toy shop	oyuncakçı	o·yoon·jak·chuh
Do you sell ...?	Bebekler için ... satıyor musunuz?	be·bek·ler ee·cheen ... sa·tuh·yor moo·soo·nooz
baby wipes	ıslak mendil	uhs·lak men·deel
disposable diapers/nappies	bez	bez
infant painkillers	ağrı kesici	a·ruh ke·see·jee
tissues	kutu mendil	koo·too men·deel

Are there any good places to take children around here?

Burada çocukları götürecek iyi yerler var mı?	boo·ra·da cho·jook·la·ruh ger·tew·re·jek ee·yee yer·ler var muh

Is there space for a pram?

Çocuk arabası için yer var mı?	cho·jook a·ra·ba·suh ee·cheen yer var muh

Are children allowed?

Çocuklar girebilir mi?	cho·jook·lar gee·re·bee·leer mee

Where can I change a nappy/diaper?

Bebeğin bezini nerede değiştirebilirim?	be·be·een be·zee·nee ne·re·de de·eesh·tee·re·bee·lee·reem

Do you mind if I breast-feed here?

Burada çocuk emzirmemin bir sakıncası var mı?	boo·ra·da cho·jook em·zeer·me·meen beer sa·kuhn·ja·suh var muh

Is this suitable for (three)-year-old children?

Bu (üç) yaşındaki çocuklar için uygun mu?	boo ewch ya·shuhn·da·kee cho·jook·lar ee·cheen ooy·goon moo

Do you know a dentist/doctor who is good with children?
   Çocuklar için iyi bir   cho·jook·*lar* ee·*cheen* ee·*yee* beer
   dişçi/doktor biliyor   deesh·*chee*/dok·*tor* bee·*lee*·yor
   musunuz?   moo·soo·*nooz*

If your child is sick, see **health**, page 191.

talking with children

What's your name?
   Adın ne?   a·*duhn* ne

How old are you?
   Kaç yaşındasın?   kach ya·shuhn·da·*suhn*

When's your birthday?
   Doğum günün ne zaman?   do·*oom* gew·*newn* ne za·*man*

Do you go to school/kindergarten?
   Okula/anaokuluna   o·koo·*la*/a·na·o·koo·loo·*na*
   gidiyor musun?   gee·*dee*·yor moo·*soon*

What grade are you in?
   Kaçıncı sınıftasın?   ka·chuhn·*juh* suh·nuhf·ta·suhn

Do you like (sport)?
   (Okulu) seviyor musun?   (o·koo·*loo*) se·*vee*·yor moo·*soon*

What do you do after school?
   Okuldan sonra   o·kool·*dan* son·ra
   neler yapıyorsun?   ne·*ler* ya·puh·yor·soon

Do you learn (English)?
   (İngilizce) öğreniyor   (een·gee·*leez*·je) er·re·*nee*·yor
   musun?   moo·*soon*

grandma & grandpa

In chitchat with Turkish kids, you could ask them about their *dede* de·de (grandpa) or *nine* nee·ne (grandma).

talking about children

When's the baby due?
Doğum ne zaman? — do·*oom* ne za·*man*

What are you going to call the baby?
Bebeğe ne isim — be·be·*e* ne ee·*seem*
vereceksiniz? — ve·re·*jek*·see·neez

Is this your first child?
İlk çocuğunuz mu? — eelk cho·joo·oo·*nooz* moo

Is it a boy or a girl?
Erkek mi kız mı? — er·*kek* mee kuhz muh

How many children do you have?
Kaç çocuğunuz var? — kach cho·joo·oo·*nooz* var

What a beautiful child!
Ne şirin şey! — ne shee·*reen* shay

What's his/her name?
Adı ne? — a·*duh* ne

How old is he/she?
Kaç yaşında? — kach ya·shuhn·*da*

Does he/she go to school?
Okula gidiyor mu? — o·koo·*la* gee·*dee*·yor moo

He ...	*Oğlunuz ...*	oo·loo·*nooz* ...
She ...	*Kızınız ...*	kuh·zuh·*nuhz* ...
has your eyes	*gözlerini*	gerz·le·ree·*nee*
	sizden almış	seez·*den* al·*muhsh*
looks like you	*size benziyor*	see·ze ben·*zee*·yor

tempting fate

Turkish parents don't want evil spirits paying attention to their kids, so to praise a child to its parents say *Maşallah!* ma·*shal*·lah (May God preserve him/her from evil!) before or after your compliment to ward the spirits off.

In this chapter, phrases are in the formal *siz* seez (you) form unless otherwise marked. If you're not sure what this means, see the box on page 30.

basics

temel sözcükler & cümleler

Yes.	*Evet.*	e-*vet*
No.	*Hayır.*	ha-yuhr
Please.	*Lütfen.*	lewt-fen
Thank you (very much). pol	*(Çok) Teşekkür ederim.*	(chok) te-shek-*kewr* e-de-reem
Thanks. inf	*Teşekkürler.*	te-shek-kewr-*ler*
You're welcome.	*Birşey değil.*	beer-*shay* de-*eel*
Excuse me. (to get attention)	*Bakar mısınız?*	ba-*kar* muh-suh-*nuhz*
Excuse me. (to get past)	*Affedersiniz.*	a-fe-der-see-neez
Sorry.	*Özür dilerim.*	er-*zewr* dee-*le*-reem
Be my guest.	*Benim misafirim olun.*	be-*neem* mee-sa-fee-*reem* o-loon
Let's go!	*Gidelim!*	gee-de-*leem*
Of course.	*Tabi.*	ta-*bee*

sex, religion & politics

Avoid asking questions about someone's age, religion or sexual preference, as the Turkish prefer not to discuss these topics openly. They love talking about politics, but exercise a little caution when expressing your opinion – some Turks verge on the fanatical when it comes to the 'p' word.

meeting people

greetings & goodbyes

| Hello. | Merhaba. | mer·ha·ba |
| Hi. | Selam. | se·lam |

Good ...		
afternoon	Tünaydın	tew·nai·duhn
day	İyi günler	ee·yee gewn·ler
morning	İyi sabahlar	ee·yee sa·bah·lar
evening	İyi akşamlar	ee·yee ak·sham·lar

How are you?
Nasılsın/Nasılsınız? inf/pol   na·suhl·suhn/na·suhl·suh·nuhz

Fine. And you?
İyiyim. Ya sen/siz? inf/pol   ee·yee·yeem ya sen/seez

What's your name?
Adınız ne? inf   a·duh·nuhz ne
Adınız nedir? pol   a·duh·nuhz ne·deer

My name is ...
Benim adım ...   be·neem a·duhm ...

I'd like to introduce you to ...
Sizi ... ile tanıştırmak   see·zee ... ee·le ta·nuhsh·tuhr·mak
istiyorum.   ees·tee·yo·room

This is my ...	Bu benim ...	boo be·neem ...
colleague	iş arkadaşım	eesh ar·ka·da·shuhm
daughter	kızım	kuh·zuhm
friend	arkadaşım	ar·ka·da·shuhm
husband	kocam	ko·jam
partner (intimate)	partnerim	part·ne·reem
son	oğlum	o·loom
spouse	eşim	e·sheem
wife	karım	ka·ruhm

I'm pleased to meet you.
Tanıştığımıza   ta·nuhsh·tuh·uh·muh·za
memnun oldum.   mem·noon ol·doom

When Turks are introduced to each other, they shake hands and/or kiss on both cheeks. At other meetings women kiss women and men kiss men, but kissing the opposite sex is only common between close friends. When you meet someone of the opposite sex who has strong religious beliefs, avoid shaking their hands or kissing them. Instead, greet them with the Arabic words *selamın aleyküm* se·*la*·muhn a·*lay*·kewm (lit: may peace be upon you).

See you later.
    Sonra görüşürüz.   son·ra ger·rew·*shew*·rewz

Goodbye. (by person leaving)
    Hoşçakal. inf   hosh·*cha*·kal
    Hoşçakalın. pol   hosh·*cha*·ka·luhn

Goodbye. (by person staying)
    Güle güle.   gew·*le* gew·*le*

Bye.
    Bay bay.   bai bai

Good night.
    İyi geceler.   ee·*yee* ge·je·*ler*

Bon voyage!
    İyi yolculuklar!   ee·*yee* yol·joo·look·*lar*

addressing people

hitap

Polite forms of address are used to show courtesy and acknowledge status, so use the polite *siz* seez (you) form with anyone you don't know well. In informal situations and with friends, use people's first names and address them in the *sen* sen (you) form. For more details see the box on page 30.

Mr/Sir	*Bay*	bai
Ms/Mrs/Miss/Madam	*Bayan*	ba·*yan*

Titles are also used to show respect. Address men as *bey* bay (sir) and women as *hanım* ha-*nuhm* (madam), preceded by their profession if appropriate – the taxi driver is *Şoför Bey* sho-*fer* bay (lit: driver sir) and a female doctor is *Doktor Hanım* dok-*tor* ha-*nuhm* (lit: doctor madam). Here are some titles for people with other occupations:

conductor m	*Kondaktör Bey*	kon-dak-*ter* bay
director f	*Müdire Hanım*	mew-dee-*re* ha-*nuhm*
official m (police or civil)	*Memur Bey*	me-*moor* bay
principal m	*Müdür Bey*	mew-*dewr* bay
waiter m	*Garson Bey*	gar-*son* bay

making conversation

sohbet ederken

What a beautiful day!
Ne güzel bir gün!
ne gew-*zel* beer gewn

Nice/Awful weather, isn't it?
Çok güzel/berbat bir hava, değil mi?
chok gew-*zel*/ber-*bat* beer ha-*va* de-*eel* mee

That's (beautiful), isn't it?
Şu çok (güzel), değil mi?
shoo chok (gew-*zel*) de-*eel* mee

What's this called?
Buna ne deniyor?
boo-*na* ne de-*nee*-yor

Can I help you?
Size yardım edebilir miyim?
see-*ze* yar-*duhm* e-de-bee-leer mee-*yeem*

What are you doing?
Ne yapıyorsunuz?
ne ya-*puh*-yor-soo-nooz

Where are you going?
Nereye gidiyorsunuz? ne·re·ye gee·dee·yor·soo·nooz

Thanks, I don't smoke.
Teşekkürler, te·shek·kewr·ler
kullanmıyorum. kool·lan·muh·yo·room

How do you like Turkey?
Türkiye'yi nasıl tewr·kee·ye·yee na·suhl
buldunuz? bool·doo·nooz

Do you like it here?
Burayı seviyor boo·ra·yuh se·vee·yor
musunuz? moo·soo·nooz

I love it here.
Ben burayı seviyorum. ben boo·ra·yuh se·vee·yo·room

Do you live here?
Burada mı boo·ra·da muh
oturuyorsunuz? o·too·roo·yor·soo·nooz

Are you here on holiday?
Buraya tatile mi boo·ra·ya ta·tee·le mee
geldiniz? gel·dee·neez

How long are you here for?

Ne kadar süre için buradasınız?	ne ka·*dar* sew·re ee·*cheen* boo·ra·*da*·suh·nuhz

I'm here for (four) weeks/days.

(Dört) hafatlığına/ günlüğüne buradayım.	(dert) haf·ta·luh·uh·*na*/ gewn·lew·ew·*ne* boo·ra·*da*·yuhm

I'm here ... ... *buradayım.* ... boo·ra·*da*·yuhm

for a holiday	*Tatil için*	*ta*·teel ee·*cheen*
on business	*İş için*	eesh ee·*cheen*
to study	*Öğrenim görmek için*	er·re·*neem* ger·*mek* ee·*cheen*

nationalities

To say where you're from, add *-lıyım* ·luh·yuhm, *-liyim* ·lee·yeem, *-luyum* ·loo·yoom or *-lüyüm* ·lew·yewm to your country's name. This choice depends on vowel harmony (see page 13).

Where are you from?	*Nerelisiniz?* pol	ne·re·lee·see·neez
	Nerelisin? inf	ne·re·lee·seen
I'm from ...	*Ben ...*	ben ...
Australia	*Avustralya'lıyım*	a·voos·*tral*·ya·luh·yuhm
China	*Çin'liyim*	cheen·*lee*·yeem
Jordan	*Ürdün'lüyüm*	ewr·dewn·lew·yewm
Singapore	*Singapur'luyum*	seen·ga·poor·loo·yoom

For more countries, see the **dictionary**.

age

How old ...?	*Kaç ...?*	kach ...
are you	*yaşındasınız* pol	ya·shuhn·*da*·suh·nuhz
	yaşındasın inf	ya·shuhn·*da*·suhn
is your son	*yaşında oğlunuz*	ya·shuhn·da o·loo·*nooz*
is your	*yaşında*	ya·shuhn·*da*
daughter	*kızınız*	kuh·zuh·*nuhz*

I'm ... years old.
Ben ... yaşındayım.　ben ... ya·shuhn·*da*·yuhm

He/She is ... years old.
O ... yaşında.　o ... ya·shuhn·*da*

Too old!
Çok yaşlı!　chok yash·*luh*

I'm younger than I look.
Göründüğümden　ger·rewn·dew·ewm·*den*
daha gencim.　da·*ha* gen·*jeem*

For your age, see **numbers & amounts**, page 35.

occupations & studies

What's your occupation?

Mesleğiniz nedir? pol		mes·le·ee·*neez* ne·deer
Mesleğin nedir? inf		mes·le·*een* ne·deer

I'm a/an ...	*Ben ...*	ben ...
chef	*ahçıyım*	ah·*chuh*·yuhm
engineer	*mühendisim*	mew·hen·*dee*·seem
hairdresser	*kuaförüm*	koo·a·*fer*·rewm
janitor	*kapıcıyım*	ka·puh·*juh*·yuhm
journalist	*gazeteciyim*	ga·ze·te·*jee*·yeem
labourer	*işçiyim*	eesh·*chee*·yeem
nurse	*hemşireyim*	hem·shee·*re*·yeem
official	*memurum*	me·*moo*·room
taxi driver	*taksi şoförüyüm*	tak·*see* sho·fer·*rew*·yewm
teacher	*öğretmenim*	er·ret·*me*·neem
tea seller	*çaycıyım*	chai·*juh*·yuhm

I work in ...	*... işinde*	... ee·sheen·*de*
	çalışıyorum.	cha·luh·*shuh*·yo·room
an office	*Ofis*	o·*fees*
health	*Sağlık*	sa·*luhk*
sales and	*Satış ve*	sa·*tuhsh* ve
marketing	*pazarlama*	pa·zar·la·*ma*

---

well-wishing

In your honour!	*Şerefinize!*	she·re·fee·nee·*ze*
To your health!	*Sağlığınıza!*	sa·luh·uh·nuh·*za*
Congratulations!	*Tebrikler!*	teb·*reek*·ler
Good luck!	*İyi şanslar!*	ee·*yee* shans·*lar*
Happy Birthday!	*Doğum günün*	do·*oom* gew·*newn*
	kutlu olsun!	koot·*loo* ol·*soon*
Merry Christmas!	*Yeni yılınız*	ye·*nee* yuh·luh·*nuhz*
	kutlu olsun!	koot·*loo* ol·*soon*

I'm ...	*Ben ...*	ben ...
retired	*emekliyim*	e·mek·*lee*·yeem
self-employed	*kendi işimin*	ken·*dee* ee·shee·*meen*
	sahibiyim	sa·hee·*bee*·yeem
unemployed	*işsizim*	eesh·*see*·zeem

What are you studying?	*Ne üzerine öğrenim görüyorsunuz?*	ne ew·ze·ree·*ne* er·re·*neem* ger·*rew*·yor·soo·nooz

I'm studying ...	*... öğreniyorum.*	... er·re·*nee*·yo·room
humanities	*Uygarlık tarihi*	ooy·gar·*luhk* ta·ree·*hee*
science	*Fen*	fen
Turkish	*Türkçe*	tewrk·che

family

Do you have (a) ...?	*... var mı?*	... var muh
brother	*Kardeşiniz*	kar·de·shee·*neez*
children	*Çocuklarınız*	cho·jook·la·ruh·*nuhz*
daughter	*Kızınız*	kuh·zuh·*nuhz*
family	*Aileniz*	a·ee·le·*neez*
granddaughter	*Kız torununuz*	kuhz to·roo·noo·*nooz*
grandson	*Erkek torununuz*	er·*kek* to·roo·noo·*nooz*
partner (intimate)	*Partneriniz*	part·ne·ree·*neez*
sister	*Kız kardeşiniz*	kuhz kar·de·shee·*neez*
son	*Oğlunuz*	o·loo·*nooz*
spouse	*Eşiniz*	e·shee·*neez*

For more kinship terms, see the **dictionary**.

I have (a) ...	... var.	... var
I don't have (a) ...	... yok.	... yok
brother	Kardeşim	kar·de·sheem
children	Çocuğum	cho·joo·oom
daughter	Kızım	kuh·zuhm
family	Ailem	a·ee·lem
granddaughter	Kız torunum	kuhz to·roo·noom
grandson	Erkek torunum	er·kek to·roo·noom
partner (intimate)	Partnerim	part·ne·reem
sister	Kız kardeşim	kuhz kar·de·sheem
son	Oğlum	o·loom
spouse	Eşim	e·sheem

| Are you married? | Evli misiniz? | ev·lee mee·see·neez |

| I live with | Birisiyle | bee·ree·seey·le |
| someone. | yaşıyorum. | ya·shuh·yo·room |

I'm ...	Ben ...	ben ...
divorced	boşandım	bo·shan·duhm
married	evliyim	ev·lee·yeem
separated	ayrıldım	ay·ruhl·duhm
single	bekarım	be·ka·ruhm

farewells

Tomorrow is my last day here.

Yarın benim burada   ya·ruhn be·neem boo·ra·da
son günüm.   son gew·newm

If you come to (Scotland) you can stay with me.

Eğer (İskoçya'ya) yolunuz   e·er (ees·koch·ya·ya) yo·loo·nooz
düşerse bende   dew·sher·se ben·de
kalabilirsiniz.   ka·la·bee·leer·see·neez

why oh why

Every time you see a y in the pronunciation guide, pronounce it like the 'y' in 'yes'.

Birader bee-*ra*-der (taken from English 'brother'), *dostum* dos-*toom* (my friend) and *cankuş* jan-*koosh* (mate) are some common terms that men use to address each other. As a sign of respect, men will address their friends' wives as *yenge* yen-*ge* (lit: sister-in-law or aunt). Until you're invited to address your mate's wife by her first name, you should call her *yenge*, too. If your friends are quite a lot older than you, you can call your male friend *abi* a-bee (lit: big brother) and your female friend *abla* ab-*la* (lit: big sister).

Unlike Turkish men, most Turkish women don't use similar terms of endearment among themselves or to men. In some rural and eastern regions the friend's husband would be *enişte* e-neesh-*te* (lit: brother-in-law or uncle), but this isn't very common.

Keep in touch!
   Haberleşelim.   ha-ber-le-she-*leem*

It's been great meeting you.
   Tanıştığımıza çok   ta-nuhsh-tuh-uh-muh-*za* chok
   memnun oldum.   mem-*noon* ol-*doom*

Here's my ...	*İşte benim ...*	eesh-*te* be-*neem* ...
address	*adresim*	ad-re-*seem*
email address	*e-posta adresim*	e-pos-ta ad-re-*seem*
phone number	*telefon*	te-le-fon
	numaram	noo-ma-*ram*

What's your ...?	*Sizin ... nedir?*	see-*zeen* ... *ne*-deer
address	*adresiniz*	ad-re-see-*neez*
email address	*e-posta adresiniz*	e-pos-ta ad-re-see-*neez*
phone number	*telefon*	te-le-*fon*
	numaranız	noo-ma-ra-*nuhz*

Tongue twisters are called *tekerlemeler* te·ker·le·me·*ler* in Turkish, meaning 'roll round' or 'repeat the same thing over and over again'. Give your tongue a workout with this pair:

> *Karaağaç, karaağaç,*
> *kabuğu kara karaağaç,*
> *kabuğu kurumuş kara kuru karaağaç.*
>
> ka·*ra*·a·ach ka·*ra*·a·ach
> ka·boo·*oo* ka·*ra* ka·*ra*·a·ach
> ka·boo·*oo* koo·roo·*moosh* ka·*ra* koo·*roo* ka·*ra*·a·ach
> Elm tree, elm tree;
> its bark, black tree;
> its bark dried-up, black withered elm tree.

> *Hakkı Hakkı'nın hakkını yemiş.*
> *Hakkı Hakkı'dan hakkını istemiş.*
> *Hakkı Hakkı'ya hakkını vermeyince,*
> *Hakkı da haklı olarak Hakkı'nın hakkından gelmiş.*
>
> hak·*kuh* hak·kuh·*nuh* hak·kuh·*nuh* ye·*meesh*
> hak·*kuh* hak·kuh·*dan* hak·kuh·*nuh* ees·te·*meesh*
> hak·*kuh* hak·kuh·*ya* hak·kuh·*nuh* ver·me·yeen·je
> hak·*kuh* da hak·*luh* o·la·*rak* hak·kuh·*nuh*
> hak·kuhn·*dan* gel·*meesh*
> Hakkı cheated Hakkı of his rights.
> Hakkı asked Hakkı for his rights.
> As Hakkı didn't give Hakkı his due,
> Hakkı rightfully paid Hakkı back.

In this chapter, phrases are in the informal *sen* sen (you) form unless otherwise marked. For more detail, see the box on page 30.

common interests

ortak noktalar

What do you do in your spare time?

Boş zamanlarında neler yaparsın?		bosh za·man·la·ruhn·*da* ne·ler ya·*par*·suhn

Do you like …?	… *sever misin?*	… se·*ver* mee·*seen*
I like …	… *seviyorum.*	… se·*vee*·yo·room
I don't like …	… *sevmiyorum.*	… sev·mee·yo·room
calligraphy	*Hat sanatını*	hat sa·na·tuh·*nuh*
cooking	*Yemek pişirmeyi*	ye·mek pee·sheer·me·*yee*
films	*Sinemaya gitmeyi*	see·ne·ma·*ya* geet·me·*yee*
gardening	*Bahçe işlerini*	bah·*che* eesh·le·ree·*nee*
hiking	*Yürüyüş yapmayı*	yew·rew·*yewsh* yap·ma·*yuh*
marbling paper	*Ebru sanatını*	eb·*roo* sa·na·tuh·*nuh*
photography	*Fotoğrafçılığı*	fo·to·raf·chuh·luh·*uh*
reading	*Okumayı*	o·koo·ma·*yuh*
shopping	*Alış-veriş yapmayı*	a·luhsh·ve·*reesh* yap·ma·*yuh*
sport	*Sporu*	spo·*roo*
travelling	*Seyahat etmeyi*	se·ya·*hat* et·me·*yee*
watching TV	*Televizyon seyretmeyi*	te·le·veez·*yon* say·ret·me·*yee*

For types of sports, see **sport**, page 141, and the **dictionary**.

music

Do you ...?	*... misin?* inf	... mee-*seen*
	... misiniz? pol	... mee-see-*neez*
dance	*Dans eder*	dans e-*der*
go to concerts	*Konserlere gider*	kon-ser-le-*re* gee-*der*
listen to music	*Müzik dinler*	mew-*zeek* deen-*ler*
play an	*Müzik aleti*	mew-*zeek* a-le-*tee*
instrument	*çalmayı bilir*	chal-ma-*yuh* bee-*leer*
sing	*Şarkı söyler*	shar-*kuh* say-*ler*
What ...	*Hangi ...*	*han*-gee ...
do you like?	*seversin?* inf	se-*ver*-seen
	Hangi ...	*han*-gee ...
	seversiniz? pol	se-*ver*-see-neez
bands	*gurupları*	goo-*roop*-la-*ruh*
music	*müziği*	mew-zee-*ee*
singers	*şarkıcıları*	shar-*kuh*-juh-la-*ruh*
blues	*blues*	blooz
classical music	*klasik müzik*	kla-*seek* mew-*zeek*
electronic music	*elektronik müzik*	e-lek-tro-*neek* mew-*zeek*
jazz	*caz*	jaz
Ottoman	*klasik Türk*	kla-*seek* tewrk
classical music	*musikisi*	moo-see-kee-*see*
pop	*pop*	pop
rock	*rok*	rok
... music	*... müziği*	... mew-zee-*ee*
Ottoman	*tasavvuf*	ta-sav-*voof*
religious		
traditional	*geleneksel Türk*	ge-le-nek-*sel* tewrk
Turkish		
Turkish folk	*Türk halk*	tewrk halk
world	*dünya*	dewn-*ya*

Planning to go to a concert? See **tickets**, page 49, and **going out**, page 125.

116

cinema & theatre

I feel like going to a ...	*Canım ... izlemeye gitmek istiyor.*	ja·*nuhm* ... eez·le·me·*ye* geet·*mek* ees·*tee*·yor
The ... was good, wasn't it?	*... güzeldi, değil mi?*	... gew·*zel*·dee de·*eel* mee
ballet	*bale*	ba·*le*
film	*film*	feelm
play	*oyun*	o·*yoon*

I thought it was ...	*Bence ...*	ben·*je* ...
excellent	*mükemmeldi*	mew·kem·*mel*·dee
long	*çok uzundu*	chok oo·*zoon*·doo
OK	*fena değildi*	fe·*na* de·*eel*·dee

What's showing at the cinema/theatre tonight?
Bu akşam sinemada/ tiyatroda ne oynuyor?
boo ak·*sham* see·ne·ma·*da*/ tee·yat·ro·*da* ne oy·*noo*·yor

Is it in (English)?
(İngilizce) mi?
(een·gee·*leez*·je) mee

Does it have (English) subtitles?
(İngilizce) Alt yazısı var mı?
(een·gee·*leez*·je) alt ya·zuh·*suh* var muh

Have you seen (Firuze)?
(Firuze'yi) izlediniz mi?
(fee·*roo*·ze·yee) eez·le·dee·*neez* mee

Who's in it?
Kim oynuyor?
keem oy·*noo*·yor

It stars (Demet Akbağ).
(Demet Akbağ) oynuyor.
(de·met ak·*ba*) oy·*noo*·yor

Is this seat taken?
Bu koltuk boş mu?
boo kol·*took* bosh moo

I like ...	... seviyorum.	... se·vee·yo·room
I don't like ...	... sevmiyorum.	... sev·mee·yo·room
action movies	Macera filmlerini	ma·je·ra feelm·le·ree·nee
animated films (Turkish)	Animasyonları (Türk)	a·nee·mas·yon·la·ruh (tewrk)
cinema	sinemasını	see·ne·ma·suh·nuh
comedies	Komedi filmlerini	ko·me·dee feelm·le·ree·nee
documentaries	Belgeselleri	bel·ge·sel·le·ree
drama	Dramları	dram·la·ruh
horror movies	Korku filmlerini	kor·koo feelm·le·ree·nee
sci-fi	Bilim-kurguları	bee·leem·koor·goo·la·ruh
short films	Kısa filmleri	kuh·sa fee·leem·le·ree
thrillers	Heyecan filmlerini	he·ye·jan feelm·le·ree·nee
war movies	Savaş filmlerini	sa·vash feelm·le·ree·nee

french, italian & german

As you start to learn Turkish, you'll notice that there are many words adopted from both French and Italian (and one from German). Francophones will pick up on *garson* gar·son (waiter), *plaj* plazh (beach) and *jeton* zhe·ton (token), among many others. Italian speakers will spot *banka* ban·ka (bank), *bavul* ba·vool (suitcase) and *numara* noo·ma·ra (number). German speakers will notice *otoban* o·to·ban for 'motorway'. The pronunciation of these words may have changed slightly from the original, but if you pronounce them with a French, Italian or German accent you'll be understood.

In this chapter, phrases are in the informal *sen* sen (you) form only. If you're not sure what this means, see the box on page 30.

feelings

duygular

Are you ...?

cold	*Üşüdün mü?*	ew·shew·*dewn* mew
happy	*Mutlu musun?*	moot·*loo* moo·*soon*
hot	*Sıcakladın mı?*	suh·jak·la·*duhn* muh
hungry	*Aç mısın?*	ach muh·*suhn*
thirsty	*Susadın mı?*	soo·sa·*duhn* muh
tired	*Yorgun musun?*	yor·*goon* moo·*soon*
worried	*Bir endişen mi var?*	beer en·dee·*shen* mee var

I'm ...

cold	*Üşüdüm.*	ew·shew·*dewm*
happy	*Mutluyum.*	moot·*loo*·yoom
hot	*Sıcakladım.*	suh·jak·la·*duhm*
hungry	*Açım.*	*a*·chuhm
thirsty	*Susadım.*	soo·sa·*duhm*
tired	*Yorgunum.*	yor·*goo*·noom
worried	*Biraz endişeliyim.*	*bee*·raz en·dee·she·*lee*·yeem

I'm not ...

cold	*Üşümedim.*	ew·*shew*·me·deem
happy	*Mutlu değilim.*	moot·*loo* de·ee·leem
hot	*Sıcaklamadım.*	suh·jak·*la*·ma·duhm
hungry	*Aç değilim.*	ach de·*ee*·leem
thirsty	*Susamadım.*	soo·*sa*·ma·duhm
tired	*Yorgun değilim.*	yor·*goon* de·*ee*·leem
worried	*Endişeli değilim.*	en·dee·she·*lee* de·*ee*·leem

showing your feelings		
a little	*biraz*	bee·raz
I'm a little sad.	*Biraz üzgünüm.*	bee·raz ewz·*gew*·newm
very/extremely	*çok*	chok
I feel very lucky.	*Kendimi çok şanslı hissediyorum.*	ken·dee·*mee* chok shans·*luh* hees·se·dee·yo·room

What happened?
Ne oldu? ne ol·*doo*

What's wrong with you?
Neyin var? ne·*yeen* var

If you're not feeling well, see **health**, page 191.

opinions

fikirler

Did you like it?
Beğendin mi? be·en·*deen* mee

What do you think of it?
Bunun için ne düşünüyorsun? boo·*noon* ee·*cheen* ne dew·shew·*new*·yor·soon

It's ...	*O ...*	o ...
I thought it was ...	*... olduğunu düşünüyorum.*	... ol·doo·oo·*noo* dew·shew·*new*·yo·room
awful	*korkunç*	kor·*koonch*
beautiful	*güzel*	gew·*zel*
boring	*sıkıcı*	suh·kuh·*juh*
great	*harika*	ha·ree·*ka*
interesting	*ilginç*	eel·*geench*
OK	*idare eder*	ee·da·re e·*der*
strange	*acayip*	a·ja·*yeep*
too expensive	*çok pahalı*	chok pa·ha·*luh*

SOCIAL

120

politics & social issues

Who do you vote for?
Oyunu kime verirsin?　　o·yoo·*noo* kee·me ve·*reer*·seen

I support	*... partisini*	... par·*tee*·see·*nee*
the ... party.	*destekliyorum.*	des·tek·*lee*·yo·room
I'm a member	*... parti üyesiyim.*	... par·*tee* ew·ye·see·yeem
of the ... party.		
communist	*Komünist*	ko·mew·*neest*
conservative	*Muhafazakarların*	moo·ha·fa·za·kar·la·*ruhn*
democratic	*Demokratların*	de·mok·rat·la·*ruhn*
green	*Yeşiller*	ye·sheel·*ler*
liberal	*Liberallerin*	lee·be·ral·le·*reen*
social	*Sosyal*	sos·*yal*
democratic	*demokratların*	de·mok·rat·la·*ruhn*
socialist	*Sosyalistlerin*	sos·ya·leest·le·*reen*

Do you agree with it?
Katılıyor musun?　　ka·tuh·*luh*·yor moo·*soon*

I agree with ...
... ile aynı fikirdeyim.　　... ee·le ai·*nuh* fee·keer·*de*·yeem

I don't agree with ...
... ile aynı fikirde　　... ee·le ai·*nuh* fee·keer·*de*
değilim.　　de·*ee*·leem

How do people feel about ...?
Herkes ... hakkında　　*her*·kes ... hak·kuhn·*da*
ne düşünüyor?　　ne dew·shew·*new*·yor

How can we support ...?
... konusuna nasıl　　... ko·noo·soo·*na na*·suhl
destek verebiliriz?　　des·*tek* ve·re·bee·lee·*reez*

Justice and Development Party
*AKP (Adalet ve
Kalkınma Partisi)*
a·ke·pe (a·da·*let* ve
kal·kuhn·*ma* par·tee·*see*)

Motherland Party
ANAP (Anavatan Partisi)
a·*nap* (a·*na*·va·tan par·tee·*see*)

People's Republican Party
*CHP (Cumhuriyet
Halk Partisi)*
je·he·*pe* (joom·hoo·ree·*yet*
halk par·tee·*see*)

Democratic Left Party
*DSP (Demokratik
Sol Parti)*
de·se·*pe* (de·mok·ra·*teek*
sol par·*tee*)

True Road Party
DYP (Doğru Yol Partisi)
de·ye·*pe* (do·*roo* yol par·tee·*see*)

Nationalist Movement Party
*MHP (Milliyetçi
Hareket Partisi)*
me·he·*pe* (meel·lee·yet·*chee*
ha·re·*ket* par·tee·*see*)

Social Democratic People's Party
*SHP (Sosyal Demokrat
Halk Partisi)*
se·he·*pe* (sos·*yal* de·mok·*rat*
halk par·tee·*see*)

Prosperity Party
SP (Saadet Partisi)
se·*pe* (sa·a·*det* par·tee·*see*)

abortion	*çocuk aldırma*	cho·*jook* al·duhr·*ma*
animal rights	*hayvan hakları*	hai·van hak·la·*ruh*
corruption	*yolsuzluk*	yol·sooz·*look*
crime	*suç*	sooch
discrimination	*ayrım*	ai·*ruhm*
drugs	*uyuşturucular*	oo·yoosh·too·roo·joo·*lar*
the economy	*ekonomi*	e·ko·no·*mee*
education	*eğitim*	e·ee·*teem*
the environment	*çevre*	chev·*re*
equal opportunity	*fırsat eşitliği*	fuhr·*sat* e·sheet·lee·*ee*
the European Union	*Avrupa Birliği*	av·roo·pa beer·lee·*ee*
euthanasia	*ötenazi*	er·te·na·*zee*

globalisation	globalleşme	glo·bal·lesh·me
human rights	insan hakları	een·san hak·la·ruh
immigration	göç	gerch
inequality	eşitsizlik	e·sheet·seez·leek
Kurdish separatism	kürt ayrımı	kewrt ai·ruh·muh
military intervention in government	askeri darbe	as·ke·ree dar·be
party politics	parti politikası	par·tee po·lee·tee·ka·suh
poverty	yoksulluk	yok·sool·look
privatisation	özelleştirme	er·zel·lesh·teer·me
racism	ırkçılık	uhrk·chuh·luhk
religious fundamentalism	din fanatizmi	deen fa·na·teez·mee
sexism	cins ayrımı	jeens ai·ruh·muh
social welfare	toplum refahı	top·loom re·fa·huh
terrorism	terörizm	te·rer·reezm
unemployment	işsizlik	eesh·seez·leek
the wearing of headscarves	başörtüsü takmak	bash·er·tew·sew tak·mak

the environment

Is there a ... problem here?
 *Burada bir ...
 problemi mi var?*
boo·ra·da beer ...
prob·le·mee mee var

What should be done about ...?
 *... ile ilgili ne
 yapılmalı?*
... ee·le eel·gee·lee ne
ya·puhl·ma·luh

Is this a protected (forest)?
 *Bu koruma altına
 alınmış bir (orman mı)?*
boo ko·roo·ma al·tuh·na
a·luhn·muhsh beer (or·man muh)

air pollution	hava kirliliği	ha·*va* keer·lee·lee·*ee*
conservation	koruma	ko·roo·*ma*
construction of oil pipelines	petrol boru hatlarının yapımı	pet·*rol* bo·*roo* hat·la·ruh·*nuhn* ya·puh·*muh*
dam-building projects	baraj inşa projesi	ba·*razh* een·*sha* pro·zhe·*see*
drought	kuraklık	koo·rak·*luhk*
ecosystem	ekosistem	e·ko·sees·*tem*
endangered species	nesli tükenmekte olan türler	nes·*lee* tew·ken·mek·*te* o·*lan* tewr·*ler*
GAP (South-East Anatolia dam-building project)	Güney Doğu Anadolu Projesi	gew·*nay* do·oo a·*na*·do·loo pro·zhe·*see*
genetically modified food	genetiği değiştirilmiş gıdalar	ge·ne·tee·*ee* de·eesh·tee·reel·*meesh* guh·da·*lar*
hunting	avlanma	av·lan·*ma*
hydroelectricity	hidro-elektrik	heed·*ro*·e·lek·treek
immigration	göç	gerch
irrigation	sulama	soo·la·*ma*
nuclear energy	nükleer enerji	newk·le·*er* e·ner·*zhee*
nuclear testing	nükleer denemeler	newk·le·*er* de·ne·me·*ler*
overfishing	aşırı avlanma	a·shuh·*ruh* av·lan·*ma*
ozone layer	ozon tabakası	o·*zon* ta·ba·ka·*suh*
pesticides	zirai ilaçlar	zee·ra·*ee* ee·lach·*lar*
petroleum transportation through the Bosphorus	Boğaz'da petrol taşımacılığı	bo·az·*da* pet·*rol* ta·shuh·ma·juh·luh·*uh*
pollution	kirlilik	keer·lee·*leek*
recycling	yeniden kazanım	ye·nee·*den* ka·za·*nuhm*
solar power	güneş enerjisi	gew·*nesh* e·ner·zhee·*see*
toxic waste	zehirli atıklar	ze·heer·*lee* a·tuhk·*lar*
water supply	su kaynakları	soo kai·nak·la·*ruh*

In this chapter, phrases are in the informal *sen* sen (you) form unless otherwise marked. For more details, see the box on page 30.

where to go

nereye gitmeli

What's there to do in the evenings?
Akşamları buralarda ak·sham·la·*ruh* boo·ra·lar·*da*
neler yapılabilir? ne·ler ya·puh·*la*·bee·leer

What's on …?	… *görülecek*	… ger·rew·le·*jek*
	neler var?	ne·ler var
locally	*Yerel olarak*	ye·*rel* o·la·*rak*
today	*Bugün*	boo·gewn
tonight	*Bu gece*	boo ge·*je*
this weekend	*Bu hafta sonu*	boo haf·*ta* so·*noo*

Where are the …?	*Buranın … nerede?*	boo·ra·*nuhn* … ne·re·de
clubs	*kulüpleri*	koo·lewp·le·*ree*
gay venues	*gey kulüpleri*	gay koo·lewp·le·*ree*
places to eat	*yemek*	ye·*mek*
	yenilebilecek	ye·nee·le·bee·le·jek
	yerleri	yer·le·*ree*
pubs	*birahaneleri*	bee·ra·ha·ne·le·*ree*

Is there a	*Buranın yerel …*	boo·ra·*nuhn* ye·*rel* …
local … guide?	*rehberi var mı?*	reh·be·*ree* var muh
entertainment	*eğlence*	e·len·*je*
film	*film*	feelm
music	*müzik*	mew·*zeek*

I feel like going to a/the ...	Canım ... gitmek istiyor.	ja·*nuhm* ... geet·*mek* ees·*tee*·yor
bar	bara	ba·*ra*
café	kafeye	ka·fe·*ye*
concert	konsere	kon·se·*re*
film	sinemaya	see·ne·ma·*ya*
folk dance display	halk dansları gösterisine	halk dans·la·*ruh* gers·te·ree·see·*ne*
folk music concert	halk müziği konserine	halk mew·zee·*ee* kon·se·ree·*ne*
hamam (Turkish bath)	hamama	ha·ma·*ma*
nightclub	gece kulübüne	ge·*je* koo·lew·bew·*ne*
party	partiye	par·tee·*ye*
performance	temsile	tem·see·*le*
play	oyuna	o·yoo·*na*
restaurant	restorana	res·to·ra·*na*
seaside	deniz kenarına	de·*neez* ke·na·ruh·*na*
tea house	çay bahçesine	chai bah·che·see·*ne*

invitations

What are you doing ...?	... ne yapıyorsun?	... ne ya·*puh*·yor·soon
now	Şimdi	*sheem*·dee
tonight	Bu akşam	boo ak·*sham*
this weekend	Bu haftasonu	boo haf·*ta*·so·*noo*

We're having a party.
Parti yapıyoruz.   par·*tee* ya·*puh*·yo·rooz

You should come.
Gelmelisin.   gel·me·*lee*·seen

spinning out of control

For some classic Turkish entertainment, check out a *sema ayini* se·*ma* a·yee·*nee*, which is the traditional Mevlevi worship ceremony with *dervişler* der·veesh·*ler* (whirling dervishes). A *hafız* ha·*fuhz* (person who knows the Koran by heart) will intone a prayer to Mevlana (founder of the Mevlevi order), the *ney* nay (reed flute) will be played to release its soul, and the *şeyh* shayh (sheik/master) will bow his head and lead the dervishes into their whirling ritual.

The music you'll hear during the ceremony is the slightly lugubrious *mevlevi müziği* mev·le·*vee* mew·zee·*ee* (*mevlevi* music) which uses a system of tones called *makamlar* ma·kam·*lar*, similar to Western scales. In other situations, you could find yourself listening to *türkü* tewr·*kew* (folk music) or *arabesk* a·ra·*besk*, folk music with an Arabic twist which is slowly gaining kitsch status.

Would you like to go (for a) …?	… *gitmek ister misin?*	… geet·mek ees·ter mee·seen
I feel like going (for a) …	*Canım … gitmek istiyor.*	ja·nuhm … geet·mek ees·tee·yor
coffee	*kahve içmeye*	kah·ve eech·me·ye
dancing	*dansa*	dan·sa
drink	*birşeyler içmeye*	beer·shay·ler eech·me·ye
meal	*yemeğe*	ye·me·e
out	*bir yere*	beer ye·re
tea	*çay içmeye*	chai eech·me·ye
walk	*yürüyüşe*	yew·rew·yew·she

Do you know a good restaurant?
Bildiğin iyi bir restoran var mı?
beel·dee·*een* ee·*yee* beer res·to·*ran* var muh

Do you want to come to the concert with me?
Benimle konsere gelmek ister misin?
be·*neem*·le kon·se·*re* gel·*mek* ees·ter mee·seen

For more on bars, drinks and partying, see **romance**, page 131, and **eating out**, page 155.

responding to invitations

Sure!
Elbette! — el·bet·te

Yes, I'd love to.
Evet, çok sevinirim. — e·*vet* chok se·vee·*nee*·reem

That's very kind of you.
Çok naziksin. — chok na·zeek·*seen*

Where shall we go?
Nereye gideceğiz? — ne·re·ye gee·de·*je*·eez

What about tomorrow?
Yarına ne dersin? — ya·ruh·na ne *der*·seen

No, I'm afraid I can't.
Üzgünüm ama gelemem. — ewz·*gew*·newm a·*ma* ge·*le*·mem

Sorry, I can't …	*Üzgünüm ama ben … pek bilmiyorum.*	ewz·*gew*·newm a·*ma* ben … pek *beel*·mee·yo·room
dance	*dans etmeyi*	dans et·me·*yee*
sing	*şarkı söylemeyi*	shar·*kuh* say·le·me·*yee*

arranging to meet

What time will we meet?
Saat kaçta buluşacağız? — sa·*at* kach·*ta* boo·loo·sha·*ja*·uhz

Where will we meet?
Nerede buluşacağız? — ne·re·de boo·loo·sha·*ja*·uhz

I'll pick you up.
Seni alırım. — se·*nee* a·*luh*·ruhm

Let's meet at …	*… buluşalım.*	… boo·loo·*sha*·luhm
(eight) o'clock	*Saat (sekizde)*	sa·*at* (se·keez·*de*)
the entrance	*Girişte*	gee·reesh·*te*

Are you ready?
Hazır mısın?   ha·*zuhr* muh·*suhn*

I'm ready.
Hazırım.   ha·*zuh*·ruhm

I'll be coming later.
Ben daha geç   ben da·*ha* gech
orada olacağım.   o·ra·*da* o·la·*ja*·uhm

Where will you be?
Siz nerede olacaksınız?   seez ne·re·de o·la·*jak*·suh·nuhz

If I'm not there by (nine), don't wait for me.
Eğer (dokuza) kadar   e·*er* (do·koo·*za*) ka·*dar*
orada olmazsam   o·ra·*da* ol·*maz*·sam
beni beklemeyin.   be·*nee* bek·*le*·me·yeen

I'll see you then.
O zaman görüşürüz.   o za·*man* ger·rew·*shew*·rewz

See you later/tomorrow.
Sonra/yarın görüşürüz.   *son*·ra/*ya*·ruhn ger·rew·*shew*·rewz

I'm looking forward to it.
Dört gözle bekliyorum.   dert gerz·*le* bek·*lee*·yo·room

Sorry I'm late.
Özür dilerim, geciktim.   er·*zewr* dee·*le*·reem ge·jeek·*teem*

Never mind.
Sağlık olsun.   sa·*luhk* ol·*soon*

drugs

Do you want to have a smoke?
Bir fırt çekmek ister   beer fuhrt chek·*mek* ees·*ter*
misin?   mee·*seen*

Do you have a light?
Ateşin var mı?   a·te·*sheen* var muh

I take ... occasionally.
Ara sıra ... alıyorum.   a·*ra* suh·*ra* ... a·*luh*·yo·room

I'm high.
Kafam iyi.

ka·*fam* ee·*yee*

I don't take drugs.
Uyuşturucu
kullanmıyorum.

oo·yoosh·too·roo·*joo*
kool·*lan*·muh·yo·room

If the police are talking to you about drugs, see **essentials**, page 190, for useful phrases.

sex rules

Gender boundaries in Turkey are more strictly observed in some venues than others. For women travellers who'd like to have a drink or two, the best option is the Western-style *barlar* bar·*lar* (bars) which can be found in most tourist destinations. Traditional Turkish watering holes, like the *meyhane* may·*ha*·ne (wine-house) and *birahane* bee·ra·*ha*·ne (beer-house), are all-male preserves and women generally aren't welcome. As a general rule, Turkish women don't drink because they're Muslims, and foreign women overindulging in public isn't well regarded.

The sexes are segregated when bathing at *hamamlar* ha·mam·*lar* (hamams). Sometimes baths will be designated for *erkekler* er·kek·*ler* (men) and *kadınlar* ka·duhn·*lar* (women), or separate bathing times may be posted. Both men and women are offered a *peştemal* pesh·te·*mal* (short, thin sarong), *takunya* ta·*koon*·ya (wooden clogs) and, after the bath, a *havlu* hav·*loo* (towel). Etiquette says that men keep their *peştemal* on at all times, while women could keep their underwear on beneath their *peştemal* until they've assessed the acceptable way to behave in that particular *hamam*.

When visiting mosques or temples, both men and women should wear modest clothing – no t-shirts, singlets or tatty travelling rags. Women should cover their head, arms and shoulders, and wear modest knee-length dresses. A *türban* tewr·*ban* or *eşarp* e·*sharp* (headscarf) can be borrowed (or 'rented' with a donation) at most temples if needed. Kick off your shoes as you go in.

SOCIAL

130

In this chapter, phrases are in the informal *sen* sen (you) form only. If you're not sure what this means, see the box on page 30.

asking someone out

birisine çıkma teklif ederken

Where would you like to go (tonight)?
(Bu akşam) Nereye   (boo ak·*sham*) ne·re·ye
gitmek istersin?   geet·*mek* ees·*ter*·seen

Would you like to do something (tomorrow)?
(Yarın) Birşeyler   (*ya*·ruhn) beer·shay·*ler*
yapmak ister misin?   yap·*mak* ees·ter mee·*seen*

Yes, I'd love to.
Evet, çok sevinirim.   e·*vet* chok se·vee·*nee*·reem

Sorry, I can't.
Üzgünüm, bir   ewz·*gew*·newm beer
yere gidemem.   ye·*re* gee·*de*·mem

pick-up lines

tanışma sözleri

Would you like a drink?
Bir içki ister misiniz?   beer eech·*kee* ees·ter mee·see·*neez*

You have beautiful eyes.
Ne kadar güzel   ne ka·*dar* gew·*zel*
gözleriniz var.   gerz·le·ree·*neez* var

You look like someone I know.
Tanıdığım birisine   ta·nuh·duh·*uhm* bee·ree·see·*ne*
benziyorsunuz.   ben·*zee*·yor·soo·nooz

You're a fantastic dancer.
Harika dans ediyorsunuz.   ha·ree·*ka* dans e·*dee*·yor·soo·nooz

Do you have a light?
Ateşiniz var mı?   a·te·shee·*neez* var muh

Can I ...?	... *miyim?*	... mee·*yeem*
dance with you	*Sizinle dans edebilir*	see·*zeen*·le dans e·*de*·bee·leer
sit here	*Buraya oturabilir*	boo·ra·*ya* o·too·ra·bee·leer
give you a lift home	*Sizi eve bırakabilir*	see·*zee* e·*ve* buh·ra·*ka*·bee·leer

rejections

No, thank you.
Hayır, teşekkürler.   ha·yuhr te·shek·kewr·*ler*

I'd rather not.
Hayır istemiyorum.   ha·*yuhr* ees·*te*·mee·yo·room

I'm here with my girlfriend/boyfriend.
Kız/Erkek arkadaşımla buradayım.   kuhz/er·*kek* ar·ka·da·*shuhm*·la boo·ra·*da*·yuhm

Excuse me, I have to go now.
Üzgünüm ama hemen gitmem gerekli.   ewz·*gew*·newm a·*ma* he·*men* geet·*mem* ge·rek·*lee*

local talk		
Leave me alone!	*Git başımdan!*	geet ba·shuhm·*dan*
Piss off!	*Defol!*	*de*·fol

getting closer

I like you very much.
Seni çok beğeniyorum.   se·nee chok be·e·nee·yo·room

You're great.
Harikasın.   ha·ree·ka·suhn

Can I kiss you?
Seni öpebilir miyim?   se·nee er·pe·bee·leer mee·yeem

Do you want to come inside for a while?
Biraz içeri gelmek   bee·raz ee·che·ree gel·mek
ister misin?   ees·ter mee·seen

Do you want a massage?
Sana masaj yapmamı   sa·na ma·sazh yap·ma·muh
ister misin?   ees·ter mee·seen

Can I stay over?
Bu gece burada   boo ge·je boo·ra·da
kalabilir miyim?   ka·la·bee·leer mee·yeem

local talk

He/She is ...

a babe	Bebek gibi.	be·bek gee·bee
hot	Çok seksi.	chok sek·see
an idiot	Aptalın teki o.	ap·ta·luhn te·kee o
very attractive	Çok çekici.	chok che·kee·jee
full of himself/	Kendini	ken·dee·nee
herself	beğenmiş.	be·en·meesh

He/She gets around.
İnsanı kandırmayı   een·sa·nuh kan·duhr·ma·yuh
iyi biliyor.   ee·yee bee·lee·yor

He's a bastard.
Piçin teki.   pee·cheen te·kee

She's a bitch.
Orospunun teki o.   o·ros·poo·noon te·kee o

sex

Kiss me.
Öp beni. — erp be·*nee*

I want you.
Seni istiyorum. — se·*nee* ees·*tee*·yo·room

Let's go to bed.
Hadi yatalım. — *ha*·dee ya·ta·*luhm*

Touch me here.
Dokun bana. — do·*koon* ba·*na*

Do you like this?
Hoşuna gidiyor mu? — ho·shoo·*na* gee·*dee*·yor moo

I like that.
Çok hoşuma gidiyor. — chok ho·shoo·*ma* gee·*dee*·yor

I don't like that.
Bundan hiç hoşlanmadım. — boon·*dan* heech hosh·*lan*·ma·duhm

I think we should stop now.
Daha ileri gitmeyelim. — da·*ha* e·le·*ree* geet·me·ye·leem

Do you have a (condom)?
(Prezervatifin) var mı? — (pre·zer·va·tee·*feen*) var muh

Let's use a (condom).
(Prezervatif) kullanalım. — (pre·zer·va·*teef*) kool·la·na·*luhm*

I won't do it without protection.
Korunmasız yapmam. — ko·roon·ma·*suhz yap*·mam

sweet nothings

My beauty.	*Güzelim.*	gew·ze·*leem*
My darling.	*Sevgilim.*	sev·gee·*leem*
My dear.	*Canım.*	ja·*nuhm*
My only one.	*Bir tanem.*	beer ta·*nem*
My sweetie.	*Tatlım.*	tat·*luhm*

SOCIAL

134

It's my first time.
   Bu benim ilk defam.   boo be·*neem* eelk de·*fam*

Don't worry, I'll do it myself.
   Endişelenme ben   en·dee·she·*len*·me ben
   hallederim.   hal·le·*de*·reem

Oh my god!	*Aman tanrım!*	a·man tan·*ruhm*
That's great.	*Harika!*	ha·ree·*ka*
Easy tiger!	*Yavaş ol!*	ya·*vash* ol

faster	*daha hızlı*	da·*ha* huhz·*luh*
harder	*daha kuvvetli*	da·*ha* koov·vet·*lee*
slower	*daha yavaş*	da·*ha* ya·*vash*
softer	*daha yumuşak*	da·*ha* yoo·moo·*shak*

That was ...		
amazing	*Harikaydı.*	ha·ree·*kai*·duh
romantic	*Romantikti.*	ro·man·*teek*·tee
wild	*Çılgınlıktı.*	chuhl·guhn·*luhk*·tuh

love

I think we're good together.
   Birbirimizi   beer·bee·ree·mee·*zee*
   tamamlıyoruz.   ta·mam·*luh*·yo·rooz

I love you.
   Seni seviyorum.   se·*nee* se·*vee*·yo·room

Will you ...?	*... misin?*	*... mee·seen*
go out	*Benimle*	be·*neem*·le
with me	*çıkmak ister*	chuhk·*mak* ees·*ter*
meet my	*Anne ve babamla*	an·ne ve ba·bam·*la*
parents	*tanışmak ister*	ta·nuhsh·*mak* ees·*ter*
marry me	*Benimle evlenir*	be·*neem*·le ev·le·*neer*

romance

135

problems

Are you seeing someone else?
Yoksa bir başkasıyla   *yok*·sa beer bash·ka·*suhy*·la
mı çıkıyorsun?   muh chuh·*kuh*·yor·soon

He/She is just a friend.
O sadece bir arkadaş.   o sa·de·*je* beer ar·ka·*dash*

You're just using me for sex.
Beni sadece seks   be·*nee* sa·de·*je* seks
için kullanıyorsun.   ee·*cheen* kool·la·*nuh*·yor·soon

I never want to see you again.
Seni bir daha asla   se·*nee* beer da·*ha as*·la
görmek istemiyorum.   ger·mek ees·*te*·mee·yo·room

I don't think it's working out.
Bence bu ilişki   ben·*je* boo ee·leesh·*kee*
yürümüyor.   yew·*rew*·mew·yor

We'll work it out.
Bir çözüm bulacağımıza   beer cher·*zewm* boo·la·ja·uh·muh·*za*
inanıyorum.   ee·na·*nuh*·yo·room

leaving

I have to leave (tomorrow).
(Yarın) Gitmem gerekli.   (ya·ruhn) geet·*mem* ge·rek·*lee*

I'll …	*Seni …*	se·*nee* …
keep in touch	*arayacağım*	a·ra·ya·*ja*·uhm
miss you	*özleyeceğim*	erz·le·ye·*je*·eem
visit you	*görmeye*	ger·me·*ye*
	geleceğim	ge·le·*je*·eem

SOCIAL

beliefs & cultural differences

inançlar & kültürel farklılıklar

religion

din

What's your religion?
Dininiz nedir? pol   dee·nee·*neez* ne·deer
Dinin nedir? inf   dee·*neen* ne·deer

I'm not religious.
Dindar değilim.   deen·*dar* de·ee·leem

I'm (a/an) ...	*Ben ...*	ben ...
agnostic	*agnostiğim*	ag·nos·*tee*·eem
Alevi	*Aleviyim*	a·le·*vee*·yeem
Buddhist	*Budistim*	boo·*dees*·teem
Catholic	*Katoliğim*	ka·to·*lee*·eem
Christian	*Hıristiyanım*	huh·rees·tee·*ya*·nuhm
Hindu	*Hinduyum*	heen·*doo*·yoom
Jehovah's Witness	*Yehova Şahidiyim*	ye·*ho*·va sha·hee·*dee*·yeem
Jewish	*Yahudiyim*	ya·hoo·*dee*·yeem
Muslim	*Müslümanım*	mews·lew·*ma*·nuhm
Shiite	*Şiiyim*	shee·*ee*·yeem
Sunni	*Sünniyim*	sewn·*nee*·yeem

I believe in ...	*Ben ... inanıyorum.*	ben ... ee·na·*nuh*·yo·room
I don't believe in ...	*Ben ... inanmıyorum.*	ben ... ee·*nan*·muh·yo·room
astrology	*astrolojiye*	as·tro·lo·zhee·*ye*
fate	*kadere*	ka·de·*re*
God	*Tanrıya*	tan·ruh·*ya*

Where can I ...?	*Nerede ...?*	ne·re·de
attend mass	*ayin yapabilirim*	a·yeen ya·pa·bee·lee·reem
attend a	*ibadet*	ee·ba·det
service	*edebilirim*	e·de·bee·lee·reem
pray	*dua edebilirim*	doo·a e·de·bee·lee·reem
worship	*ibadet*	ee·ba·det
	yapabilirim	ya·pa·bee·lee·reem

cultural differences

Is this a local or national custom?
Bu yerel mi yoksa   boo ye·rel mee yok·sa
ulusal bir gelenek mi?   oo·loo·sal beer ge·le·nek mee

I don't want to offend you.
Sizi kırmak istemem.   see·zee kuhr·mak ees·te·mem

I'll try it.
Deneyeceğim.   de·ne·ye·je·eem

I'd rather not join in.
Ben size katılmasam   ben see·ze ka·tuhl·ma·sam
daha iyi.   da·ha ee·yee

I'm sorry. I didn't mean to do/say anything wrong.
Özür dilerim.   er·zewr dee·le·reem
Yanlış birşey yapmak/   yan·luhsh beer·shay yap·mak/
söylemek istemedim.   say·le·mek ees·te·me·deem

I'm sorry, it's	*Üzgünüm ama*	ewz·gew·newm a·ma
against my ...	*bu benim ...*	boo be·neem ...
	aykırı.	ai·kuh·ruh
beliefs	*inançlarıma*	ee·nanch·la·ruh·ma
religion	*dinime*	dee·nee·me

This is ...	*Bu çok ...*	boo chok ...
different	*farklı*	fark·luh
fun	*eğlenceli*	e·len·je·lee
interesting	*ilginç*	eel·geench

In this chapter, phrases are in the informal *sen* sen (you) form only. If you're not sure what this means, see the box on page 30.

When's the gallery/museum open?
Galeri/Müze   ga·le·*ree*/mew·ze
ne zaman açılıyor?   ne za·*man* a·chuh·*luh*·yor

What kind of art are you interested in?
Ne tür sanattan   ne tewr sa·nat·*tan*
hoşlanırsın?   hosh·la·*nuhr*·suhn

What's in the collection?
Koleksiyonda neler var?   ko·lek·see·yon·*da* ne·ler var

What do you think of ...?
... hakkında ne   ... hak·kuhn·*da* ne
düşünüyorsun?   dew·shew·*new*·yor·soon

It's an exhibition of ...
Bu bir ... sergisi.   boo beer ... ser·gee·*see*

I'm interested in ...
Ben ... ile   ben ... ee·*lee*
ilgileniyorum.   eel·gee·le·*nee*·yo·room

I like the works of ...
... eserlerini beğeniyorum.   ... e·ser·le·ree·*nee* be·e·*nee*·yo·room

It reminds me of ...
Bana ... hatırlatıyor.   ba·*na* ... ha·tuhr·la·*tuh*·yor

graphic	*grafik*	gra·*feek*
impressionist	*izlenimci*	eez·le·neem·*jee*
Islamic	*İslamcı*	ees·lam·*juh*
modern	*modern*	mo·*dern*
nomadic	*göçebeliğe ait*	ger·che·be·lee·*e* a·*eet*
performance	*eser*	e·*ser*
Renaissance	*Rönesans*	rer·ne·*sans*
Turkish	*geleneksel Türk*	ge·le·nek·*sel* tewrk
traditional art	*sanatı*	sa·na·*tuh*

architecture	mimari	mee·ma·*ree*
art	sanat	sa·*nat*
artwork	sanat eseri	sa·*nat* e·se·*ree*
calligraphy	güzel yazı sanatı	gew·*zel* ya·*zuh* sa·na·*tuh*
carpet	halı	ha·*luh*
weaving	dokumacılığı	do·koo·ma·juh·luh·*uh*
curator	müze müdürü	mew·*ze* mew·dew·*rew*
design n	desen	de·*sen*
embroidery	nakış	na·*kuhsh*
etching	resim hakketme	re·*seem* hak·ket·*me*
	sanatı	sa·na·*tuh*
exhibit n	sergi	ser·*gee*
exhibition hall	sergi salonu	ser·*gee* sa·lo·*noo*
installation	yerleştirme	yer·lesh·teer·*me*
Islamic	İslam mimarisi	ees·*lam* mee·ma·ree·*see*
architecture		
lace-making	dantel işleme	dan·*tel* eesh·le·*me*
metalwork	metal işçiliği	me·*tal* eesh·chee·lee·*ee*
opening	açılış	a·chuh·*luhsh*
painter	ressam	res·*sam*
painting (artwork)	tablo	tab·lo
painting	boyama tekniği	bo·ya·*ma* tek·nee·*ee*
(technique)		
paper marbling	ebru sanatı	eb·*roo* sa·na·*tuh*
period	dönem	der·*nem*
permanent	daimi	da·ee·*mee*
collection	kolleksiyon	ko·lek·see·*yon*
porcelain	porselen	por·se·*len*
pottery	çömlekçilik	cherm·lek·chee·*leek*
print n	baskı	bas·*kuh*
sculptor	heykeltıraş	hay·kel·tuh·*rash*
sculpture	heykeltıraşlık	hay·kel·tuh·rash·*luhk*
statue	heykel	hay·*kel*
studio	stüdyo	stewd·yo
style n	tarz	tarz
technique	teknik	tek·*neek*
woodworking	ahşap	ah·*shap*
	işlemeciliği	eesh·le·me·jee·lee·*ee*

In this chapter, phrases are in the informal *sen* sen (you) form only. If you're not sure what this means, see the box on page 30.

sporting interests

spor merakı

What sport do you follow/play?

Hangi sporu takip ediyorsunuz/ oynuyorsunuz?		*han*·gee spo·*roo* ta·keep e·*dee*·yor·soo·nooz/ oy·*noo*·yor·soo·nooz

I follow ...	*Ben ... oyunlarını takip ederim.*	ben ... o·yoon·la·ruh·*nuh* ta·keep e·de·reem
I play ...	*Ben ... oynarım.*	ben ... oy·*na*·ruhm
football (soccer)	*futbol*	*foot*·bol
tennis	*tenis*	te·*nees*

I do ...	*Ben ... yaparım.*	ben ... ya·*pa*·ruhm
martial arts	*savunma sporları*	sa·voon·*ma* spor·la·*ruh*
scuba diving	*aletli dalış*	a·let·lee da·*luhsh*
wrestling	*güreş*	gew·*resh*

I ...	*Ben ...*	ben ...
cycle	*bisiklete binerim*	bee·seek·le·*te* bee·*ne*·reem
run	*koşarım*	ko·*sha*·ruhm

calling the game

The names and terminology of most sports have been translated into Turkish, but you'll also hear English words used. Use the English terms and you'll be clearly understood.

Do you like (cricket)?
(Kriket) sever misin?   (kree·*ket*) se·*ver* mee·*seen*

Yes, very much.
Evet, çok.   e·*vet* chok

Not really.
Pek değil.   pek de·*eel*

I like watching it.
İzlemeyi severim.   eez·le·me·*yee* se·ve·reem

Who's your favourite …?   *En sevdiğin …?*   en sev·dee·*een* …
    sportsperson   *sporcu kim*   spor·*joo* keem
    team   *takım hangisi*   ta·*kuhm* han·gee·see

going to a game

Would you like to go to a game?
Maça gitmek ister misin?   ma·*cha* geet·mek ees·*ter* mee·*seen*

Who are you supporting?
Kimi tutuyorsun?   *kee*·mee too·*too*·yor·soon

Who's playing/winning?
Kim oynuyor/kazanıyor?   keem oy·*noo*·yor/ka·za·*nuh*·yor

That was a … game!   *… bir oyundu!*   … beer o·*yoon*·doo
    bad   *Berbat*   ber·*bat*
    boring   *Sıkıcı*   suh·kuh·*juh*
    great   *Harika*   ha·ree·*ka*

scoring

What's the score?	*Skor nedir?*	skor *ne*·deer
draw/even	*berabere*	be·*ra*·be·re
love (tennis)	*sıfır sıfır*	suh·*fuhr* suh·*fuhr*
match-point	*maç sayısı*	mach sa·yuh·*suh*
nil	*sıfır*	suh·*fuhr*

playing sport

Do you want to play?
Oynamak ister misin?
oy·na·*mak* ees·*ter* mee·*seen*

Can I join in?
Ben de oynayabilir miyim?
ben de oy·na·*ya*·bee·leer mee·*yeem*

That would be great.
Çok iyi olur.
chok ee·*yee* o·*loor*

I can't.
Yapamam.
ya·*pa*·mam

I have an injury.
Sakatlığım var.
sa·kat·luh·*uhm* var

Your/My point.
Senin/Benim sayım.
se·*neen*/be·*neem* sa·*yuhm*

Kick/Pass it to me!
Bana pas ver!
ba·*na* pas ver

You're a good player.
İyi bir oyuncusun.
ee·*yee* beer o·yoon·*joo*·soon

Thanks for the game.
Oyun için teşekkürler.
o·*yoon* ee·*cheen* te·shek·kewr·*ler*

Where's a good place to ...?	... için neresi iyi?	... ee·*cheen* ne·re·see ee·*yee*
fish	*Balık avlamak*	ba·*luhk* av·la·*mak*
go horse riding	*Ata binmek*	a·*ta* been·*mek*
run	*Koşmak*	kosh·*mak*
ski	*Kayak yapmak*	ka·*yak* yap·*mak*
snorkel	*Şnorkel*	shnor·*kel*
surf	*Sörf yapmak*	serf yap·*mak*

sports talk

What a ...!	Ne ...!	ne ...
goal	goldü	gol-dew
hit/kick	vuruştu	voo-roosh-too
pass	pastı	pas-tuh
performance	oyundu	o-yoon-doo

Where's the nearest ...?	En yakın ... nerede?	en ya-kuhn ... ne-re-de
golf course	golf alanı	golf a-la-nuh
gym	jimnastik salonu	zheem-nas-teek sa-lo-noo
swimming pool	yüzme havuzu	yewz-me ha-voo-zoo
tennis court	tenis kortu	te-nees kor-too

What's the charge per ...?	... ne kadar?	... ne ka-dar
day	Günlüğü	gewn-lew-ew
game	Oyun başına ücreti	o-yoon ba-shuh-na ewj-re-tee
hour	Saati	sa-a-tee
visit	Giriş	gee-reesh

Can I hire a ...?	... kiralayabilir miyim?	... kee-ra-la-ya-bee-leer mee-yeem
ball	Top	top
bicycle	Bisiklet	bee-seek-let
court	Kort	kort
racquet	Raket	ra-ket

Do I have to be a member to attend?
Oynamak için üye — oy-na-mak ee-cheen ew-ye
olmam gerekli mi? — ol-mam ge-rek-lee mee

Is there a women-only session?
Sadece bayanlara özel — sa-de-je ba-yan-la-ra er-zel
programınız var mı? — prog-ra-muh-nuhz var muh

Where are the changing rooms?
Soyunma odaları nerede? — so-yoon-ma o-da-la-ruh ne-re-de

diving

Where's a good diving site?
Dalmak için neresi iyi?   dal·*mak* ee·*cheen* ne·re·see ee·*yee*

I'd like to ...	... *istiyorum.*	... ees·*tee*·yo·room
explore caves/	*Mağaraları/*	ma·a·ra·la·*ruh*/
wrecks	*Batıkları*	ba·tuhk·la·*ruh*
	incelemek	een·je·le·mek
go night diving	*Gece dalışına*	ge·*je* da·luh·shuh·*na*
	çıkmak	chuhk·mak
go scuba diving	*Aletli dalışa*	a·let·*lee* da·luh·*sha*
	çıkmak	chuhk·mak
go snorkelling	*Şnorkelle dalmak*	shnor·*kel*·le dal·*mak*
join a diving	*Dalış turuna*	da·*luhsh* too·roo·*na*
tour	*katılmak*	ka·tuhl·*mak*
learn to dive	*Dalmayı*	dal·ma·*yuh*
	öğrenmek	er·ren·mek

Are there ...?	... *var mı?*	... var muh
currents	*Akıntı*	a·kuhn·*tuh*
sharks	*Köpek balıkları*	ker·*pek* ba·luhk·la·*ruh*
whales	*Balinalar*	ba·lee·na·*lar*

Is the visibility good?
Görüş iyi mi?   ger·*rewsh* ee·*yee* mee

How deep is the dive?
Dalış derinliği nedir?   da·*luhsh* de·reen·lee·*ee* ne·deer

Is it a boat/shore dive?
Tekne/Kıyı dalışı mı?   tek·*ne*/kuh·*yuh* da·luh·*shuh* muh

I need an air fill.
Hava doldurmaya   ha·*va* dol·door·ma·*ya*
ihtiyacım var.   eeh·tee·*ya*·juhm var

I want to hire (a) ...	... kiralamak istiyorum.	... kee·ra·la·*mak* ees·*tee*·yo·room
buoyancy vest	Can yeleği	jan ye·le·*ee*
diving equipment	Dalış malzemeleri	da·*luhsh* mal·ze·me·le·*ree*
flippers	Palet	pa·*let*
mask	Maske	mas·*ke*
regulator	Regülatör	re·gew·la·*ter*
snorkel	Şnorkel	shnor·*kel*
tank	Hava tüpü	ha·*va* tew·*pew*
weight belt	Ağırlık kemeri	a·uhr·*luhk* ke·me·*ree*
wetsuit	Dalış elbisesi	da·*luhsh* el·bee·se·*see*

extreme sports

I'd like to go ...	... yapmak istiyorum.	... yap·*mak* ees·*tee*·yo·room
abseiling	Kaya inişi	ka·*ya* ee·nee·*shee*
caving	Mağaracılık	ma·a·ra·juh·*luhk*
canyoning	Kanyon yürüyüşü	kan·*yon* yew·rew·yew·*shew*
game fishing	Balık tutma yarışı	ba·*luhk* toot·*ma* ya·ruh·*shuh*
hang-gliding	Yelkenkanat uçuşu	yel·*ken*·ka·nat oo·choo·*shoo*
hot-air ballooning	Balon sporu	ba·*lon* spo·*roo*
mountain biking	Dağ bisikleti	da bee·seek·le·*tee*
paragliding	Yamaç paraşütü uçuşu	ya·*mach* pa·ra·shew·*tew* oo·choo·*shoo*
rock climbing	Kaya tırmanışı	ka·*ya* tuhr·ma·nuh·*shuh*
skydiving	Serbest paraşüt uçuşu	ser·*best* pa·ra·*shewt* oo·choo·*shoo*
snowboarding	Board kayağı	bord ka·ya·*uh*
white-water rafting	Rafting	raf·teeng

Is the equipment secure?
Teçhizat emniyetli mi? tech·hee·*zat* em·nee·yet·*lee* mee

Is this safe?
Bu emniyetli mi? boo em·nee·yet·*lee* mee

This is insane.
Delilik bu. de·lee·*leek* boo

For words or phrases you might need while hiking or trekking,
see **outdoors**, page 151, and **camping**, page 71.

fishing

balık avlarken

Where are the good spots?
Balık avlamak için neresi iyi? ba·*luhk* av·la·*mak* ee·*cheen* ne·re·see ee·*yee*

Do I need a fishing permit?
Balık avlama iznine ihtiyacım var mı? ba·*luhk* av·la·*ma* eez·nee·*ne* eeh·tee·ya·*juhm* var muh

Do you do fishing tours?
Balık avlama turları düzenliyor musunuz? ba·*luhk* av·la·*ma* toor·la·*ruh* dew·zen·*lee*·yor moo·soo·*nooz*

What's the best bait?
En iyi yem hangisi? en ee·*yee* yem *han*·gee·see

Are they biting?
Isırırlar mı? uh·suh·*ruhr*·lar muh

What kind of fish are you landing?
Ne tür balık çıkarıyorsunuz? ne tewr ba·*luhk* chuh·ka·*ruh*·yor·soo·nooz

How much does it weigh?
Ağırlığı nedir? a·uhr·luh·*uh* ne·deer

football/soccer

Who plays for (Galatasaray)?
(Galatasaray'da)   (ga·la·*ta*·sa·rai·da)
kimler oynuyor?   *keem*·ler oy·*noo*·yor

He's a great (player).
O çok iyi bir (oyuncu).   o chok ee·*yee* beer (o·yoon·*joo*)

He played brilliantly in the match against (Italy).
(İtalya) maçında   (ee·*tal*·ya) ma·chuhn·*da*
muhteşem oynadı.   mooh·te·*shem* oy·na·*duh*

Which team is at the top of the league?
Hangi takım lig   *han*·gee ta·*kuhm* leeg
birincisi?   bee·reen·jee·*see*

Off to see a match? Check out **going to a game**, page 142.

skiing

How much is a pass?
Giriş ne kadar? — gee·*reesh* ne ka·*dar*

Can I take lessons?
Ders alabilir miyim? — ders a·*la*·bee·leer mee·*yeem*

I'd like to hire …	… kiralamak istiyorum.	… kee·ra·la·*mak* ees·*tee*·yo·room
boots	Kayak ayakkabısı	ka·*yak* a·yak·ka·buh·*suh*
gloves	Kayak eldiveni	ka·*yak* el·dee·ve·*nee*
goggles	Kayak gözlüğü	ka·*yak* gerz·lew·*ew*
poles	Baton	ba·*ton*
skis	Kayak takımı	ka·*yak* ta·kuh·*muh*
a ski suit	Kayak elbisesi	ka·*yak* el·bee·se·*see*
Is it possible to go …?	… yapmak mümkün mü?	… yap·*mak* mewm·*kewn* mew
Alpine skiing	Alp kayağı	alp ka·ya·*uh*
cross-country skiing	Kayaklı koşu	ka·yak·*luh* ko·*shoo*
snowboarding	Board kayağı	bord ka·ya·*uh*
tobogganing	Kar kızağı ile kayak	kar kuh·za·*uh* ee·*le* ka·*yak*
What are the conditions like …?	… kayak koşulları nelerdir?	… ka·*yak* ko·shool·la·*ruh* ne·ler·deer
at Palandöken	Palandöken'de	pa·*lan*·der·ken·de
higher up	Yukarı kısımlarda	yoo·ka·*ruh* kuh·suhm·lar·*da*
on that run	Bu inişin	boo ee·*nee*·sheen

Which are the ... slopes?	Hangi kayak pisti ... kayakçılar için?	han·gee ka·yak pees·tee ... ka·yak·chuh·lar ee·cheen
beginner	amatör	a·ma·ter
intermediate	az deneyimli	az de·ne·yeem·lee
advanced	deneyimli	de·ne·yeem·lee

What level is that slope?
Yamaç yüksekliği nedir?　　ya·mach yewk·sek·lee·ee ne·deer

For more skiing vocabulary, see the **dictionary**.

water sports

su sporları

Can I book a lesson?
Ders için randevu　　ders ee·cheen ran·de·voo
alabilir miyim?　　a·la·bee·leer mee·yeem

Can I hire (a) ...?	... kiralayabilir miyim?	... kee·ra·la·ya·bee·leer mee·yeem
boat	Tekne	tek·ne
canoe	Kano	ka·no
kayak	Kayak	ka·yak
life jacket	Can yeleği	jan ye·le·ee
scuba gear	Dalış malzemeleri	da·luhsh mal·ze·me·le·ree
snorkelling gear	Şnorkel	shnor·kel
water-skis	Su kayağı	soo ka·ya·uh
wetsuit	Dalış elbisesi	da·luhsh el·bee·se·see

Are there any ...?	... var mı?	... var muh
reefs	Kayalıklar	ka·ya·luhk·lar
rips	Anafor	a·na·for
water hazards	Herhangi bir su tehlikesi	her·han·gee beer soo teh·lee·ke·see

For the names of water sports, see the **dictionary**.

hiking

Where can I ...?	Nereden ...?	ne-re-den ...
buy supplies	erzak alabilirim	er-*zak* a-*la*-bee-lee-reem
find someone	bu bölgeyi bilen	boo berl-ge-*yee* bee-*len*
who knows	birisini	bee-ree-see-*nee*
this area	bulabilirim	boo-*la*-bee-lee-reem
get a map	harita	ha-ree-*ta*
	alabilirim	a-*la*-bee-lee-reem
hire hiking	yürüyüş	yew-rew-*yewsh*
gear	malzemeleri	mal-ze-me-le-*ree*
	kiralayabilirim	kee-ra-la-*ya*-bee-lee-reem

How ...?	... nedir?	... ne-deer
high is the	Tırmanış	tuhr-ma-*nuhsh*
climb	yüksekliği	yewk-sek-lee-*ee*
long is the	Patikanın	pa-tee-ka-*nuhn*
trail	uzunluğu	oo-zoon-loo-oo

Is it safe?
Emniyetli mi? em-nee-yet-*lee* mee

Do we need a guide?
Rehbere ihtiyacımız reh-be-*re* eeh-tee-ya-*juh*-muhz
var mı? var muh

Are there guided treks?
Rehberli yürüyüşleriniz reh-ber-*lee* yew-rew-yewsh-le-ree-*neez*
var mı? var muh

Is there a hut?
Orada kulübe var mı? o-ra-*da* koo-lew-*be* var muh

When does it get dark?
Hava ne zaman ha-*va* ne za-*man*
kararıyor? ka-ra-*ruh*-yor

Do we need to take ...?	... almamıza gerek var mı?	... al·ma·muh·za ge·rek var muh
bedding	Uyku tulumu	ooy·koo too·loo·moo
food	Yiyecek	yee·ye·jek
water	Su	soo

Is the track ...?	Patika ...?	pa·tee·ka ...
(well) marked	(iyice) işaretli mi	(ee·yee·je) ee·sha·ret·lee mee
open	açık mı	a·chuhk muh
scenic	manzarası güzel mi	man·za·ra·suh gew·zel mee

Which is the ... route?	En ... yol hangisi?	en ... yol han·gee·see
easiest	kolay	ko·lai
most interesting	ilginç	eel·geench
shortest	kısa	kuh·sa

Where can I find the ...?	... nerede?	... ne·re·de
camping ground	Kamp alanı	kamp a·la·nuh
nearest village	En yakın köy	en ya·kuhn kay
showers	Duşlar	doosh·lar
toilets	Tuvaletler	too·va·let·ler

Where have you come from?
Nereden geliyorsunuz?   ne·re·den ge·lee·yor·soo·nooz

How long did it take?
Yol ne kadar sürdü?   yol ne ka·dar sewr·dew

Does this path go to (Alandız)?
Bu patika (Alandız'a) gider mi?   boo pa·tee·ka (a·lan·duh·za) gee·der mee

Can I go through here?
Buradan geçebilir miyim?   boo·ra·dan ge·che·bee·leer mee·yeem

Is the water OK to drink?
Su içilebilir mi?   soo ee·chee·le·bee·leer mee

I'm lost.
Kayboldum.   kai·bol·doom

beach

plajda

Where's the ... beach?	... nerede?	... ne·re·de
best	En iyi plaj	en ee·yee plazh
nearest	En yakın plaj	en ya·kuhn plazh
nudist	Çıplaklar plajı	chuhp·lak·lar pla·zhuh
public	Halk plajı	halk pla·zhuh

Is it safe to dive/swim here?
Burada dalmak/yüzmek emniyetli mi?   boo·ra·da dal·mak/yewz·mek em·nee·yet·lee mee

Is the water polluted?
Su kirli mi?   soo keer·lee mee

Are there dangerous currents?
Tehlikeli akıntılar var mı?   teh·lee·ke·lee a·kuhn·tuh·lar var muh

What time is high/low tide?
Deniz ne zaman kabarıyor/alçalıyor?   de·neez ne za·man ka·ba·ruh·yor/al·cha·luh·yor

Do we have to pay?
Ödeme yapmamız gerekli mi?   er·de·me yap·ma·muhz ge·rek·lee mee

How much for a/an ...?	... ne kadar?	... ne ka·dar
chair	Şezlong	shez·long
hut	Kalif	ka·leef
umbrella	Şemsiye	shem·see·ye

outdoors

153

weather

What's the weather like?
Hava nasıl?　　　　　ha·*va* na·suhl

It's …	*Hava …*	ha·*va* …
cloudy	*bulutlu*	boo·loot·*loo*
cold	*soğuk*	so·*ook*
freezing	*buz gibi*	booz gee·*bee*
hot	*sıcak*	suh·*jak*
raining	*yağmurlu*	ya·moor·*loo*
snowing	*kar yağışlı*	kar ya·uhsh·*luh*
sunny	*güneşli*	gew·nesh·*lee*
windy	*rüzgarlı*	rewz·gar·*luh*

flora & fauna

bitki & hayvanlar

What … is that?	*Bu hangi …?*	boo *han*·gee …
animal	*hayvan*	hai·*van*
flower	*çiçek*	chee·*chek*
plant	*bitki*	beet·*kee*
tree	*ağaç*	a·*ach*

For geographical and agricultural terms, and names of animals and plants, see the **dictionary**.

local animals & plants

Ankara cat	*Ankara kedisi*	an·ka·ra ke·dee·*see*
bald ibis	*kelaynak*	kel·ai·nak
Caretta turtle	*Caretta Caretta*	ka·ret·ta ka·ret·ta
Kangal dog	*Kangal köpeği*	kan·gal ker·pe·ee
partridge	*keklik*	kek·leek
poppy	*gelincik*	ge·leen·jeek
Van cat	*Van kedisi*	van ke·dee·see

basics

breakfast	kahvaltı	kah·val·*tuh*
lunch	öğle yemeği	er·*le* ye·me·*ee*
dinner	akşam yemeği	ak·*sham* ye·me·*ee*
snack n	hafif yemek	ha·*feef* ye·*mek*
eat v	yemek	ye·*mek*
drink v	içmek	eech·*mek*

I'd like ...	... istiyorum.	... ees·*tee*·yo·room
I'm starving!	Açlıktan ölüyorum!	ach·luhk·*tan* er·*lew*·yo·room

finding a place to eat

Can you recommend a ...?	İyi bir ... tavsiye edebilir misiniz?	ee·*yee* beer ... tav·see·ye e·de·bee·leer mee·see·*neez*
bar	bar	bar
café	kafe	ka·*fe*
fireside kebab restaurant	ocakbaşı kebabçısı	o·*jak*·ba·shuh ke·bab·chuh·*suh*
kebab restaurant	kebabçı	ke·bab·*chuh*
ready-food restaurant	lokanta	lo·*kan*·ta
restaurant	restoran	res·to·*ran*

listen for ...		
Bir dakika.	beer da·kee·*ka*	One moment.
Doluyuz.	do·*loo*·yooz	We're full.
Kapalıyız.	ka·pa·*luh*·yuhz	We're closed.

eating out

155

Where would you go for (a) ...?	... için nereye gidilebilir?	... ee·cheen ne·re·ye gee·dee·le·bee·leer
celebration	Kutlama yapmak	koot·la·ma yap·mak
cheap meal	Ucuz bir yemek yemek	oo·jooz beer ye·mek ye·mek
local specialities	Bu yöreye özgü birşeyler yemek	boo yer·re·ye erz·gew beer·shay·ler ye·mek
I'd like to reserve a table for ...	... bir masa ayırtmak istiyorum.	... beer ma·sa a·yuhrt·mak ees·tee·yo·room
(two) people	(İki) kişilik	(ee·kee) kee·shee·leek
(eight) o'clock	Saat (sekiz) için	sa·at (se·keez) ee·cheen

Are you still serving food?

Yemek servisi halen devam ediyor mu?   ye·mek ser·vee·see ha·len de·vam e·dee·yor moo

How long is the wait?

Ne kadar bekleriz?   ne ka·dar bek·le·reez

---

listen for ...

Afiyet olsun. a·fee·yet ol·soon	**Enjoy your meal.**
Buyurun! boo·yoo·roon	**Here you go!**
Nasıl pişmesini istersiniz? na·suhl peesh·me·see·nee ees·ter·see·neez	**How would you like that cooked?**
Ne arzu edersiniz? ne ar·zoo e·der·see·neez	**What can I get for you?**
Nerede oturmak istersiniz? ne·re·de o·toor·mak ees·ter·see·neez	**Where would you like to sit?**
... sever misiniz? ... se·ver mee·see·neez	**Do you like ...?**
... tavsiye ederim. ... tav·see·ye e·de·reem	**I suggest the ...**

restaurant

I'd like (a/the)...	... istiyorum.	... ees·tee·yo·room
children's menu	Çocuk menüsünü	cho·jook me·new·sew·new
drink list	İçecek listesini	ee·che·jek lees·te·see·nee
half portion	Yarım porsiyon	ya·ruhm por·see·yon
menu (in English)	(İngilizce) menüyü	(een·gee·leez·je) me·new·yew
nonsmoking	Sigara içilmeyen bir yer	see·ga·ra ee·cheel·me·yen beer yer
smoking	Sigara içilen bir yer	see·ga·ra ee·chee·len beer yer
table for (five)	(Beş) kişilik bir masa	(besh) kee·shee·leek beer ma·sa

What would you recommend?
Ne tavsiye edersiniz?   ne tav·see·ye e·der·see·neez

What's in that dish?
Bu yemekte neler var?   boo ye·mek·te ne·ler var

What's that called?
Şuna ne deniliyor?   shoo·na ne de·nee·lee·yor

I'll have that.
Şunu alayım.   shoo·noo a·la·yuhm

Does it take long to prepare?
Hazırlanması uzun sürer mi?   ha·zuhr·lan·ma·suh oo·zoon sew·rer mee

Is it self-serve?
Self servis mi?   self ser·vees mee

Is there a cover charge?
Fiks menü fiyatınız var mı?   feeks me·new fee·ya·tuh·nuhz var muh

Is service included in the bill?
Hesaba servis dahil mi?   he·sa·ba ser·vees da·heel mee

Are these complimentary?

Bunlar müessesenin   boon·*lar* mew·es·se·se·*neen*
ikramı mı?   eek·ra·*muh* muh

How much is that dish?

Şu yemek ne kadar?   shoo ye·*mek* ne ka·*dar*

Can you recommend a good local wine?

Güzel bir yöre şarabı   gew·*zel* beer yer·re sha·ra·*buh*
tavsiye eder misiniz?   tav·see·*ye* e·der mee·see·*neez*

I'd like (a/the)...	... istiyorum.	... ees·tee·yo·room
local	*Bu yöreye özgü*	boo yer·re·ye erz·gew
speciality	*bir yemek*	beer ye·mek
meal fit for	*Krallara layık*	kral·la·ra la·yuhk
a king	*bir yemek*	beer ye·mek
that dish	*Şu yemeği*	shoo ye·me·ee

I'd like it with/	*Yemeğimi*	ye·me·ee·mee
without ...	*... istiyorum.*	... ees·tee·yo·room
black pepper	*kara biberli/*	ka·ra bee·ber·lee/
	kara bibersiz	ka·ra bee·ber·seez
cheese	*peynirli/*	pay·neer·lee/
	peynirsiz	pay·neer·seez
chilli	*acılı/acısız*	a·juh·luh/a·juh·suhz
chilli sauce	*acı soslu/*	a·juh sos·loo/
	acı sossuz	a·juh sos·sooz
garlic	*sarımsaklı/*	sa·ruhm·sak·luh/
	sarımsaksız	sa·ruhm·sak·suhz
ketchup	*ketçaplı/*	ket·chap·luh/
	ketçapsız	ket·chap·suhz
nuts	*fıstıklı/*	fuhs·tuhk·luh/
	fıstıksız	fuhs·tuhk·suhz
oil	*yağlı/yağsız*	ya·luh/ya·suhz
salt	*tuzlu/tuzsuz*	tooz·loo/tooz·sooz
tomato sauce	*domates soslu/*	do·ma·tes sos·loo/
	domates sossuz	do·ma·tes sos·sooz
vinegar	*sirkeli/sirkesiz*	seer·ke·lee/seer·ke·seez

For other specific meal requests, see **vegetarian & special meals**, page 173.

It's considered rude to ask the price of the meal before you've ordered it, and you should always order your drinks while you're contemplating what you'd like to eat. With some foods, such as chicken, it's acceptable to eat with your fingers.

at the table

masada

Please bring (a/the) ...	Lütfen ... getirir misiniz?	lewt·fen ... ge·tee·reer mee·see·neez
bill	hesabı	he·sa·buh
glass	bir bardak	beer bar·dak
serviette	peçete	pe·che·te
cloth	bir masa silme bezi	beer ma·sa seel·me be·zee
wineglass	bir şarap bardağı	beer sha·rap bar·da·uh

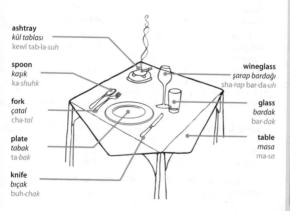

ashtray
kül tablası
kewl tab·la·suh

spoon
kaşık
ka·shuhk

fork
çatal
cha·tal

plate
tabak
ta·bak

knife
bıçak
buh·chak

wineglass
şarap bardağı
sha·rap bar·da·uh

glass
bardak
bar·dak

table
masa
ma·sa

eating out

159

talking food

I love this dish.
Bu yemeğe bayılıyorum.   boo ye·me·*e* ba·yuh·*luh*·yo·room

I love the local cuisine.
Buranın yemeklerine   boo·ra·*nuhn* ye·mek·le·ree·*ne*
bayılıyorum.   ba·yuh·*luh*·yo·room

That was delicious!
Nefisti!   ne·*fees*·tee

I'm full.
Doydum.   doy·*doom*

look for ...

Mezeler	me·ze·*ler*	Appetisers
Çorbalar	chor·ba·*lar*	Soups
Ordövler	or·derv·*ler*	Entrées
Salatalar	sa·la·ta·*lar*	Salads
Ana Yemekler	a·*na* ye·mek·*ler*	Main Courses
Yan Yemekler	yan ye·mek·*ler*	Side Dishes
Tatlılar	tat·luh·*lar*	Desserts
Dondurmalar	don·door·ma·*lar*	Ice Cream
İçecekler	ee·che·jek·*ler*	Drinks
Alkolsüz	al·kol·*sewz*	Soft Drinks
İçecekler	ee·che·jek·*ler*	
Alkollü	al·kol·*lew*	Spirits
İçecekler	ee·che·jek·*ler*	
Bira Çeşitleri	*bee*·ra che·sheet·le·*ree*	Beers
Köpüklü	ker·pewk·*lew*	Sparkling Wines
Şaraplar	sha·rap·*lar*	
Beyaz Şaraplar	be·*yaz* sha·rap·*lar*	White Wines
Kırmızı	kuhr·muh·*zuh*	Red Wines
Şaraplar	sha·rap·*lar*	
Tatlı Şaraplar	tat·*luh* sha·rap·*lar*	Dessert Wines

For more words you might see on a menu, see the **culinary reader**, page 175.

This is ...	Bu ...	boo ...
burnt	*yanık*	ya·*nuhk*
(too) cold	*(çok) soğuk*	(chok) so·*ook*
(too) spicy	*(çok) acı*	(chok) a·*juh*
spoiled	*bozulmuş*	bo·zool·*moosh*
stale	*bayat*	ba·*yat*
superb	*enfes*	en·*fes*
undercooked	*az pişmiş*	az peesh·*meesh*

methods of preparation

I'd like it ...	... *istiyorum.*	... ees·*tee*·yo·room
I don't want it ...	... *istemiyorum.*	... ees·*te*·mee·yo·room
boiled	*Haşlanmış*	hash·lan·*muhsh*
broiled	*Izgara*	uhz·*ga*·ra
fried	*Kızarmış*	kuh·zar·*muhsh*
grilled	*Izgara*	uhz·*ga*·ra
mashed	*Püre*	pew·*re*
medium	*Orta karar*	or·*ta* ka·*rar*
	pişmiş	peesh·*meesh*
rare	*Az pişmiş*	az peesh·*meesh*
reheated	*Isıtılmış*	uh·suh·tuhl·*muhsh*
steamed	*Buharda*	boo·har·*da*
	pişmiş	peesh·*meesh*
well-done	*İyi pişmiş*	ee·*yee* peesh·*meesh*
with the dressing	*Sosunu*	so·soo·*noo*
on the side	*yanında*	ya·nuhn·*da*

on the streets

When roaming Turkey's streets you'll find a great variety of kebabs, burgers and sandwiches to snack on. Try the dainties below, or the round bagel with sesame seeds known as *simit* see·*meet* or *gevrek* gev·*rek*.

balık ekmek	ba·*luhk* ek·*mek*	**fish and bread**
köfte ekmek	kerf·*te* ek·*mek*	**meatballs and bread**

nonalcoholic drinks

tea

Contrary to popular belief, the must-have drink in Turkey is *çay* chai (tea), not *kahve* kah·ve (coffee). You may be offered lemon, but don't expect any milk. Order your tea either *açık* a·chuhk (light) or *koyu* ko·yoo (dark) according to taste. Fruit, flower and herb teas are drunk for their health properties and are usually unsweetened.

cup of tea	*bir fincan çay*	beer feen·*jan* chai
glass of tea	*bir bardak çay*	beer bar·*dak* chai
tall glass of tea	*büyük bardak çay*	bew·*yewk* bar·*dak* chai
apple tea	*elma çayı*	el·*ma* cha·*yuh*
chamomile tea	*papatya çayı*	pa·*pat*·ya cha·*yuh*
cinnamon tea	*tarçın çayı*	tar·*chuhn* cha·*yuh*
fruit tea	*meyve çayı*	may·*ve* cha·*yuh*
island tea (sage)	*ada çayı*	a·*da* cha·*yuh*
lemon tea	*limon çayı*	lee·*mon* cha·*yuh*
linden-flower tea	*ıhlamur çayı*	uh·la·*moor* cha·*yuh*
orange tea	*portakal çayı*	por·ta·*kal* cha·*yuh*
peppermint tea	*nane çayı*	na·ne cha·*yuh*
thyme tea	*kekik çayı*	ke·*keek* cha·*yuh*

coffee

To get a classic 'melt your teaspoon' Turkish coffee, ask for a *Türk kahvesi* tewrk kah·ve·see. Each brew is made with different amounts of sugar – you don't put it in yourself – so order using the phrases on the next page. In the eastern parts of Turkey you can also order *mırra* muhr·ra, 'old-fashioned coffee' flavoured with *kakule* ka·koo·le (cardamom).

(cup of) coffee ...	... bir (fincan) kahve	... beer (feen·jan) kah·ve
with milk	sütlü	sewt·lew
with a little sugar	az şekerli	az she·ker·lee
with some sugar	orta şekerli	or·ta she·ker·lee
with a lot of sugar	çok şekerli	chok she·ker·lee
without sugar	şekersiz/sade	she·ker·seez/sa·de

If European coffee is your poison, try the words below:

... coffee	... bir kahve	... beer kah·ve
black	sütsüz	sewt·sewz
decaffeinated	kafeinsiz	ka·fe·een·seez
iced	buzlu	booz·loo
strong	sert	sert
white	sütlü	sewt·lew

local brews

ayran   ai·ran
A refreshing cold drink made of yogurt, water (or soda water) and salt, usually drunk at mealtimes.

boza   bo·za
A hot, creamy drink made of grain (such as chickpea, bulgur, millet) mixed with cinnamon. It's not drunk with meals and is sold by *bozacı* bo·za·juh (*boza* vendors) who walk the streets at night-time selling their brew.

gül şerbeti   gewl sher·be·tee
A summer drink made with rose-water, water and sugar – a specialty of Sivas.

sahlep   sah·lep
A hot drink of milk and crushed tapioca root extract, usually available in winter. It has a mild, nutty flavour and is drunk mostly for its health and aphrodisiac properties.

şalgam suyu   shal·gam soo·yoo
Juice of dark turnips, served cold and often with a piece of turnip in the glass – a specialty of the Adana region.

under the influence

Turks call 'breakfast' *kahvaltı* kah·val·*tuh*, which literally means 'under coffee' or 'before coffee'.

cold drinks

orange juice	*portakal suyu*	por·ta·*kal* soo·*yoo*
soft drink	*alkolsüz içecek*	al·kol·*sewz* ee·che·*jek*
(hot) water	*(sıcak) su*	(suh·*jak*) soo
... mineral water	*maden ...*	ma·*den* ...
sparkling	*sodası*	so·da·*suh*
still	*suyu*	soo·*yoo*

alcoholic drinks

alkollü içecekler

brandy	*brendi*	*bren*·dee
champagne	*şampanya*	sham·*pan*·ya
cocktail	*kokteyl*	kok·*tayl*
local/imported ...	*... yerli/ithal*	... yer·*lee*/eet·*hal*
vermouth	*vermut*	ver·*moot*
vodka	*votka*	*vot*·ka
whisky	*viski*	*vees*·kee
a shot/glass of ...	*bir tek/bardak ...*	beer tek/bar·*dak* ...
(five-star)	*(beş yıldızlı)*	(besh yuhl·duhz·*luh*)
cognac	*konyak*	kon·*yak*
fruit brandy	*meyveli brendi*	may·ve·*lee* bren·dee
gin	*cin*	jeen
rum	*rom*	rom
a ... of beer	*bir ... bira*	beer ... bee·ra
can	*kutu*	koo·*too*
glass	*bardak*	bar·*dak*
jug	*sürahi*	sew·ra·*hee*
small bottle	*küçük şişe*	kew·*chewk* shee·*she*
large bottle	*büyük şişe*	bew·*yewk* shee·*she*

a bottle/glass	bir şişe/bardak	beer shee·*she*/bar·*dak*
of ... wine	... şarap	... sha·*rap*
dessert	tatlı	tat·*luh*
red	kırmızı	kuhr·muh·*zuh*
rosé	pembe	pem·*be*
sparkling	köpüklü	ker·pewk·*lew*
white	beyaz	be·*yaz*

in the bar

barda

Excuse me!
  Affedersiniz!   a·fe·*der*·see·neez

I'm next.
  Benim sıram.   be·*neem* suh·*ram*

I'll have ...
  ... alayım.   ... a·la·*yuhm*

rakı

Rakı ra·*kuh* is the Turkish national drink, made from fermented grapes flavoured with anise. Naturally a strong, clear alcohol, it becomes cloudy white once you mix it. The traditional *meze* me·*ze* (snack) served with *rakı* is *beyaz peynir* be·*yaz* pay·*neer* (white cheese). It's nicknamed *aslan sütü* as·*lan* sew·*tew*, which means 'lion's milk' and it's apparently considered as mere 'milk to strong, powerful lions like Turkish men'. (Think of the lion-god Aslan in the *Chronicles of Narnia* by C.S. Lewis.)

As befits such a prestigious drink, certain rituals must be followed. *Rakı* should be cooled to 8–10°C before being served, and sipped from a tall cylindrical glass. On no account should you knock it back from a shot glass, and mixing *rakı* with other alcohol is done only at your own peril. Never put ice in the glass before you add the *rakı*, as this changes the taste. It's permitted to mix it with water or soda water, or alternate sips of *rakı* with sips of your mixer of choice. True *rakı* drinkers establish their preferred blend, as personal and ingrained as a signature.

To make toasts with *rakı*, wait until everyone has been served and try not to raise your glass higher than anyone else's. Join in the toast of *Şerefe!* she·re·*fe* (Cheers!) and have fun!

Same again, please.
  Aynısından lütfen.　　　　ai·nuh·suhn·*dan lewt*·fen

No ice, thanks.
  Buz koymayın lütfen.　　　booz koy·ma·yuhn *lewt*·fen

I'll buy you a drink.
  Sana içecek alayım.　　　sa·*na* ee·che·*jek* a·la·*yuhm*

What would you like?
Ne alırsınız?　　　　　　ne a·*luhr*·suh·nuhz

I don't drink alcohol.
Alkol kullanmıyorum.　　al·*kol* kool·*lan*·muh·yo·room

It's my round.
Benim sıram.　　　　　　be·*neem* suh·*ram*

Do you serve meals here?
Yemek servisi　　　　　　ye·mek ser·vee·*see*
yapılıyor mu?　　　　　　ya·puh·*luh*·yor moo

drinking up

The drinks are on me.
İçkiler benden.　　　　　eech·kee·*ler* ben·*den*

Cheers!
Şerefe!　　　　　　　　she·re·*fe*

This is hitting the spot.
Bu çok makbule geçti.　　boo chok mak·boo·*le* gech·*tee*

I feel fantastic!
Kendimi harika　　　　　ken·dee·*mee* ha·ree·*ka*
hissediyorum!　　　　　hees·se·*dee*·yo·room

I think I've had one too many.
Sanırım çok içtim.　　　　sa·*nuh*·ruhm chok eech·*teem*

I'm feeling drunk.
   Sarhoş oldum.   sar·*hosh* ol·*doom*

I'm pissed.
   Zil zurna sarhoşum.   zeel zoor·*na* sar·*ho*·shoom

I feel ill.
   Kendimi kötü   ken·dee·*mee* ker·*tew*
   hissediyorum.   hees·se·*dee*·yo·room

Where's the toilet?
   Tuvalet nerede?   too·va·*let* ne·re·de

I'm tired, I'd better go home.
   Yorgunum, eve gitsem   yor·*goo*·noom e·ve geet·sem
   daha iyi olur.   da·*ha* ee·*yee* o·*loor*

Can you call a taxi for me?
   Bana bir taksi   ba·*na* beer tak·*see*
   çağırır mısınız?   cha·uh·*ruhr* muh·suh·*nuhz*

I don't think you should drive.
   Araba kullanmamalısın. a·ra·*ba* kool·*lan*·ma·ma·luh·suhn

---

what a cucumber!

One Turkish word for 'dickhead' is *hıyar* huh·*yar*, which also
means 'cucumber'.

buying food

What's the local speciality?
*Bu yöreye has
yiyecekler neler?*
boo yer·re·ye has
yee·ye·jek·ler ne·ler

What's that?
Bu nedir?
boo ne·deer

What's pestil?
Pestil nedir?
pes·teel ne·deer

Can I taste it?
*Tadına bakabilir
miyim?*
ta·duh·na ba·ka·bee·leer
mee·yeem

How much (is a kilo of cheese)?
*(Bir kilo peynir)
Ne kadar?*
(beer kee·lo pay·neer)
ne ka·dar

I'd like ...	... istiyorum.	... ees·tee·yo·room
(200) grams	*(İkiyüz) gram*	(ee·kee·yewz) gram
half a dozen	*Yarım düzine*	ya·ruhm dew·zee·ne
a dozen	*Bir düzine*	beer dew·zee·ne
half a kilo	*Yarım kilo*	ya·ruhm kee·lo
a kilo	*Bir kilo*	beer kee·lo
(two) kilos	*(İki) kilo*	(ee·kee) kee·lo
a bottle	*Bir şişe*	beer shee·she
a jar	*Bir kavanoz*	beer ka·va·noz
a packet	*Bir paket*	beer pa·ket
a piece	*Bir parça*	beer par·cha
(three) pieces	*(Üç) parça*	(ewch) par·cha
a slice	*Bir dilim*	beer dee·leem
(six) slices	*(Altı) dilim*	(al·tuh) dee·leem
a tin	*Bir kutu*	beer koo·too

I'd like …	… istiyorum.	… ees·tee·yo·room
(just) a little	(sadece) biraz	(sa·de·je) bee·raz
more	daha fazla	da·ha faz·la
some …	biraz …	bee·raz …
that one	şunu	shoo·noo
this one	bunu	boo·noo

Less.	Daha az.	da·ha az
A bit more.	Biraz daha fazla.	bee·raz da·ha faz·la
Enough.	Yeterli.	ye·ter·lee

Do you have …?	… var mı?	… var muh
anything	Daha ucuz	da·ha oo·jooz
cheaper	birşey	beer·shay
other kinds	Başka	bash·ka
	çeşitleriniz	che·sheet·le·ree·neez

Where can I find the … section?	… reyonu nerede?	… re·yo·noo ne·re·de
dairy	Süt mamülleri	sewt ma·mewl·le·ree
fish	Balık	ba·luhk
frozen goods	Donmuş gıda	don·moosh guh·da
fruit and vegetable	Sebze meyve	seb·ze may·ve
meat	Et	et
poultry	Kümes	kew·mes
	hayvanları et	hai·van·la·ruh et

For food items, see the **culinary reader** and the **dictionary**.

food stuff

cooked	pişmiş	peesh·meesh
cured	terbiye edilmiş	ter·bee·ye e·deel·meesh
dried	kuru	koo·roo
fresh	taze	ta·ze
frozen	donmuş	don·moosh
raw	çiğ	chee
smoked	dumanda	doo·man·da
	kurutulmuş	koo·roo·tool·moosh

meze

Meze me·ze is the Turkish equivalent of Spanish tapas – a selection of small, tasty nibbles served in bars, restaurants and homes. Here's a list of some you're likely to find in your travels:

ançüez	an·chew·ez	pickled anchovy
barbunya pilaki	bar·boon·ya pee·la·kee	red bean salad
beyaz peynir	be·yaz pay·neer	white goat's cheese
beyin salatası	be·yeen sa·la·ta·suh	sheep's brain salad
biber dolması	bee·ber dol·ma·suh	stuffed capsicum
cacık	ja·juhk	yogurt with cucumber and mint
çerkez tavuğu	cher·kez ta·voo·oo	Circassian chicken, made with bread, walnuts, salt and garlic
enginar	en·gee·nar	cooked artichoke
fava	fa·va	mashed broad bean paste
haydari	hai·da·ree	yogurt with roasted eggplant and garlic
humus	hoo·moos	chickpea, tahini and lemon dip
kalamar	ka·la·mar	fried calamari
kısır	kuh·suhr	bulgur salad
lakerda	la·ker·da	sliced and salted tuna
mücver	mewj·ver	deep-fried zucchini fritters
pastırma	pas·tuhr·ma	air-dried beef
patlıcan kızartması	pat·luh·jan kuh·zart·ma·suh	fried eggplant with tomatoes
peynirli börek	pay·neer·lee ber·rek	cheese pastry
yaprak sarma	yap·rak sar·ma	vine leaves stuffed with rice, herbs and pine nuts

cooking utensils

Could I please borrow a ...?	Bir ... ödünç alabilir miyim lütfen?	beer ... er·dewnch a·la·bee·leer mee·yeem lewt·fen
chopping board	kesme tahtası	kes·me tah·ta·suh
frying pan	tava	ta·va
knife	bıçak	buh·chak
saucepan	tencere	ten·je·re
I need a ...	... ihtiyacım var.	... eeh·tee·ya·juhm var
chopping board	Kesme tahtasına	kes·me tah·ta·suh·na
frying pan	Tavaya	ta·va·ya
knife	Bıçağa	buh·cha·a
saucepan	Tencereye	ten·je·re·ye

For more cooking implements, see the **dictionary**.

---

listen for ...

Başka birşey var mı? bash·ka beer·shay var muh		**Anything else?**
Kalmadı. kal·ma·duh		**There isn't any.**
Ne arzu edersiniz? ne ar·zoo e·der·see·neez		**What would you like?**
Yardımcı olabilir miyim? yar·duhm·juh o·la·bee·leer mee·yeem		**Can I help you?**

vegetarian & special meals
vejeteryan & özel yemekler

ordering food

Where's a ...	Buralarda ...	boo·ra·lar·da ...
restaurant?	restoran var mı?	res·to·ran var muh
Do you have	... yiyecekleriniz	... yee·ye·jek·le·ree·neez
... food?	var mı?	var muh
halal	helal	he·lal
kosher	koşer	ko·sher
vegetarian	vejeteryan	ve·zhe·ter·yan

I don't eat ...	... yemiyorum.	... ye·mee·yo·room
Is it cooked	İçinde ... var mı?	ee·cheen·de... var muh
with ...?		
butter	Tereyağ	te·re·ya
eggs	Yumurta	yoo·moor·ta
fish	Balık	ba·luhk
fish stock	Balık suyu	ba·luhk soo·yoo
meat stock	Et suyu	et soo·yoo
oil	Yağ	ya
pork	Domuz eti	do·mooz e·tee
poultry	Tavuk eti	ta·vook e·tee
red meat	Kırmızı et	kuhr·muh·zuh et

I can't eat meat.
Et yiyemiyorum.　　　et yee·ye·mee·yo·room

Do you have any dishes without meat?
Etsiz yemekleriniz var mı?　et·seez ye·mek·le·ree·neez var muh

asking about msg

Use the words *lezzet artırıcılar* lez·zet ar·tuh·ruh·juh·lar (fla-vour enhancers) to ask about MSG. The phrase *monosodyum glutamat* mo·no·sod·yoom gloo·ta·mat does exist but it isn't very well-known.

Is this ...?	Bu ...?	boo ...
decaffeinated	kafeinsiz mi	ka·fe·een·seez mee
free of animal produce	hayvansal ürünler içermiyor, değil mi	hai·van·sal ew·rewn·ler ee·cher·mee·yor de·eel mee
gluten-free	gluten içermiyor, değil mi	gloo·ten ee·cher·mee·yor de·eel mee
low in sugar	az şekerli mi	az she·ker·lee mee
organic	organik mi	or·ga·neek mee
salt-free	tuzsuz mu	tooz·sooz moo

special diets & allergies

I'm a vegan.
Sadece bitkisel besinler yiyorum.
sa·de·je beet·kee·sel be·seen·ler yee·yo·room

I'm (a) ...	Ben ...	ben ...
Buddhist	Budistim	boo·dees·teem
Hindu	Hinduyum	heen·doo·yoom
Jewish	Yahudiyim	ya·hoo·dee·yeem
Muslim	Müslümanım	mews·lew·ma·nuhm
vegetarian	vejeteryanım	ve·zhe·ter·ya·nuhm

I'm allergic to ...	... alerjim var.	... a·ler·zheem var
dairy produce	Süt ürünlerine	sewt ew·rewn·le·ree·ne
eggs	Yumurtaya	yoo·moor·ta·ya
gelatine	Jelatine	zhe·la·tee·ne
gluten	Glutene	gloo·te·ne
honey	Bala	ba·la
nuts	Çerezlere	che·rez·le·re
peanuts	Fıstığa	fuhs·tuh·a
seafood	Deniz ürünlerine	de·neez ew·rewn·le·ree·ne
shellfish	Kabuklu su ürünlerine	ka·book·loo soo ew·rewn·le·ree·ne

This miniguide to Turkish cuisine lists dishes and ingredients in Turkish alphabetical order. It's designed to help you get the most out of your gastronomic experience by providing you with food terms that you may see on menus. For certain dishes we've marked the region or city where they're most popular.

A

acı a-juh hot (spicy)
— **badem** ba-dem bitter almond
— **badem kurabiyesi** ba-dem koo-ra-bee-ye-see almond cookie
acur a-joor gherkin
Adana kebab a-da-na ke-bab spicy meat patty grilled on a poker (Adana)
ağ kabak a ka-bak squash
ağaç çileği a-ach chee-le-ee raspberry
ahlat ah-lat wild pear
ahtapot ah-ta-pot octopus
— **kavurma** ka-voor-ma fried octopus with lemon & parsley
ahtapotlu pilav ah-ta-pot-loo pee-lav rice pilau with sliced octopus (Muğla)
ahududu a-hoo-doo-doo raspberry
akciğer ak-jee-er lung
akıtma a-kuht-ma pancake dessert similar to yassı kadayıf
alacatane a-la-ja-ta-ne starter of onions with lentils & bulgur (Uşak)
alafranga a-la-fran-ga European-style
alaturka a-la-toor-ka Turkish-style
alinazik a-lee-na-zeek eggplant purée with yogurt & meat köfte
alkazar al-ka-zar red wine & lemon drink
Amerikan salatası a-me-ree-kan sa-la-ta-suh Turkish 'Russian salad' – with mayonnaise, chilli sauce & gherkins
ananas a-na-nas pineapple
ançüez an-chew-ez pickled anchovy
Ankara tavası an-ka-ra ta-va-suh lamb with pilau
Antalya piyazı an-tal-ya pee-ya-zuh type of **piyaz** with beans, tahini, capsicum & lemon (Antalya)
Antep fıstığı pilavı an-tep fuhs-tuh-uh pee-la-vuh pilau with pistachios

arabaşı çorbası a-rab-a-shuh chor-ba-suh spicy chicken soup
araka a-ra-ka large peas
armut ar-moot pear
Arnavut biberi ar-na-voot bee-be-ree cayenne • Albanian red capsicum
Arnavut ciğeri ar-na-voot jee-e-ree Albanian fried liver
arpa ar-pa barley
arpacık soğanı ar-pa-juhk so-a-nuh small onion used in soups or casseroles
asma kabağı as-ma ka-ba-uh squash
asma yaprağında sardalya as-ma yap-ra-uhn-da sar-dal-ya sardines in grapevine leaves
aşure a-shoo-re fruit pudding
av eti av e-tee game meat
av kuşu av koo-shoo game bird
ay çöreği ai cher-re-ee croissant
ayşekadın ai-she-ka-duhn green bean
ayşe kızın düğün çorbası ai-she kuh-zuhn dew-ewn chor-ba-suh soup of wheat, meat, yogurt & corn meal
ayva ai-va quince
az pişmiş az peesh-meesh rare (steak)

B

bacak ba-jak leg
badem ba-dem almond
— **ezmesi** ez-me-see almond paste • marzipan
— **şekeri** she-ke-ree sugared almonds
bademli ba-dem-lee with almonds
bakla bak-la broad bean
baklava bak-la-va triangular dessert of pastry stuffed with pistachio & walnuts
bakliyat bak-lee-yat legumes • pulses
bal bal honey
— **kabağı** ka-ba-uh pumpkin

balcan söğürmesi bal-jan ser-ewr-me-see eggplant cooked over hot coals (Konya)

balık ba-luhk fish
— **buğulama** boo-oo-la-ma steamed fish stew
— **tavası** ta-va-suh fried fish platter
— **yahni** yah-nee fish ragout
— **yumurtası** yoo-moor-ta-suh fish roe

bamya bam-ya okra

bamyalı tavuk bam-ya-luh ta-vook chicken with okra

barbunya bar-boon-ya pinto bean
— **pilaki** pee-la-kee red bean salad
— **tava** ta-va fried red mullets

bastı bas-tuh vegetable stew

bazlama baz-la-ma flat baked bread

beğendi be-en-dee puréed eggplant sauce

beğendili tas kebabı be-en-dee-lee tas ke-ba-buh see hünkar beğendi

beğendili tavuk be-en-dee-lee ta-vook chicken with puréed eggplant

benekli çorba be-nek-lee chor-ba lentil soup

benli pilav ben-lee pee-lav pilau dish of rice & lentils (Yozgat)

beyaz be-yaz white
— **fıstık** fuhs-tuhk pine nuts
— **İspanyol şarabı** ees-pan-yol sha-ra-buh sherry
— **lahana** la-ha-na white cabbage
— **muhallebi** moo-hal-le-bee white pudding
— **peynir** pay-neer white cheese like feta
— **peynirli omlet** pay-neer-lee om-let omelette with white cheese
— **peynirli sandviç** pay-neer-lee sand-veech white cheese sandwich

beyin be-yeen brain

beyti kebab bay-tee ke-bab Adana-style meat kebab, rolled in thin bread & sliced

bezelye be-zel-ye pea

bıldırcın buhl-duhr-juhn quail
— **kebabı** ke-ba-buh quail with potato, tomato & green capsicum (Bilecik)
— **yumurtası** yoo-moor-ta-suh quail eggs

biber bee-ber bell pepper • capsicum
— **dolması** dol-ma-suh stuffed capsicum
— **gibi** gee-bee hot • capsicum
— **kızartması** kuh-zart-ma-suh fried capsicum
— **tanesi** ta-ne-see peppercorn
— **turşusu** toor-shoo-soo pickled capsicum

biftek beef-tek steak

bira bee-ra beer

bisküvi bees-kew-vee biscuit

bitkisel beet-kee-sel vegetable
— **çay** chai herbal tea

bizon bee-zon bison • buffalo

boğa bo-a bull

bonbon bon-bon candy • lollies • sweets

bonfile bon-fee-le sirloin steak

böbrek berb-rek kidney

böğürtlen ber-ewrt-len blackberry • dewberry

börek ber-rek various sweet or savoury dishes with a thin crispy pastry
— **çorbası** chor-ba-suh thick soup of mincemeat, bones, tomato & mint (Antep)

börülce ber-rewl-je black-eyed pea • cow pea
— **pilavı** pee-la-vuh pilau dish of rice & black-eyed peas (Aydın & Muğla)
— **salatası** sa-la-ta-suh salad of black-eyed peas, mushrooms, onion & parsley
— **teletoru** te-le-to-roo black-eyed pea salad with flour & lemon (Muğla)

bulamaç çorbası boo-la-mach chor-ba-suh soup of flour, semolina & margarine (Eskişehir)

bulgur bool-goor cracked wheat
— **köftesi** kerf-te-see meatballs of bulgur & mincemeat
— **pilavı** pee-la-vuh bulgur pilau

bumbar boom-bar sausage made of rice & meat stuffed in a large sheep or lamb gut

burma kadayıf boor-ma ka-da-yuhf shredded wheat bun with pistachios

Bursa kebabı boor-sa ke-ba-buh döner kebab with tomato & butter on pitta bread

bülbül yuvası bewl-bewl yoo-va-suh shredded wheat with pistachios & syrup

C

cacık ja-juhk yogurt, mint & cucumber mix

ceviz je-veez walnut
— **gibi kabuklu bir yemiş** gee-bee ka-book-loo beer ye-meesh pecan

cevizli bat je-veez-lee bat salad of bulgur, green lentils, tomato paste & walnuts

cevizli kek je-veez-lee kek walnut cake

cevizli sucuk je-veez-lee soo-jook walnuts on a string dipped in pekmez

cezeriye je-ze-ree-ye sweet of carrot & nuts

cızbız köfte juhz-buhz kerf-te grilled mincemeat ovals

Ç

çağanoz cha-a-*noz* green crab
çala cha-*la* seasoned bread & cheese
çalı fasulyesi cha-*luh* fa-sool-ye-*see* string beans
çamfıstığı cham-fuhs-tuh-*uh* pine nut
çarliston biber char-lees-ton bee-*ber* long, light-green sweet capsicum
çayüzümü chai-ew-zew-mew blueberry
çene çarpan çorbası che-ne char-*pan* chor-ba-*suh* 'jaw-bumping' soup of flour, water, egg, milk & lemon (Tekirdağ)
Çerkez peyniri cher-*kez* pay-nee-*ree* Circassian cheese, similar to **dil peynir**
Çerkez tavuğu cher-*kez* ta-voo-oo Circassian chicken with bread, walnuts & cayenne pepper (Sakarya & Adapazarı)
çevirme che-veer-me eggplant, chicken, rice, onion, pistachios & allspice dish — **çorbası** chor-ba-*suh* soup of egg, rice, yogurt, butter & red capsicum (Kütahya)
çılbır chuhl-*buhr* eggs poached in vinegary water topped with yogurt sauce
çıtırmak chuh-tuhr-*mak* boiled honey & roasted sesame seed sweet (Muğla)
çifte kavrulmuş lokum cheef-te kav-rool-moosh lo-koom Turkish delight
çiğ börek chee ber-*ek* fried **börek** made with ground meat, onions & spices
çiğ köfte chee kerf-te raw lamb, bulgur, clove, cinnamon, black & red capsicum
ciğer tava jee-er ta-*va* fried liver & onions
çilek chee-*lek* strawberry
çipura chee-poo-ra sea bream
çirli et cheer-*lee* et dish of seasoned beef chunks & dried apricot (Sivas)
çiroz chee-*roz* kipper • mackerel
çoban salatası cho-*ban* sa-la-ta-*suh* salad of tomato, cucumber & capsicum
çomak cho-*mak* stuffed flat **bazlama** bread
çorba chor-*ba* soup
çökelekli biber dolması cher-le-lek-*lee* bee-*ber* dol-ma-*suh* **dolma** dish of capsicums with cheese, & tomato (Antalya)
çökelekli zeytin cher-le-lek-*lee* zay-teen cottage cheese & green olive salad (Hatay)
çökelek peynir cher-ke-*lek* pay-neer cottage cheese
çökertme cher-kert-me sliced steak served on potatoes with yogurt sauce (Muğla)
çöp şiş kebab cherp sheesh ke-*bab* meat-only kebab
çörek cher-*rek* sweet biscuit
çullama chool-la-*ma* pancake dish of sliced quail, butter & flour (Muğla)

D

dağ domuzu da do-moo-zoo mountain boar
dağ keçisi da ke-chee-*see* mountain goat
dana eti da-*na* e-*tee* veal
delice de-lee-*je* cockle
deniz tarağı de-*neez* ta-ra-*uh* clam • scallop
deniz ürünü de-*neez* ew-rew-new seafood
dereotu de-*re*-o-too dill
dible deeb-*le* cold vegetable dish with beans
diken dutu dee-*ken* doo-too blackberry
dil deel tongue
dilber dudağı deel-*ber* doo-da-*uh* sweet pastry in the shape of a lip
dil peynir deel pay-*neer* mozzarella-like cheese
diş deesh clove
divriği alatlı pilavı deev-ree-*ee* a-lat-*luh* pee-la-*vuh* pilau with rice, lamb, bouillon, chickpeas & seedless grapes (Sivas)
dolma dol-*ma* vine or cabbage leaves stuffed with rice
domates do-ma-tes tomato
domatesli patlıcan kızartması do-ma-tes-lee pat-luh-*jan* kuh-zart-ma-*suh* fried eggplant with tomato
domatesli patlıcan çarliston biber kızartması do-ma-tes-lee pat-luh-*jan* char-lees-ton bee-*ber* kuh-zart-ma-*suh* fried eggplant with tomato & capsicum
domatesli pilav do-ma-tes-lee pee-*lav* tomato pilau
domatesli şehriye çorbası do-ma-tes-lee sheh-ree-ye chor-ba-*suh* tomato soup with vermicelli
domuz do-*mooz* pig
— **eti** e-*tee* bacon • pork
— **sosisi** so-see-*see* pork sausages
dondurma don-door-ma ice cream
döner der-*ner* slices of meat stacked on a vertical skewer, grilled and shaved off
— **kebab** ke-*bab* kebab (usually lamb or chicken) cooked on a rotating spit
dövme etli karalahana sarması derv-me et-*lee* ka-*ra*-la-ha-na sar-ma-*suh* lamb strips, rice & tomato paste wrapped in **karalahana** leaves (Rize)

dul avrat çorbası dool av·*rat* chor·ba·*suh* 'widow soup' of chickpeas, lentils, lamb, tomato paste, capsicum & mint (Adana)

dut doot *mulberry*

düğün çorbası dew·*ewn* chor·ba·*suh* wedding soup with ground meat, carrot & lemon or vinegar

düğün pilavı dew·*ewn* pee·la·*vuh* 'wedding pilau' – rice, chickpeas & meat (Kayseri) • chicken & *yarma* (Sakarya)

dürüm dew·*rewm* kebab in pitta bread

E

ekmek ek·*mek* bread
— **böreği** ber·re·*ee* oven-baked stale bread & melted *kaşar* cheese (Izmir)

ekmekkadayıf ek·*mek*·ka·da·*yuhf* dessert of baked *kadayıf* bread rusks soaked in thick syrup & topped with *kaymak*

ekşili ıspanak başı ek·shee·lee uhs·pa·*nak* ba·*shuh* spinach & lentil stew (Tarsus)

ekşili nohutlu bamya ek·shee·lee no·*hoot*·loo bam·*ya* mutton stew with okra & chickpeas (Mersin & İçel)

ekşili patlıcan dolması ek·shee·lee pat·luh·*jan* dol·ma·*suh* eggplant *dolma*

ekşili taraklık tavası ek·shee·lee ta·rak·*luhk* ta·va·*suh* sour lamb cutlets with quince

elbasan el·ba·*san* open-faced pie with fried lamb chunks, eggs & yogurt (Manisa)
— **dolması** dol·ma·*suh* dolma with artichoke, rice & mincemeat
— **şarabı** sha·ra·*buh* apple cider

erik e·*reek* plum
— **aşı** a·*shuh* plum dish with prunes, rice & sugar (Tekirdağ)

erikli biber dolması e·reek·lee bee·ber dol·ma·*suh* capsicum stuffed with eggplant, tomato, walnuts & kızılcık (Bilecik)

erikli tavşan e·reek·lee tav·*shan* rabbit with plums

erikli tavuk dolması e·reek·lee ta·*vook* dol·ma·*suh* stuffed chicken with plums

erişte e·reesh·te noodles • pasta

Erzincan piyazı er·zeen·jan pee·ya·*zuh* salad with cucumber, tomato, cheeses, capsicum & herbs (Erzincan)

etli et·lee with meat
— **bohça böreği** boh·*cha* ber·re·*ee* delicate *börek* filled with beef

— **bulgur pilavı** bool·*goor* pee·la·*vuh* bulgur pilau with meat & chickpeas
— **dolma** dol·*ma* meat-stuffed vegetables
— **dövme pilavı** derv·*me* pee·la·*vuh* pilau with chickpeas, bulgur & lamb
— **ekmek** ek·*mek* bread topped with meat
— **enginar** en·gee·*nar* stew of artichoke, meat or lamb chunks, onion & tomato
— **enginar dolması** en·gee·*nar* dol·ma·*suh* artichokes stuffed with meat
— **kabak dolması** ka·*bak* dol·ma·*suh* zucchini stuffed with meat
— **kabak ve biber dolması** ka·*bak* ve bee·*ber* dol·ma·*suh* zucchini & capsicum stuffed with meat
— **kereviz dolması** ke·re·*veez* dol·ma·*suh* celery stuffed with meat
— **kuru fasulye** koo·roo fa·*sool*·ye haricot or butter beans & meat
— **lahana dolması** la·*ha*·na dol·ma·*suh* cabbage leaves stuffed with meat
— **marul dolması** ma·*rool* dol·ma·*suh* lettuce leaves stuffed with rice, tomato, parsley, cumin & meat (Edirne)
— **nohut** no·*hoot* chickpeas in meat sauce
— **patlıcan dolması** pat·luh·*jan* dol·ma·*suh* eggplant stuffed with meat
— **pide** pee·*de* Turkish 'pizza' with ground meat
— **sebzeli güveç** seb·ze·lee gew·*vech* stewed meat with vegetables
— **yaprak dolması** yap·*rak* dol·ma·*suh* vine leaves with meat stuffing
— **yeşil mercimek** ye·*sheel* mer·jee·*mek* lentils with meat, onion & tomato paste

etyemez et·ye·*mez* vegetarian

ezme lahana ez·me la·*ha*·na flat vegetable 'pie' made of karalahana, chard, suet, cornflour, tomato & red capsicum (Rize)

ezme salata ez·me sa·la·*ta* tomato salad or cold tomato soup, like gazpacho (Antep)

ezo gelin çorbası e·zo ge·*leen* chor·ba·*suh* red lentil 'bride' soup

F

fasulye fa·*sool*·ye bean
— **filizi** fee·lee·*zee* beansprout

fındık fuhn·*duhk* hazelnut

fıstık fuhs·*tuhk* peanut

fosul fo·*sool* lamb or mutton kebab

francala fran·ja·la long narrow loaf of bread

G

gerdan dolması ger-dan dol-ma-suh lamb neck stuffed with rice, mince, almonds, tomato paste & spiced **köfte** (Adana)

gerdaniye ger-da-nee-ye neck of lamb with plum & sugar (Edirne)

geyik eti ge-yeek e-tee venison

gökkuşağı salatası gerk-koo-sha-uh sa-la-ta-suh 'rainbow salad' – macaroni, capsicum, mushrooms, pickles & salami

gül reçeli gewl re-che-lee rose jam

gül şerbeti gewl sher-be-tee nonalcoholic drink of rose-water, water & sugar (Sivas)

gül tatlısı gewl tat-luh-suh fried rose-shaped pastry covered in lemon sherbet

güneşte kurutulmuş domates gew-nesh-te koo-roo-tool-moosh do-ma-tes sun-dried tomato

güveçte kıymalı yumurta gew-vech-te kuhy-ma-luh yoo-moor-ta casseroled eggs with minced meat

güveçte türlü gew-vech-te tewr-lew mixed vegetable casserole with chicken

güvercin gew-ver-jeen pigeon

H

Halep işi kebap ha-lep ee-shee ke-bap grilled meatballs, onions & spices

halim aşı ha-leem a-shuh soup of chickpeas, meaty bones, wheat & tomato

hamburger ekmeği ham-boor-ger ek-me-ee bread roll

hamsi ham-see anchovies

— **böreği** ber-re-ee layers of breaded fried anchovies & seasoned rice (Giresun)

— **buğulaması** boo-oo-la-ma-suh anchovies with tomato & capsicum

— **çorbası** chor-ba-suh anchovy & tomato soup (Trabzon)

— **ekşilisi** ek-shee-lee-see 'anchovy sour' with capsicum & tomato salad (Rize)

— **ızgara** uhz-ga-ra grilled anchovies served with raw onion & lemon

— **kuşu** koo-shoo anchovies fried with tomato & green capsicum

— **salamura** sa-la-moo-ra pickled anchovy, rock salt & bay leaf

— **tatlısı** tat-luh-suh jellied sweet made from anchovy (Rize)

— **tava** ta-va fried, corn-breaded anchovies served with onion & lemon

hamsikoli ham-see-ko-lee bread with chard, mint, corn meal & anchovies (Rize)

hamsili pilav ham-see-lee pee-lav oven-baked anchovy pilau (Rize)

hamur işleri ha-moor eesh-le-ree pastries

hamur tatlısı ha-moor tat-luh-suh pastry

hamurlu çorba ha-moor-loo chor-ba dark soup of **erişte** dough, lentils & meat

hamurlu yeşil mercimek çorbası ha-moor-loo ye-sheel mer-jee-mek chor-ba-suh lentil soup with dumplings

hanibana ha-nee-ba-na **köfte** cooked with capsicum, carrot, tomato & peas

hardal har-dal mustard

hardallı patlıcan kızartması har-dal-luh pat-luh-jan kuh-zart-ma-suh fried eggplant & mustard

haşhaş hash-hash poppyseed

haşhaşlı gözleme hash-hash-luh gerz-le-me savoury pancake with poppy seed (Eskişehir & Edirne)

haşlama hash-la-ma steamed lamb & vegetables in broth

havuç ha-vooch carrot

havyar hav-yar caviar

haydari hai-da-ree yogurt with roasted eggplant & garlic

hırtlama köfte huhrt-la-ma kerf-te **köfte** of veal, cornflour & thyme (Trabzon)

hıyar huh-yar cucumber

hibeş hee-besh **meze** spread of tahini & red capsicum flakes (Antalya)

hindi heen-dee turkey

hindiba heen-dee-ba chicory • endive

Hindistan cevizi heen-dees-tan je-vee-zee coconut

hingel heen-gel dish of thin pastry layers & crumbled cottage cheese (Yozgat)

Hint cevizi heent je-vee-zee nutmeg

Hint fıstığı heent fuhs-tuh-uh cashew

Hint kirazı heent kee-ra-zuh mango

hörre her-re soup of butter, flour & tomato

höşmerim hersh-me-reem classic Anatolian pudding with walnuts & pistachios

humus hoo-moos humus – finely mashed chickpeas with sesame oil, lemon & spices

hurma hoor-ma date

— **tatlısı** tat-luh-suh semolina & date cake

hülüklü düğün çorbası hew-lewk-lew dew-ewn chor-ba-suh hearty soup with tripe, meatballs, chickpeas & rice (Adana)

hünkar beğendi hewn-kar be-en-dee 'sultan's delight' – lamb stew on eggplant

I

ısırganotu ezmesi uh-suhr-*gan*-o-too ez-me-*see* stinging nettle purée (Rize)

ıslama uhs-la-*ma* gravy from beef broth, red capsicum & vegetable oil
— **köfte** kerf-*te* meat patties on toasted bread, doused in **ıslama** juice (Sakarya)

ıspanak uhs-pa-*nak* spinach

ızgara uhz-*ga*-ra barbecue • grill
— **köfte** kerf-*te* grilled meatballs

i

içi dolmuş ee-*chee* dol-*moosh* eggplant with **beyaz peynir**, tomato & egg

içli köfte eech-*lee* kerf-*te* **köfte** with bulgur covering (Antep, Diyarbakır & Adana)

iç pilav eech pee-*lav* rice with currants, nuts & onions

imambayıldı ee-mam-ba-yuhl-*duh* 'the imam fainted' – famous dish of eggplant, tomato & onion

incir een-*jeer* fig
— **uyuşturması** oo-yoosh-toor-ma-*suh* 'fig narcotic' – dessert of milk & figs

İnegöl köfte ee-*ne*-gerl kerf-*te* **köfte** dish made with mincemeat

irmik eer-*meek* semolina

İskender kebab ees-ken-*der* ke-bab **döner** kebab on flat bread, covered in tomato sauce & hot butter sauce

isotreçeli ee-sot-re-che-*lee* preserve made of 'Urfa' capsicum & cinnamon (Urfa)

istakoz ees-ta-*koz* lobster

istiridye ees-tee-*reed*-ye oyster

işkembe eesh-kem-*be* tripe

İzmir köfte eez-*meer* kerf-*te* **köfte** with mincemeat, egg, breadcrumbs & tomato

K

kabak ka-*bak* courgette • zucchini
— **pane** pa-*ne* crumbed fried zucchini
— **tatlısı** tat-luh-*suh* dessert of pumpkin, sweet syrup & walnuts

kabaklı pirinç çorbası ka-bak-luh pee-*reench* chor-ba-*suh* zucchini & rice soup

kabuklular ka-book-loo-*lar* shellfish

kadayıf ka-da-*yuhf* dessert of dough soaked in syrup with a layer of **kaymak**

kadınbudu köfte ka-duhn-boo-doo kerf-*te* **köfte** of ground meat mixed with cooked rice & fried in batter (İzmir)

kağıt kebabı ka-*uht* ke-ba-*buh* lamb chunks & vegetables baked in wax paper (Manisa)

kağıtta barbunya ka-uht-*ta* bar-*boon*-ya baked **barbunya**

kağıtta pastırma ka-uht-*ta* pas-tuhr-*ma* **pastırma** cooked in foil with vegetables

kahırtlak hamuru ka-huhrt-*lak* ha-moo-*roo* fried dough used in soup (Adana)

kalburabastı kal-boo-ra-*bas*-tuh baked eggshaped dessert topped with lemon syrup

kapalı kıymalı pide ka-pa-*luh* kuhy-ma-*luh* pee-*de* **pide** filled with mincemeat & tomato (Samsun, Bafra & Giresun)

kapama ka-pa-*ma* boiled chicken & rice

kaplumbağa kap-loom-ba-*a* turtle

karaçuval helvası ka-*ra*-choo-val hel-va-*suh* sweet potato-shaped pastries served with **pekmez** (Çorum)

karalahana ka-*ra*-la-ha-na dark cabbage
— **çorbası** chor-ba-*suh* **karalahana**, carrot, zucchini, **çarliston biber** & potato soup (Rize)
— **dible** deeb-*le* **karalahana**, Albanian red capsicum, **barbunya** & rice salad
— **sarma karalahana** sar-*ma* ka-*ra*-la-ha-na **dolma** with veal & rice wrapped in **karalahana** (Rize)

karaş ka-*rash* pudding dessert of blackberries, grapes & hazelnuts

karides ka-ree-*des* prawn

karışık ızgara ka-ruh-*shuhk* uhz-*ga*-ra mixed grill

karışık dolma ka-ruh-*shuhk* dol-*ma* **dolma** of grape leaves, capsicum & eggplant

karışık meyve ka-ruh-*shuhk* may-*ve* mixed fruit

karışık pide ka-ruh-*shuhk* pee-*de* Turkish 'pizza' with tomato, green capsicum, mincemeat, **pastırma** sausage & **kaşar**

karnabahar kar-*na*-ba-har cauliflower
— **kızartması** kuh-zart-ma-*suh* fried cauliflower

karnıyarık kar-nuh-ya-*ruhk* 'split belly' – eggplant stuffed with seasoned ground beef

karpuz kar-*pooz* watermelon

kaşar ka-shar sheep's milk
— **peyniri** pay-nee-ree sheep's cheese similar to mild cheddar
— **peynirli omlet** pay-neer-lee om-let omelette with kaşar peyniri

kaşık börek çorbası ka-shuhk ber-rek chor-ba-suh egg, yogurt & tomato soup

katıklı aş ka-tuhk-luh ash soup of bulgur, water, butter & süzme yoğurt (Aksaray)

katmerli pazı böreği kat-mer-lee pa-zuh ber-re-ee savoury börek of flour, chard, onion, egg yolk & sesame seeds (Edirne)

katmerli saç böreği kat-mer-lee saj ber-re-ee börek of pitta bread filled with spinach, cheese & onion (Muğla)

kavun ka-voon melon • rockmelon

kavunağacı ka-voon-a-a-juh papaya

kavurma erişte pilavı ka-voor-ma e-reesh-te-see pee-la-vuh pilau dish of home-made noodles & rice (Sivas)

kayısı ka-yuh-suh apricot
— **yahnisi** yah-nee-see stew with apricots, meat chunks & **pekmez** (Nevşehir)

kaymak kai-mak sour cream

kaynamış kai-na-muhsh boiled

kaz kaz goose

kebab/kebap ke-bab/ke-bap skewered meat & vegetables cooked on an open fire

keçi ke-chee goat

kepekli ekmek ke-pek-lee ek-mek wholemeal bread

kepir dolması ke-peer dol-ma-suh dolma of kepir & mincemeat wrapped in karalahana & topped with yogurt (Ordu)

kerbel ker-bel fragrant herb from the parsley family used with fish & salads

kerevit ke-re-veet crawfish • crayfish • prawn

kereviz ke-re-veez celeriac • celery root

kesme çorbası kes-me chor-ba-suh black lentils, **köfte** & macaroni soup (Erzurum) • mincemeat & tomato soup (Kayseri) • egg, ayran & salt soup (Erzincan)

kestane kes-ta-ne chestnut

kestaneli hindi kes-ta-ne-lee heen-dee roast turkey with chestnuts

kestane yemeği kes-ta-ne ye-me-ee dish of chestnuts & mincemeat (Sinop)

keşkek kesh-kek ground wheat • wedding dish of mutton & ground wheat (Denizli)

keşkül kesh-kewl pudding of ground almonds, coconut & milk

kete ke-te roll with spinach & nuts (Kars)

kiraz kee-raz cherry

kırmızı biber salatası kuhr-muh-zuh bee-ber sa-la-ta-suh capsicum, garlic, lemon & olive oil salad (Adana)

kırmızı turp kuhr-muh-zuh toorp radish

kısır kuh-suhr bulgur salad with onion, parsley, lemon, cucumber & tomato

kişniş hoşafı keesh-neesh ho-sha-fuh raisins, sugar & water drink (Sivas)

kıtır patlıcan kuh-tuhr pat-luh-jan crispy eggplant

kıvırcık salata kuh-vuhr-juhk sa-la-ta lettuce with very crinkly leaves

kıyma kuhy-ma ground meat • mincemeat

kızarmış kuh-zar-muhsh fried • roasted
— **ekmek** ek-mek toasted bread
— **patates** pa-ta-tes fried potato

kızılcık kuh-zuhl-juhk cranberry
— **tarhana çorbası** tar-ha-na chor-ba-suh soup of tarhana and kızılcık

kokoreç ko-ko-rech seasoned grilled lamb or mutton intestines (Tekirdağ)

kolay tatlı ko-lai tat-luh dessert with apricots & sugar water

kornişon kor-nee-shon gherkin

koyun ko-yoon mutton

koz helvası koz hel-va-suh nougat

köfte kerf-te small mincemeat or bulgur balls

köleş ker-lesh salad with cucumber, melon, tomato, capsicum & yogurt (Eskişehir)

köpek balığı ker-pek ba-luh-uh shark

köpüklü şarap ker-pewk-lew sha-rap sparkling wine

közleme biber salatası kerz-le-me bee-ber sa-la-ta-suh capsicum salad

Kudüs enginarı koo-dews en-gee-na-ruh Jerusalem artichoke

kulak çorbası koo-lak chor-ba-suh 'ear soup' – meat dumplings boiled in stock • chickpeas & meat (Antalya)

kurbağa koor-ba-a frog

kuru erik koo-roo e-reek prune

kuru köfte koo-roo kerf-te fried meat patty

kuru mantı koo-roo man-tuh meat dumplings with garlicky broth (Çorum)

kuru meyve koo-roo may-ve dried fruit

kuru üzüm koo-roo ew-zewm raisin

kuşkonmaz koosh-kon-maz asparagus

kuzu koo-zoo lamb • mutton

kümes hayvanları kew-mes hai-van-la-ruh poultry

L

labne *lab*-ne mild cream cheese
lahana la-*ha*-na cabbage
lahmacun lah-ma-*joon* Turkish 'pizza' (also **pide**)
lahusa şekeri la-*hoo*-sa she-ke-*ree* slabs of sugar flavoured with spices & dyed red
lahusa şerbeti la-*hoo*-sa sher-be-*tee* sherbet to celebrate a birth
lakerda la-*ker*-da salted tuna fish salad
lebeniyeli köfte le-be-nee-ye-*lee* kerf-te bulgur **köfte** stuffed with meat (Adana)
levrek lev-*rek* sea bass
loğusa tatlısı lo-*oo*-sa tat-luh-*suh* sweet of sugar, lemon powder & red food dye (see **lahusa şekeri**)
lokma lok-*ma* yeast fritters with syrup
lokum lo-*koom* Turkish delight • sweet pastry
— **pilavı** pee-la-*vuh* noodles & mincemeat
lop lop 'big, tender & round' – sometimes used to describe a cut of meat like **nuar**
löbye *lerb*-ye cold bean salad (İstanbul)

M

maden suyu ma-*den* soo-*yoo* mineral water
madımak ma-duh-*mak* green vegetable
— **yemeği** ye-me-*ee* stew of **madımak**, **pastırma**, bulgur & spring onion
mafiş tatlısı ma-*feesh* tat-luh-*suh* savoury pastry dessert (Balıkesir)
mahaleb ma-ha-*leb* St Lucie cherry • cordial made from St Lucie cherry
mahallebi ma-hal-le-*bee* sweet rice flour & milk pudding
makarna ma-*kar*-na noodles • pasta
mandalina man-da-*lee*-na mandarin • tangerine
mantar man-*tar* mushroom
Maraş dondurması ma-*rash* don-door-ma-*suh* stringy, chewy & delicious ice cream
Maraş tarhanası ma-*rash* tar-ha-na-*suh* **tarhana** used in stuffing or as is' in soup
maraska ma-ras-*ka* sour cherry
marul ma-*rool* lettuce
menemen me-ne-*men* eggs with green capsicum, tomato & cheese
mercimek mer-jee-*mek* lentil
meşhur Karadeniz kavurması mesh-*hoor* ka-*ra*-de-neez ka-voor-ma-*suh* baked 'pizza' topped with fried meat

meyan me-*yan* liquorice
meyve may-*ve* fruit
meze me-*ze* Turkish hors d'oeuvres
mıhlama muh-la-*ma* egg dish • **pastırma**, onions & egg dish • cheese & corn dish
mısır muh-*suhr* corn
— **çorbası** chor-ba-*suh* soup of corn kernels, **barbunya** & meat chunks (Sinop)
midye *meed*-ye mussel
— **pilavı** pee-la-*vuh* pilau of rice, mussels, seedless grapes & nuts (Balıkesir)
misket limonu mees-*ket* lee-mo-*noo* lime
morina mo-*ree*-na cod
muammara moo-am-ma-*ra* **meze** or salad of walnuts, breadcrumbs & tahini (Adana)
musakka moo-sak-*ka* vegetable & ground meat pie
muska böreği moos-*ka* ber-re-*ee* **börek** of potato, cheese & mincemeat (Uşak)
muz mooz banana

N

nar nar pomegranate
nevzine nev-zee-*ne* savoury **börek** with eggs, tahini, yogurt & walnuts (Kayseri)
Niğde tavası *nee*-de ta-va-*suh* lamb with tomato, capsicum & rice (Niğde)
nohut no-*hoot* chickpea
nohutlu kuskus pilavı no-hoot-*loo* koos-koos pee-la-*vuh* couscous with boiled chickpeas & butter (İstanbul)
nokul no-*kool* meat pie with seasoned mincemeat, parsley & walnuts (Sinop)
nuar noo-*ar* tender cut of veal, boiled & sliced thinly for sandwiches & cold cuts

O

orfoz fileto or-*foz* fee-le-*to* fillet of groper garnished with rocket (Mediterranean)
orman kebabı or-*man* ke-ba-*buh* roast lamb & onions

Ö

öğmeç çorbası er-*mech* chor-ba-*suh* soup of flour, eggs & tomato paste (Burdur)
öküz er-*kewz* ox
ördek er-*dek* duck
örgülü makarna er-gew-*lew* ma-kar-*na* noodles, chicken, peas, carrot & almonds

P

paça çorbası pa·cha chor·ba·suh *sheep trotter soup*

pancar pan·jar *beetroot*
— **cacığı** ja·juh·uh *beet, bulgur, yogurt & garlic cacık (Yozgat)*

papaz yahnisi pa·paz yah·nee·see *'priest's stew' with beef, vinegar & cumin (Izmir)*

pastırma pas·tuhr·ma *pressed beef preserved in spices • Turkish pastrami*

pastırmalı kuru fasulye pas·tuhr·ma·luh koo·roo fa·sool·ye *pastırma & bean casserole*

pastırmalı omlet pas·tuhr·ma·luh om·let *omelette with pastırma*

pastırmalı sigara böreği pas·tuhr·ma·luh see·ga·ra ber·re·ee *pastry of yufka, pastırma, tomato & capsicum (Kayseri)*

paşa pilavı pa·sha pee·la·vuh *'Sultan's pilau' – salad of potato, eggs & capsicum*

patates pa·ta·tes *potato*
— **kaygana** kai·ga·na *fried potato pancake • mixture of potato, parsley & red capsicum (Kastamonu)*

patlıcan pat·luh·jan *aubergine • eggplant*
— **biber tava** bee·ber ta·va *fried eggplant & capsicum with tomato paste*
— **böreği** ber·re·ee *sliced eggplant prepared with mincemeat & onion (Afyon)*
— **islim kebabı** ees·leem ke·ba·buh *baked lamb wrapped in eggplant*
— **karnıyarık** kar·nuh·ya·ruhk *eggplant stuffed with minced meat*
— **pane** pa·ne *fried eggplant covered with crumbled bread*
— **reçeli** re·che·lee *sweet eggplant preserves (Adana)*

patlıcanlı köfte pat·luh·jan·luh kerf·te *meatballs with eggplant*

patlıcanlı köy dolması pat·luh·jan·luh kay dol·ma·suh *mincemeat & bulgur served on eggplant slices (Karaman)*

patlıcanlı pilav pat·luh·jan·luh pee·lav *eggplant pilau*

pavruya pav·roo·ya *hermit crab*

pazı pa·zuh *chard*
— **kavurma** ka·voor·ma *fried eggs & chard, with onions & barbunya (Rize)*
— **kavurması** ka·voor·ma·suh *chard & onion served cold (Kastamonu)*
— **pilakisi** pee·la·kee·see *pilaki with chard, rice & salted anchovy (Trabzon)*

pekmez pek·mez *grape molasses*

peynir pay·neer *cheese*
— **helvası** hel·va·suh *dessert of cheese, flour, eggs, butter & granulated sugar*
— **tatlısı** tat·luh·suh *cheesecake • cookies*

peynirli börek pay·neer·lee ber·rek *pastry filled with peynir*

peynirli pide pay·neer·lee pee·de *cheese Turkish pizza*

pırasa puh·ra·sa *leek*
— **dolması** dol·ma·suh *leeks stuffed with mincemeat, rice & tomato (Kastamonu)*

pide pee·de *thin pitta-like bread used to make Turkish pizza or döner kebab*
— **ekmek** ek·mek *unleavened bread available during the month of Ramazan*

pilaki pee·la·kee *cold stew with vegetables & beans, black-eyed peas, rice or fish*

pilav pee·lav *pilau of rice, bulgur or lentils*

pilavlı hindi pee·lav·luh heen·dee *roast turkey with rice*

pilavlı tas kebabı pee·lav·luh tas ke·ba·buh *'kebab' with lamb chunks & red capsicum (Çorum)*

piliç pee·leech *chicken*

pirpirim çorbası peer·pee·reem chor·ba·suh *chickpea, bean & lentil soup*

piruhi pee·roo·hee *meat, flour & yogurt dish*

pirzola peer·zo·la *chops (lamb)*

pişmaniye peesh·ma·nee·ye *dessert made of sugar, flour & soapwort (Kocaeli)*

piyaz pee·yaz *white bean salad*

portakal por·ta·kal *orange (fruit or flavour)*

pürçüklü pewr·chewk·lew *purple carrot*

R

ravent ra·vent *rhubarb*

reçel re·chel *jam*

revani re·va·nee *sweet cake with semolina, vanilla & clotted cream*

ringa balığı reen·ga ba·luh·uh *herring*

S

saçaklı mantı sa·chak·luh man·tuh *chicken spread over seasoned pastry*

sahanda pirzola sa·han·da peer·zo·la *lamb cutlets with tomato sauce*

sakızlı bakla çorbası sa·kuhz·luh bak·la chor·ba·suh *soup with bakla (Bolu)*

salam sa·lam *salami*

salatalık sa·la·ta·luhk *cucumber*

salçalı köfte sal-cha-*luh* kerf-*te* *meat patties in seasoned tomato sauce*

samsa tatlısı sam-*sa* tat-luh-*suh* *sweet pastry soaked in syrup (Isparta)*

Samsun köfte sam-soon kerf-*te* *meat loaf*

samut salatası sa-*moot* sa-la-ta-*suh* *salad with dill, parsley & red capsicum*

sap kerevizi sap ke-re-vee-*zee* *celery*

sardalya sar-*dal*-ya *sardine*

sarmısak sar-muh-*sak* *garlic*

— **börülce salatası** ber-*rewl*-je sa-la-ta-*suh* *black-eyed pea salad*

— **köfte** kerf-*te* *meatless köfte with tomato sauce (Adana)*

— **tavuk dolması** ta-*vook* dol-ma-*suh* *stuffed chicken with garlic*

sebzeler seb-ze-*ler* *vegetables*

sebzeli bulgur pilavı seb-ze-*lee* bool-*goor* pee-la-*vuh* *pilau of bulgur & vegetables*

sebzeli kapama seb-ze-*lee* ka-pa-*ma* *lamb & vegetable stew*

sebzeli kuzu kızartma seb-ze-*lee* koo-zoo kuh-*zart*-ma *roast lamb with vegetables*

sebzeli piliç dolması seb-ze-*lee* pee-*leech* dol-ma-*suh* *baked chicken with potato, peas, okra & tomato (İstanbul)*

sebzeli tavuk çorbası seb-ze-*lee* ta-*vook* chor-ba-*suh* *vegetable & chicken soup*

sığır dili suh-*uhr* dee-*lee* *ox tongue*

sığır eti suh-*uhr* e-*tee* *beef*

sığır filetosu suh-*uhr* fee-le-to-soo *sirloin*

sıkıcık çorbası suh-kuh-*juhk* chor-ba-*suh* *bulgur, tarhana & meat soup (Kütahya)*

sıkma suhk-*ma* **börek** *filled with onion, beyaz peynir & parsley (Adana)*

sigara böreği see-ga-*ra* ber-re-ee *cigar-shaped pastries filled with beyaz peynir*

simit see-*meet* *crispy roll with sesame seed*

sinarit ızgara see-na-*reet* uhz-ga-*ra* *grilled sea bream with dill & lemon juice sauce*

sini köfte see-*nee* kerf-*te* *bulgur & meat köfte*

sirke seer-*ke* *vinegar*

soğan so-*an* *onion*

— **aşı** a-*shuh* *dish with meaty bones, spring onion, potato & tomato (Tekirdağ)*

— **kebabı** ke-ba-*buh* *meat chunks with arpacık soğanı & tomato paste (Niğde)*

soğanlama so-an-la-*ma* *mincemeat with onion & tomato paste (Aksaray)*

soğanlı et so-an-*luh* et *meat & onion stew*

soğuk çorba so-ook chor-*ba* *cold soup of yogurt, rice & capsicum (Kayseri)*

som balığı som ba-luh-*uh* *salmon*

somun ekmek so-moon ek-*mek* *bread rolls*

soya peyniri so-ya pay-nee-*ree* *tofu*

söğüş ser-*ewsh* *boiled meat served cold • cold cuts • sliced uncooked vegetables*

su soo *water*

— **böreği** ber-re-*ee* *flaky pastry sometimes filled with mincemeat (Edirne)*

— **kabağı** ka-ba-*uh* *water squash*

— **mahallebisi** ma-hal-le-bee-*see* *milk pudding with rose-water*

— **teresi** te-re-*see* *watercress*

sucuk soo-*jook* *spicy sausage*

susam soo-*sam* *sesame*

susamlı köfte soo-sam-*luh* kerf-*te* *meatless köfte with bulgur & tomato*

susamlı şeker soo-sam-*luh* she-*ker* *sugar-coated peanuts & almonds • hazelnuts & walnuts covered in sesame seeds*

susam yağı soo-sam ya-*uh* *sesame oil*

sülün sew-*lewn* *pheasant*

süt sewt *milk*

— **danası** da-na-*suh* *veal*

sütlaç sewt-*lach* *rice pudding*

süzme yoğurt sewz-*me* yo-*oort* *yogurt strained to remove water*

Ş

şalgam shal-*gam* *swede • turnip*

— **pilavı** pee-la-*vuh* *pilau dish of turnip, mincemeat & bulgur (Sivas)*

şamfıstığı sham-fuhs-tuh-*uh* *pistachio*

şeftali shef-*ta*-lee *peach*

şehriye sheh-ree-*ye* *noodles used in soups*

şeker she-*ker* *sugar • candy • lollies • sweets*

— **böreği** ber-re-*ee* *sweet biscuit, taken with lemon sherbet (Niğde)*

şekerpare she-ker-pa-*re* *sweet biscuit topped with lemon & sugar syrup*

şiş kebab sheesh ke-*bab* *skewered meat prepared on an open fire*

şiş köfte sheesh kerf-*te* *grilled meatballs*

T

tahinli lahana sarması ta-heen-*lee* la-*ha*-na sar-ma-*suh* *cabbage with rice, chickpeas, tahini & tomato (Adana)*

tahinli maydanoz ta-heen-*lee* mai-da-*noz* *salad of parsley, garlic & tahini (Hatay)*

tahinli patlıcan ta-heen-*lee* pat-luh-*jan* *mashed eggplant & tahini salad (Hatay)*

tahinli soğan ta-heen-lee so-an *onion, mayonnaise, lemon & tahini salad (Hatay)*

talaş böreği ta-lash ber-re-ee *meat pastry*

talaş kebabı ta-lash ke-ba-buh *meat pieces cooked then baked in pastry*

tandır kebabı tan-duhr ke-ba-buh *kebab roasted in an oven in a clay-lined pit*

tantuni kebab tan-too-nee ke-bab *dish of sliced veal & mutton on flat bread*

tarhana tar-ha-na *yogurt, onion, flour & chilli mix*

— **çorbası** chor-ba-suh **tarhana,** *yogurt, black-eyed pea & meat soup (Muğla)*

tas kebabı tas ke-ba-buh *veal & vegetable stew served on rice (Kütahya)*

tas kebaplı pilav tas ke-bap-luh pee-lav *lamb & vegetable stew (Samsun)*

tatlı biber tat-luh bee-ber *sweet capsicum*

tatlı mısır tat-luh muh-suhr *sweetcorn*

tatlı dürümü tat-luh dew-rew-mew *dessert of milk, yufka, walnuts & pekmez (Niğde)*

tatlıpatates tat-luh-pa-ta-tes *sweet potato*

tavşan tav-shan *hare • rabbit*

tavuk ta-vook *chicken*

— **dolması** dol-ma-suh *stuffed chicken*

— **göğsü** ger-sew *chicken breast*

— **kızartması** kuh-zart-ma-suh *roast chicken*

tavuklu zarf böreği ta-vook-loo zarf ber-re-ee *börek stuffed with chicken*

taze bezelye ta-ze be-zel-ye *snow pea*

Tekirdağ köftesi te-keer-da kerf-te-see *mincemeat with rice & capsicum*

tekke çorbası tek-ke chor-ba-suh *flour, meat, tomato & capsicum soup (Kütahya)*

telkadayıf tel-ka-da-yuhf *dessert of baked kadayıf dough with walnuts & kaymak*

tel şehriye tel sheh-ree-ye *thin delicate noodle, similar to vermicelli*

tel şehriyeli tavuk çorbası tel sheh-ree-ye-lee ta-vook chor-ba-suh *chicken vermicelli soup*

terbiye ter-bee-ye *sauce of lemon & egg*

terbiyeli ekşili köfte ter-bee-ye-lee ek-shee-lee kerf-te *meatballs with egg & lemon sauce*

terbiyeli işkembe çorbası ter-bee-ye-lee eesh-kem-be chor-ba-suh *tripe soup with terbiye*

terbiyeli kalkan balığı ter-bee-ye-lee kal-kan ba-luh-uh *turbot with sauce*

terbiyeli kuzu etli kereviz ter-bee-ye-lee koo-zoo et-lee ke-re-veez *celeriac with lamb in lemon sauce*

terbiyeli süt kuzusu kapaması ter-bee-ye-lee sewt koo-zoo-soo ka-pa-ma-suh *spring lamb with lettuce*

tere çorbası te-re chor-ba-suh *watercress & chicken broth soup (İzmir & Aydın)*

tereyağ te-re-ya *butter*

testi kebabı tes-tee ke-ba-buh *meat kebab in a mushroom & onion sauce (Anatolia)*

tıntış çorbası tuhn-tuhsh chor-ba-suh *corn meal soup (Zonguldak)*

ton balığı ton ba-luh-uh *tuna*

topik to-peek *chickpeas, pistachios, flour & currants topped with sesame sauce*

toyga çorbası toy-ga chor-ba-suh *soup of yogurt, hazelnut, rice, egg & mint (Konya)*

Trabzon hurması trab-zon hoor-ma-suh *persimmon*

Trabzon peynirlisi trab-zon pay-neer-lee-see *baked pizza made with 'Trabzon' cheese*

tulumba tatlısı too-loom-ba tat-luh-suh *fluted fritters served in sweet syrup*

turşu toor-shoo *pickled vegetable*

tuzlu domates ve fasulye kavurması tooz-loo do-ma-tes ve fa-sool-ye ka-voor-ma-suh *tomato & green beans*

tuzlu domuz eti tooz-loo do-mooz e-tee *salted pork*

türlü tewr-lew *stew*

U

un çorbası oon chor-ba-suh *'flour soup' – flour, meat, tomato & capsicum (Muğla)*

Urfa kebabı oor-fa ke-ba-buh *grilled lamb on skewers*

Ü

üzüm ew-zewm *grapes*

üzümlü kek ew-zewm-lew kek *cake or pie with dried grapes*

V

vartabit paçası var-ta-beet pa-cha-suh *seasoned white beans on Turkish bread*

vişneli ekmek tatlısı veesh-ne-lee ek-mek tat-luh-suh *cherry bread pudding*

Y

yaban havucu ya·ban ha·voo·joo *parsnip*
yabani pirinç ya·ba·nee pee·reench *wild rice*
yabani yeşil yapraklı sebzeler ya·ba·nee ye·sheel yap·rak·luh seb·ze·ler *wild greens*
yağsız ya·suhz *without fat • without oil*
— **kıyma** kuhy·ma *lean ground beef*
yahni yah·nee *meat & vegetable stew*
yarma yar·ma *coarsely ground wheat*
yassı kadayıf yas·suh ka·da·yuhf *baked kadayıf pancakes topped with kaymak*
yavan çorbası ya·van chor·ba·suh *'flavourless soup' with wheat, chickpeas, lentils, beans, meat & capsicum (Malatya)*
yayla çorbası yai·la chor·ba·suh *'highland' yogurt soup with mint*
yaz türlüsü yaz tewr·lew·sew *summer vegetable stew*
yengeç yen·gech *crab*
yermantarı yer·man·ta·ruh *truffle*
yeşil ye·sheel *green*
— **biber** bee·ber *green capsicum*
— **mercimekli bulgur pilavı** mer·jee·mek·lee bool·goor pee·la·vuh *pilau of green lentils & bulgur (Tokat)*
— **mercimekli erişteli çorba** mer·jee·mek·lee e·reesh·te·lee chor·ba *green lentil & noodle soup (Urfa)*
— **salata** sa·la·ta *green salad*
— **soğan** so·an *chives • spring onion*
— **zeytin** zay·teen *green olive*
yeşillikler ye·sheel·leek·ler *mixed greens*
yılanbalığı yuh·lan·ba·luh·uh *eel*
yufka yoof·ka *dough used in sweets*
yoğurt yo·oort *yogurt*
— **çorbası** chor·ba·suh *yogurt soup*
yoğurtlu fıstıklı köfte yo·oort·loo fuhs·tuhk·luh kerf·te *köfte dish of bulgur, yogurt, tomato & capsicum flakes*
yoğurtlu patlıcan salatası yo·oort·loo pat·luh·jan sa·la·ta·suh *eggplant salad with yogurt*
yoğurtlu pazı yo·oort·loo pa·zuh *chard in garlicky yogurt sauce (Kastamonu)*
yörük kebabı yer·rewk ke·ba·buh *'nomad's kebab' – lamb, mushroom, capsicum, artichoke, tomato, beans & macaroni*
yulaf yoo·laf *oats*
yumurta yoo·moor·ta *egg*
yuvarlama yoo·var·la·ma *soup with chickpeas & small mince dumplings*

yüksük çorbası yewk·sewk chor·ba·suh *soup of chickpeas & mincemeat*
yüksük makarna yewk·sewk ma·kar·na *short, fat macaroni*
yürek yew·rek *heart*

Z

zerdali zer·da·lee *wild apricots*
zencefil zen·je·feel *ginger*
zerde zer·de *dessert of rice, almonds, pistachios & pomegranate*
zeytin zay·teen *olive*
— **piyazı** pee·ya·zuh *salad of green olives, walnuts, capsicum & pomegranate*
zeytinyağı zay·teen·ya·uh *olive oil*
zeytinyağlı biber dolması zay·teen·ya·luh bee·ber dol·ma·suh *rice-stuffed capsicum*
zeytinyağlı dolma içi zay·teen·ya·luh dol·ma ee·chee *seasoned rice used for stuffing vegetables*
zeytinyağlı domates dolması zay·teen·ya·luh do·ma·tes dol·ma·suh *stuffed tomato with rice*
zeytinyağlı pilaki zay·teen·ya·luh pee·la·kee *pilaki of black-eyed peas, spring onion, carrot & potato (Aydın)*
zeytinyağlı pırasa zay·teen·ya·luh puh·ra·sa *leeks in olive oil with carrot, rice, sugar, salt & lemon*
zeytinyağlı pırasa böreği zay·teen·ya·luh puh·ra·sa ber·re·ee *leek pie in olive oil*
zeytinyağlı taze bakla zay·teen·ya·luh ta·ze bak·la *whole broad beans in olive oil*
zeytinyağlı taze fasulye zay·teen·ya·luh ta·ze fa·sool·ye *green beans in olive oil*
zeytinyağlı yaprak dolması zay·teen·ya·luh yap·rak dol·ma·suh *stuffed vine leaves with rice in olive oil*
zeytinyağlı yaz türlüsü zay·teen·ya·luh yaz tewr·lew·sew *vegetables in olive oil*
zeytinyağlı yeşil fasulye zay·teen·ya·luh ye·sheel fa·sool·ye *string beans in olive oil*
zeytinyağlılar zay·teen·ya·luh·lar *cold vegetables in olive oil*
zile pekmezi zee·le pek·me·zee *pekmez whipped with egg white (Tokat)*
zırz zuhrz *salad with fresh onion, spinach, süzme yoğurt, olive oil & boiled eggs*

emergencies

acil durumlar

Help!	*İmdat!*	*eem*·dat
Stop!	*Dur!*	door
Go away!	*Git burdan!*	geet boor·*dan*
Thief!	*Hırsız var!*	huhr·*suhz* var
Fire!	*Yangın var!*	*yan*·guhn var
Watch out!	*Dikkat et!*	*deek*·kat et

Call the police.
Polis çağırın.   po·*lees* cha·*uh*·ruhn

Call a doctor.
Doktor çağırın.   dok·*tor* cha·*uh*·ruhn

Call an ambulance.
Ambulans çağırın.   am·boo·*lans* cha·*uh*·ruhn

It's an emergency.
Bu acil bir durum.   boo a·*jeel* beer *doo*·room

There's been an accident.
Bir kaza oldu.   beer ka·*za* ol·*doo*

Could you please help?
Yardım edebilir   yar·*duhm* e·*de*·bee·leer
misiniz lütfen?   mee·see·*neez* lewt·fen

Can I use your phone?
Telefonunuzu   te·le·fo·noo·noo·*zoo*
kullanabilir miyim?   kool·la·*na*·bee·leer mee·*yeem*

signs

Acil Servis	a·*jeel* ser·*vees*	**Emergency Department**
Hastane	has·*ta*·ne	**Hospital**
Polis	po·*lees*	**Police**
Polis Karakolu	po·*lees* ka·ra·ko·*loo*	**Police Station**

I'm lost.
Kayboldum. kai·bol·*doom*

Where are the toilets?
Tuvaletler nerede? too·va·let·*ler* ne·re·de

Is it safe ...?	... *güvenli mi?*	... gew·ven·*lee* mee
at night	*Geceleyin*	ge·je·le·*yeen*
for gay	*Homoseksüeller*	ho·mo·sek·sew·el·*ler*
people	*için*	ee·*cheen*
for travellers	*Seyahat edenler*	se·ya·*hat* e·den·*ler*
	için	ee·*cheen*
for women	*Bayanlar için*	ba·yan·*lar* ee·*cheen*
on your own	*Yalnız başına*	yal·*nuhz* ba·shuh·*na*

police

polis

Where's the police station?
Polis karakolu nerede? po·*lees* ka·ra·ko·*loo* ne·re·de

Please telephone the Tourist Police.
Lütfen turizm polisini *lewt*·fen too·*reezm* po·lee·see·*nee*
arayın. a·*ra*·yuhn

I want to report an offence.
Şikayette bulunmak shee·ka·yet·*te* boo·loon·*mak*
istiyorum. ees·*tee*·yo·room

I've been ...	*Ben ...*	ben ...
assaulted	*saldırıya uğradım*	sal·duh·ruh·*ya* oo·ra·*duhm*
raped	*tecavüze uğradım*	te·ja·vew·*ze* oo·ra·*duhm*
robbed	*soyuldum*	so·yool·*doom*

He/She has been ...	*O ...*	o ...
assaulted	*saldırıya uğradı*	sal·duh·ruh·*ya* oo·ra·*duh*
raped	*tecavüze uğradı*	te·ja·vew·*ze* oo·ra·*duh*
robbed	*soyuldu*	so·yool·*doo*

SAFE TRAVEL

He/She tried to … me.	… çalıştı.	… cha·luhsh·tuh
assault	Bana saldırmaya	ba·na sal·duhr·ma·ya
rape	Bana tecavüz etmeye	ba·na te·ja·vewz et·me·ye
rob	Beni soymaya	be·nee soy·ma·ya

I've lost my …	… kayıp.	… ka·yuhp
My … was/were stolen.	… çalındı.	… cha·luhn·duh
backpack	Sırt çantası	suhrt chan·ta·suh
bags	Çantalar	chan·ta·lar
credit card	Kredi kartı	kre·dee kar·tuh
handbag	El çantası	el chan·ta·suh
jewellery	Mücevherler	mew·jev·her·ler
money	Para	pa·ra
papers	Evraklar	ev·rak·lar
travellers cheques	Seyahat çekleri	se·ya·hat chek·le·ree
passport	Pasaport	pa·sa·port
wallet	Cüzdan	jewz·dan

I've been drugged.
Bana uyuşturucu verildi.
ba·na oo·yoosh·too·roo·joo ve·reel·dee

He/She has been drugged.
Ona uyuşturucu verildi.
o·na oo·yoosh·too·roo·joo ve·reel·dee

It was him/her.
Oydu.
oy·doo

I have insurance.
Sigortam var.
see·gor·tam var

What am I accused of?
Neyle suçlanıyorum?
nay·le sooch·la·nuh·yo·room

I didn't realise I was doing anything wrong.
Yanlış birşey yaptığımın farkında değildim.
yan·luhsh beer·shay yap·tuh·uh·muhn far·kuhn·da de·eel·deem

I didn't do it.
Ben yapmadım.
ben yap·ma·duhm

... suçlanıyorsunuz.		
... sooch·la·nuh·yor·soo·nooz		**You're charged with ...**
... suçlanıyor.		
... sooch·la·nuh·yor		**He/She is charged with ...**
Hırsızlıkla	huhr·suhz·*luhk*·la	**theft**
Saldırıda	sal·duh·ruh·*da*	**assault**
bulunmakla	boo·loon·*mak*·la	
Vize süresini	vee·*ze* sew·re·see·*nee*	**overstaying a**
aşmakla	ash·*mak*·la	**visa**
Vizesiz	vee·ze·*seez*	**not having a**
seyahat etmekle	se·ya·*hat* et·*mek*·le	**visa**
Yasa dışı	ya·*sa* duh·*shuh*	**possession**
uyuşturucu	oo·yoosh·too·roo·*joo*	**(of illegal**
madde	mad·*de*	**substances)**
bulundurmakla	boo·loon·door·*mak*·la	
... cezası.	... je·za·*suh*	**It's a ... fine.**
Hız	huhz	**speeding**
Park	park	**parking**

I want to contact my embassy/consulate.

Konsoloslukla görüşmek istiyorum. kon·so·los·*look*·la ger·rewsh·*mek* ees·*tee*·yo·room

Can I make a phone call?

Bir telefon edebilir miyim? beer te·le·*fon* e·*de*·bee·leer mee·*yeem*

Can I have a lawyer (who speaks English)?

(İngilizce konuşan) Bir avukat istiyorum. (een·gee·*leez*·je ko·noo·*shan*) beer a·voo·*kat* ees·*tee*·yo·room

Can I pay an on-the-spot fine?

Cezayı hemen ödeyebilir miyim? je·za·*yuh* he·*men* er·de·*ye*·bee·leer mee·*yeem*

I have a prescription for this drug.

Bu ilaç için reçetem var. boo ee·*lach* ee·*cheen* re·che·*tem* var

doctor

doktorda

Where's the nearest ...?	En yakın ... nerede?	en ya·*kuhn* ... *ne*·re·de
dentist	dişçi	deesh·*chee*
doctor	doktor	dok·*tor*
emergency department	acil servis	a·*jeel* ser·*vees*
hospital	hastane	has·*ta*·ne
medical centre	poliklinik	po·*lee*·klee·neek
optometrist	gözlükçü	gerz·lewk·*chew*
(night) pharmacist	(nöbetçi) eczane	(ner·bet·*chee*) ej·*za*·ne

I need a doctor (who speaks English).
(İngilizce konuşan) (een·gee·*leez*·je ko·noo·*shan*)
Bir doktora ihtiyacım var. beer dok·to·*ra* eeh·tee·ya·*juhm* var

Could I see a female doctor?
Bayan doktora ba·*yan* dok·to·*ra*
görünebilir miyim? ger·rew·*ne*·bee·leer mee·*yeem*

Could the doctor come here?
Doktor buraya dok·*tor* boo·ra·*ya*
gelebilir mi? ge·*le*·bee·leer mee

Is there an after-hours emergency number?
Mesai saatleri harici acil me·sa·*ee* sa·at·le·*ree* ha·ree·*jee* a·*jeel*
telefon numarası var mı? te·le·*fon* noo·ma·ra·*suh* var muh

I've run out of my medication.
İlacım bitti. ee·la·*juhm* beet·*tee*

This is my usual medicine.
Bu benim daimi ilacım. boo be·*neem* da·ee·mee ee·la·*juhm*

My child weighs (20) kilos.
Çocuğumun ağırlığı cho·joo·oo·*moon* a·uhr·luh·*uh*
(yirmi) kilodur. (yeer·*mee*) kee·*lo*·door

hepatitis or *sarılık*

If you're speaking to a medical professional, you can say *hepatit A/B/C* he·pa·*teet* a/be/je for 'hepatitis A/B/C'. For non-medical people, use the word *sarılık* sa·ruh·*luhk*, the general term for all three kinds of hepatitis.

What's the correct dosage?
Kullanılması gereken   kool·la·nuhl·ma·*suh* ge·re·*ken*
dozaj nedir?   do·*zazh* ne·deer

My prescription is …
Benim reçetem …   be·*neem* re·che·*tem* …

How much will it cost?
Ne kadar eder?   ne ka·*dar* e·*der*

Can I have a receipt for my insurance?
Sağlık sigortam için   sa·*luhk* see·*gor*·tam ee·*cheen*
makbuz alabilir miyim?   mak·*booz* a·la·bee·leer mee·*yeem*

I don't want a blood transfusion.
Kan nakli istemiyorum.   kan nak·*lee* ees·te·mee·yo·room

Please use a new syringe.
Lütfen yeni bir iğne   *lewt*·fen ye·*nee* beer ee·*ne*
kullanın.   kool·*la*·nuhn

I have my own syringe.
Benim kendi   be·*neem* ken·*dee*
şırıngam var.   shuh·ruhn·*gam* var

I've been	*Ben … aşısı*	ben … a·shuh·*suh*
vaccinated against …	*oldum.*	ol·*doom*
He/She has been	*O … aşısı*	o … a·shuh·*suh*
vaccinated against …	*oldu.*	ol·*doo*
tetanus	*tetanoz*	te·ta·*noz*
typhoid	*tifo*	tee·*fo*

I need new …	*Yeni …*	ye·*nee* …
	ihtiyacım var.	eeh·tee·ya·*juhm* var
contact	*kontakt*	kon·*takt*
lenses	*lenslere*	lens·le·*re*
glasses	*gözlüğe*	gerz·lew·*e*

symptoms & conditions

belirtiler & sağlık durumu

I'm sick.
   Hastayım.   has·*ta*·yuhm

My friend/child is (very) sick.
   Arkadaşım/çocuğum   ar·ka·da·*shuhm*/cho·joo·*oom*
   (çok) hasta.   (chok) *has*·ta

He/She is **having a/an …**	*O …*	o …
allergic reaction	*alerjili*	a·ler·zhee·lee
asthma attack	*astım krizi*	as·*tuhm* kree·*zee*
	geçiriyor	ge·chee·*ree*·yor
baby	*doğurmak üzere*	do·oor·*mak* ew·ze·re
heart attack	*kalp krizi*	kalp kree·*zee*
	geçiriyor	ge·chee·*ree*·yor

I've been …	*Ben …*	ben …
bitten by	*bir hayvan*	beer hai·*van*
an animal	*tarafından*	ta·ra·fuhn·*dan*
	ısırıldım	uh·suh·ruhl·*duhm*
injured	*yaralandım*	ya·ra·lan·*duhm*
vomiting	*kusuyorum*	koo·soo·yo·room

He/She has been …	*O …*	o …
bitten by	*bir hayvan*	beer hai·*van*
an animal	*tarafından*	ta·ra·fuhn·*dan*
	ısırıldı	uh·suh·ruhl·*duh*
injured	*yaralandı*	ya·ra·lan·*duh*
vomiting	*kusuyor*	koo·*soo*·yor

sick as a dog

If you're not feeling well, try not to use the English word
'sick' – the Turkish word *sik* seek means 'fuck' or 'dick' so you
could get a slightly unexpected response to your death-
bed cries. Say *hastayım* has·*ta*·yuhm (lit: sick-I-am) instead,
or 'I'm ill' if you can only choke out an English phrase.

health

193

Ne şikayetiniz var?
ne shee·ka·ye·tee·*neez* var — What's the problem?

Nereniz ağrıyor?
ne·re·neez a·*ruh*·yor — Where does it hurt?

Ateşiniz var mı?
a·te·shee·*neez* var muh — Do you have a temperature?

Ne kadar zamandır bu durumdasınız?
ne ka·*dar* za·*man*·duhr boo doo·room·*da*·suh·nuhz — How long have you been like this?

Daha önce böyle bir şikayetiniz oldu mu?
da·*ha* ern·je bay·*le* beer shee·ka·ye·tee·*neez* ol·*doo* moo — Have you had this before?

Cinsel hayatınızda aktif misiniz?
jeen·*sel* ha·ya·tuh·nuhz·*da* ak·*teef* mee·see·*neez* — Are you sexually active?

Korunmasız cinsel ilişkide bulundunuz mu?
ko·roon·ma·*suhz* jeen·*sel* ee·leesh·kee·*de* boo·loon·doo·*nooz* moo — Have you had unprotected sex?

... kullanıyor musunuz? — ... kool·la·*nuh*·yor moo·soo·*nooz* — Do you ...?
  İçki — eech·*kee* — drink
  Sigara — see·*ga*·ra — smoke
  Uyuşturucu — oo·yoosh·too·roo·*joo* — take drugs

... var mı? — ... var muh — Are you ...?
  Herhangi — her·*han*·gee — allergic to
  birşeye — beer·she·*ye* — anything
  alerjiniz — a·ler·jee·*neez*
  Sürekli — sew·rek·*lee* — on medication
  kullandığınız — kool·lan·duh·uh·*nuhz*
  bir ilaç — beer ee·*lach*

the doctor may say ...

Ne kadar zaman burada kalacaksınız?
ne ka·*dar* za·*man* boo·ra·*da*
ka·la·*jak*·suh·nuhz
How long are you travelling for?

Ülkenize döndüğünüz zaman bir doktora görünmelisiniz.
ewl·ke·nee·ze dern·dew·ew·*newz*
za·*man* beer dok·to·*ra*
ger·rewn·me·*lee*·see·neez
You should have it checked when you go home.

Tedavi için ülkenize dönmeniz gerekli.
te·da·*vee* ee·*cheen* ewl·ke·nee·ze
dern·me·*neez* ge·rek·*lee*
You should return home for treatment.

Hastaneye yatırılmanız gerekli.
has·ta·ne·*ye* ya·tuh·ruhl·ma·*nuhz*
ge·rek·*lee*
You need to be admitted to hospital.

Çok evhamlısınız.
chok ev·ham·*luh*·suh·nuhz
You're a hypochondriac.

I feel ...	... hissediyorum.	... hees·se·*dee*·yo·room
anxious	*Endişeli*	en·dee·she·*lee*
better	*Daha iyi*	da·*ha* ee·*yee*
depressed	*Depresif*	dep·re·*seef*
dizzy	*Başımın*	ba·shuh·*muhn*
	döndüğünü	dern·dew·ew·*new*
hot and cold	*Bir sıcak bir soğuk*	beer suh·*jak* beer so·*ook*
nauseous	*Kusacak gibi*	koo·sa·*jak* gee·*bee*
shivery	*Üşüdüğümü*	ew·shew·dew·ew·*mew*
strange	*Tuhaf*	too·*haf*
weak	*Halsiz*	hal·*seez*
worse	*Daha kötü*	da·*ha* ker·*tew*

It hurts here.
Burası ağrıyor.   boo·ra·*suh* a·*ruh*·yor

I'm dehydrated.
Vücudum susuz kaldı.   vew·joo·*doom* soo·*sooz* kal·*duh*

I can't sleep.
Uyuyamıyorum.   oo·yoo·*ya*·muh·yo·room

I think it's the medication I'm on.
Sanırım kullandığım   sa·nuh·*ruhm* kool·lan·duh·*uhm*
ilaçtan kaynaklanıyor.   ee·lach·*tan* kai·nak·la·*nuh*·yor

I'm on medication for ...
... için ilaç   ... ee·*cheen* ee·*lach*
kullanıyorum.   kool·la·*nuh*·yo·room

I have (a/an) ...
Bende ... var.   ben·*de* ... var

He/She is on medication for ...
O ... için ilaç   o ... ee·*cheen* ee·*lach*
kullanıyor.   kool·la·*nuh*·yor

He/She has (a/an) ...
Onda ... var.   on·*da* ... var

asthma	*astım*	as·*tuhm*
cold n	*soğuk algınlığı*	so·*ook* al·guhn·luh·*uh*
constipation	*kabızlık*	ka·buhz·*luhk*
cough n	*öksürük*	erk·sew·*rewk*
diabetes	*şeker hastalığı*	she·*ker* has·ta·luh·*uh*
diarrhoea	*ishal*	ees·*hal*
fever	*ateş*	a·*tesh*
headache	*baş ağrısı*	bash a·ruh·*suh*
intestinal worms	*bağırsak kurdu*	ba·uhr·*sak* koor·*doo*
migraine	*migren*	meeg·*ren*
nausea	*bulantı*	boo·lan·*tuh*
pain	*ağrı*	a·*ruh*
sore throat	*boğaz ağrısı*	bo·*az* a·ruh·*suh*
sunburn	*güneş yanığı*	gew·*nesh* ya·nuh·*uh*

I've recently	*Yakın zamanda*	ya·*kuhn* za·man·*da*
had ...	*... geçirdim.*	... ge·cheer·*deem*
He/She has	*O yakın zamanda*	o ya·*kuhn* za·man·*da*
recently had ...	*... geçirdi.*	... ge·cheer·*dee*
(amoebic)	*(amibik)*	(a·mee·*beek*)
dysentery	*dizanteri*	dee·zan·te·*ree*
giardiasis	*giardiyaz*	gee·ar·dee·*yaz*
malaria	*sıtma*	suht·*ma*
rabies	*kuduz*	koo·*dooz*

women's health

(I think) I'm pregnant.
(Sanırım) Hamileyim.   (sa·*nuh*·ruhm) ha·mee·*le*·yeem

I'm on the pill.
Doğum kontrol hapı   do·*oom* kon·*trol* ha·*puh*
kullanıyorum.   kool·la·*nuh*·yo·room

I haven't had my period for (six) weeks.
(Altı) haftadır   (al·*tuh*) haf·ta·*duhr*
adet görmedim.   a·det *ger*·me·deem

I've noticed a lump here.
Burada bir şişlik   boo·ra·*da* beer sheesh·*leek*
fark ettim.   fark et·*teem*

Do you have something for (period pain)?
(Adet ağrısı) için   (*a*·det a·ruh·*suh*) ee·*cheen*
ilacınız var mı?   ee·la·juh·*nuhz* var muh

the doctor may say …

Adet halinde misiniz?
   a·det ha·leen·*de* mee·see·*neez*   **Are you menstruating?**

Doğum kontrol hapı kullanıyor musunuz?
   do·*oom* kon·*trol* ha·*puh*
   kool·la·*nuh*·yor moo·soo·*nooz*   **Are you using contraception?**

En son ne zaman adet gördünüz?
   en son ne za·man *a*·det
   ger·*dew*·newz   **When did you last have your period?**

Hamile misiniz?
   ha·mee·*le* mee·see·*neez*   **Are you pregnant?**

Hamilesiniz.
   ha·mee·*le*·see·neez   **You're pregnant.**

health

197

I have a ...	... var.	... var
urinary tract infection	İdrar yolları iltihabım	eed·rar yol·la·ruh eel·tee·ha·buhm
yeast infection	Mantar enfeksiyonum	man·tar en·fek·see·yo·noom

I need ...	... ihtiyacım var.	... eeh·tee·ya·juhm var
contraception	Doğum kontrol hapına	do·oom kon·trol ha·puh·na
the morning-after pill	İlişki sonrası kullanılabilen doğum kontrol ilacına	ee·leesh·kee son·ra·suh kool·la·nuh·la·bee·len do·oom kon·trol ee·la·juh·na
a pregnancy test	Hamilelik testine	ha·mee·le·leek tes·tee·ne

allergies

I'm allergic to ...	... alerjim var.	... a·ler·zheem var
He/She is allergic to ...	... alerjisi var.	... a·ler·zhee·see var
antibiotics	Antibiyotiklere	an·tee·bee·yo·teek·le·re
anti-inflammatories	Anti-emflamatuarlara	an·tee· em·fla·ma·too·ar·la·ra
aspirin	Aspirine	as·pee·ree·ne
bees	Arılara	a·ruh·la·ra
codeine	Kodeine	ko·de·ee·ne
penicillin	Penisiline	pe·nee·see·lee·ne
pollen	Polenlere	po·len·le·re
sulphur-based drugs	Sülfür bazlı ilaçlara	sewl·fewr baz·luh ee·lach·la·ra

I have a skin allergy.

Alerjik bir cildim var.   a·ler·zheek beer jeel·deem var

If you suffer from food allergies, see **special diets & allergies**, page 174.

When a friend is sorry about a promise they couldn't keep, or has had an accident or material loss but suffered no real harm, you can bid them *Canın sağ olsun!* ja·*nuhn* sa ol·*soon* (May your soul be safe from harm!)

To commiserate a friend who has suffered illness or injury, or has a sudden, troubling problem, the appropriate phrase is *Geçmiş olsun!* gech·*meesh* ol·*soon* (May it be in your past!). If there has been a death in the family, wish them *Başınız sağ olsun!* ba·shuh·*nuhz* sa ol·soo·*nooz* (May your life be spared!).

In many of these phrases the giveaway is the last word *olsun* ol·*soon* (may it be). If you hear that, and the context seems right, say *sağol* sa·*ol* (thanks) in response.

alternative treatments

alternatif tedavi yöntemleri

I don't use (Western medicine).
(Batı tıbbına) ait ilaç ve tedavi yöntemlerini kullanmıyorum.
(ba·*tuh* tuhb·buh·*na*) a·*eet* ee·*lach* ve te·da·*vee* yern·tem·le·ree·*nee* kool·*lan*·muh·yo·room

I prefer ...	*... tedavi yöntemini tercih ediyorum.*	... te·da·*vee* yern·te·mee·*nee* ter·*jeeh* e·*dee*·yo·room
Can I see someone who practises ...?	*... ile uğraşan birisini görebilir miyim?*	... ee·*le* oo·ra·*shan* bee·ree·see·*nee* ger·re·bee·leer mee·*yeem*
acupuncture	*Akupunktur*	a·koo·*poonk*·toor
naturopathy	*Natüropati*	na·tew·ro·pa·*tee*
reflexology	*Refleksoloji*	ref·lek·so·lo·*zhee*

parts of the body

My ... hurts.
  Benim ... ağrıyor.   be·*neem* ... a·*ruh*·yor

I can't move my ...
  ... hareket ettiremiyorum.   ... ha·re·*ket* et·tee·*re*·mee·yo·room

I have a cramp in my ...
  ... kramp girdi.   ... kramp geer·*dee*

My ... is swollen.
  ... şişti.   ... sheesh·*tee*

For other parts of the body, see the **dictionary**.

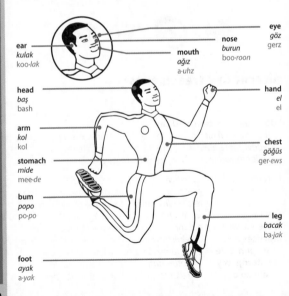

eye
göz
gerz

nose
burun
boo·*roon*

ear
kulak
koo·*lak*

mouth
ağız
a·*uhz*

head
baş
bash

hand
el
el

arm
kol
kol

chest
göğüs
ger·ews

stomach
mide
mee·de

bum
popo
po·po

leg
bacak
ba·jak

foot
ayak
a·yak

pharmacist

I need something for (a headache).
*(Baş ağrısı) için
birşey almak istiyorum.*
(bash a·ruh·*suh*) ee·*cheen*
beer·*shay* al·*mak* ees·*tee*·yo·room

Do I need a prescription for (antihistamines)?
*(Antihistamin) almak
için reçeteye
ihtiyacım var mı?*
(*an*·tee·hees·ta·meen) al·*mak*
ee·*cheen* re·che·te·*ye*
eeh·tee·ya·*juhm* var muh

I have a prescription.
Reçetem var.
re·che·*tem* var

How many times a day?
Günde kaç kez almalıyım?
gewn·*de* kach kez al·ma·luh·*yuhm*

Will it make me drowsy?
Uyku verir mi?
ooy·koo ve·*reer* mee

antiseptic n	*antiseptik*	an·tee·sep·*teek*
gut blockers (for diarrhoea)	*müsil ilacı*	mew·seel ee·la·*juh*
painkillers	*ağrı kesici*	a·ruh ke·see·*jee*
thermometer	*termometre*	ter·mo·*met*·re
rehydration salts	*rehidrasyon tuzları*	re·heed·ras·*yon* tooz·la·*ruh*

the pharmacist may say ...

Bunu daha önce kullandınız mı?
boo·*noo* da·*ha* ern·je
kool·lan·*duh*·nuhz muh
Have you taken this before?

Günde iki kez (yemekle birlikte).
gewn·*de* ee·*kee* kez
(ye·*mek*·le beer·*leek*·te)
Twice a day (with food).

İlacı bitirene kadar kullanmalısınız.
ee·la·*juh* bee·tee·re·*ne* ka·*dar*
kool·lan·ma·*luh*·suh·nuhz
You must complete the course.

dentist

I have a ...	Dişim ...	dee·*sheem* ...
broken tooth	kırıldı	kuh·ruhl·*duh*
cavity	çürüdü	chew·rew·*dew*
toothache	ağrıyor	a·*ruh*·yor

I've lost a filling.
Dolgum düştü. dol·*goom* dewsh·*tew*

My dentures are broken.
Takma dişim kırıldı. tak·*ma* dee·*sheem* kuh·ruhl·*duh*

My gums hurt.
Damaklarım ağrıyor. da·mak·la·*ruhm* a·*ruh*·yor

I don't want it extracted.
Dişimin çekilmesini dee·shee·*meen* che·keel·me·see·*nee*
istemiyorum. ees·*te*·mee·yo·room

I need (a/an) ...	... yaptırmam gerekli.	... yap·tuhr·*mam* ge·rek·*lee*
anaesthetic	Anestezi	a·nes·te·*zee*
filling	Dolgu	dol·*goo*

the dentist may say ...

Hiç acımayacak.
heech a·juh·ma·ya·*jak*

This won't hurt a bit.

Ağzınızı iyice açın.
a·zuh·nuh·*zuh* ee·yee·*je* a·chuhn

Open wide.

Hareket etmeyin.
ha·re·*ket* et·me·yeen

Don't move.

Bunu ısırın.
boo·*noo* uh·*suh*·ruhn

Bite down on this.

Ağzınızı çalkalayın!
a·zuh·nuh·*zuh* chal·ka·*la*·yuhn

Rinse!

Bitmedi, tekrar gelmelisiniz.
beet·me·dee tek·*rar*
gel·me·*lee*·see·neez

Come back, I haven't finished.

SUSTAINABLE TRAVEL

As the climate change debate heats up, the matter of sustainability becomes an important part of the travel vernacular. In practical terms, this means assessing our impact on the environment and local cultures and economies – and acting to make that impact as positive as possible. Here are some basic phrases to get you on your way …

communication & cultural differences

I'd like to learn some of your local dialects.
Bu yörelerin	boo yer·re·le·*reen*
şivesini öğrenmek	shee·ve·see·*nee* er·ren·*mek*
istiyorum.	is·*tee*·yo·room

Would you like me to teach you some English?
Size biraz İngilizce	see·ze bee·*raz* een·gee·leez·je
öğretmemi ister	er·ret·me·*mee* ees·*ter*
misiniz?	mee·see·*neez*

Is this a local or national custom?
Bu yerel mi,	boo ye·*rel* mee
yoksa ulusal	yok·*sa* oo·loo·*sal*
bir gelenek mi?	beer ge·le·*nek* mee

I respect your customs.
Geleneklerinize saygı	ge·le·nek·le·ree·nee·ze sai·*guh*
duyuyorum.	doo·*yoo*·yo·room

community benefit & involvement

What sorts of issues is this community facing?
Toplumun gündemini	top·loo·*moon* gewn·de·mee·*nee*
meşgul eden konular	mesh·*gool* e·*den* ko·noo·*lar*
nelerdir?	ne·ler·deer

drought	kuraklık	koo·rak·luhk
media control	basın yayın	ba·suhn ya·yuhn
	özgürlüğü	erz·gewr·lew·ew
political conflict	politik görüş	po·lee·teek ger·rewsh
	ayrılığı	ai·ruh·luh·uh
religious conflict	dini görüş	dee·nee ger·rewsh
	ayrılığı	ai·ruh·luh·uh

I'd like to volunteer my skills.

Gönüllü olarak	ger·newl·lew o·la·rak
çalışmak	cha·luhsh·mak
istiyorum.	ees·tee·yo·room

Are there any volunteer programs available in the area?

Bu bölgede gönüllü	boo berl·ge·de ger·newl·lew
hizmet programları	heez·met prog·ram·la·ruh
var mı?	var muh

environment

Where can I recycle this?

Bunu atabileceğim	boo·noo a·ta·bee·le·je·eem
geri dönüşüm	ge·ree der·new·shewm
kumbarası nerede var?	koom·ba·ra·suh ne·re·de var

transport

Can we get there by public transport?

Oraya toplu taşım	o·ra·ya top·loo ta·shuhm
aracıyla gidebilir	a·ra·juhy·la gee·de·bee·leer
miyiz?	mee·yeez

Can we get there by bike?

| Oraya bisikletle | o·ra·ya bee·seek·let·le |
| gidebilir miyiz? | gee·de·bee·leer mee·yeez |

I'd prefer to walk there.

| Oraya yürümeyi | o·ra·ya yew·rew·me·yee |
| tercih ederim. | ter·jeeh e·de·reem |

accommodation

I'd like to stay at a locally run hotel.

Yerel olarak işletilen bir	ye·*rel* o·la·*rak* eesh·le·tee·*len* beer
otelde kalmak istiyorum.	o·tel·*de* kal·*mak* ees·*tee*·yo·room

Can I turn the air conditioning off and open the window?

Klimayı kapatıp	klee·ma·*yuh* ka·pa·*tuhp*
pencereyi açabilir	pen·je·re·*yee* a·*cha*·bee·leer
miyim?	mee·*yeem*

Are there any ecolodges here?

Burada ekolojik	boo·ra·*da* e·ko·lo·*zheek*
konaklama yerleri var mı?	ko·nak·la·*ma* yer·le·*ree* var muh

There's no need to change my sheets.

Çarşaflarımın	char·shaf·la·ruh·*muhn*
değişmesine gerek yok.	de·eesh·me·see·*ne* ge·*rek* yok

shopping

Where can I buy locally produced goods?

Bu yöreye ait ürünler	boo yer·re·*ye* a·*eet* ew·rewn·*ler*
nereden alabilirim?	ne·re·*den* a·*la*·bee·lee·reem

Where can I buy locally produced souvenirs?

Bu yöreye ait	boo yer·re·*ye* a·*eet*
hediyelik eşyalar	he·dee·ye·*leek* esh·ya·*lar*
nereden alabilirim?	ne·re·*den* a·*la*·bee·lee·reem

Do you sell Fair Trade products?

Adil Ticaret ürünleri	a·*deel* tee·ja·*ret* ew·rewn·le·*ree*
satıyor musunuz?	sa·*tuh*·yor moo·soo·*nooz*

food

Do you sell ...?	... satıyor	... sa·*tuh*·yor
	musunuz?	moo·soo·*nooz*
locally	Yöresel	yer·re·*sel*
produced food	yiyecekler	yee·ye·jek·*ler*
organic produce	Organic ürünler	or·ga·*neek* ew·rewn·*ler*

Can you tell me what traditional foods I should try?

Hangi geleneksel   *han·gee ge·le·nek·sel*
yiyecekleri dememi   *yee·ye·jek·le·ree de·ne·me·mee*
tavsiye edersiniz?   *tav·see·ye e·der·see·neez*

sightseeing

Does your company …?	*Firmanız …?*	*feer·ma·nuhz …*
donate money to charity	*hayır kurumlarına para bağışlıyor mu*	*ha·yuhr koo·room·la·ruh·na pa·ra ba·uhsh·luh·yor moo*
hire local guides	*yerel rehberler kiralıyor mu*	*ye·rel reh·ber·ler kee·ra·luh·yor moo*
visit local businesses	*yerel işletmelere uğruyor mu*	*ye·rel eesh·let·me·le·re oo·roo·yor moo*

Are cultural tours available?

Kültürel turlar   *kewl·tew·rel toor·lar*
düzenliyor musunuz?   *dew·zen·lee·yor moo·soo·nooz*

Does the guide speak local dialects?

Rehber yerel   *reh·ber ye·rel*
şiveleri   *shee·ve·lee·ree*
konuşuyor mu?   *ko·noo·shoo·yor moo*

… dialect	… Şivesi	… she·ve·see
Aegean	*Ege*	*e·ge*
Black Sea	*Karadeniz*	*ka·ra·de·neez*
Cyprus	*Kıbrıs*	*kuhb·ruhs*
Eastern Anatolia	*Doğu Anadolu*	*do·oo a·na·do·loo*
Middle Anatolia	*Orta Anadolu*	*or·ta a·na·do·loo*
Rumelia	*Rumeli*	*roo·me·lee*
Southeastern Anatolia	*Güneydoğu Anadolu*	*gew·nay·do·oo a·na·do·loo*
Thrace	*Trakya*	*trak·ya*

You'll find words marked as adjective a, noun n, verb v, singular sg, plural pl, informal inf and polite pol where necessary. All nouns are in the nominative case. Words which take suffixes (word endings), such as the Turkish words for 'to' and 'without', are shown with their different endings separated by a slash (/). To work out which one to use, see the a–z phrasebuilder and the box on vowel harmony, page 13.

A

aboard -da/-de/-ta/-te -da/-de/-ta/-te
abortion çocuk aldırma cho·jook al·duhr·ma
about etrafında et·ra·fuhn·da
above yukarısında yoo·ka·ruh·suhn·da
abroad yurt dışı yoort duh·shuh
accident kaza ka·za
accommodation kalacak yer ka·la·jak yer
account n hesap he·sap
acropolis akropolis ak·ro·po·lees
across karşısında kar·shuh·suhn·da
activist şiddet yanlısı sheed·det yan·luh·suh
actor oyuncu o·yoon·joo
acupuncture akupunktur a·koo·poonk·toor
adaptor adaptör a·dap·ter
addiction bağımlılık ba·uhm·luh·luhk
address n adres ad·res
administration yönetim yer·ne·teem
admission (price) giriş gee·reesh
admit kabul etmek ka·bool et·mek
adult n yetişkin ye·teesh·keen
advertisement ilan ee·lan
advice tavsiye tav·see·ye
Aegean Sea Ege Denizi e·ge de·nee·zee
aerobics ayrobik ai·ro·beek
aeroplane uçak oo·chak
Africa Afrika af·ree·ka
after sonra son·ra
(this) afternoon (bu) öğleden sonra (boo) er·le·den son·ra
aftershave traş losyonu trash los·yo·noo
again tekrar tek·rar
age n yaş yash
(three days) ago (üç gün) önce (ewch gewn) ern·je
agora (open ground, town square) büyük meydan bew·yewk may·dan

agora (market place) pazar yeri pa·zar ye·ree
agree aynı fikirde olmak ai·nuh fee·keer·de ol·mak
agriculture tarım ta·ruhm
ahead ileride ee·le·ree·de
AIDS AIDS ayds
air n hava ha·va
air conditioning klima klee·ma
airline hava yolları ha·va yol·la·ruh
airmail hava yoluyla ha·va yo·looy·la
airplane uçak oo·chak
airport havaalanı ha·va·a·la·nuh
airport tax toprak bastı top·rak bas·tuh
aisle (on plane) koridor ko·ree·dor
alarm clock çalar saat cha·lar sa·at
alcohol alkol al·kol
all hepsi hep·see
allergy alerji a·ler·zhee
almond badem ba·dem
almost hemen hemen he·men he·men
alone yalnız yal·nuhz
already zaten za·ten
also bir de beer de
altar sunak soo·nak
altitude yükseklik yewk·sek·leek
always her zaman her za·man
ambassador büyükelçi bew·yewk·el·chee
ambulance ambulans am·boo·lans
American football Amerikan futbolu a·me·ree·kan foot·bo·loo
anaemia kansızlık kan·suhz·luhk
anarchist n anarşist a·nar·sheest
ancient a tarihi ta·ree·hee
and ve ve
angry kızgın kuhz·guhn
animal hayvan hai·van
ankle ayak bileği a·yak bee·le·ee
another diğer dee·er

answer n *cevap* je·*vap*
ant *karınca* ka·ruhn·*ja*
antibiotics *antibiyotik* an·tee·bee·yo·*teek*
antihistamines *antihistamin*
  an·tee·hees·ta·*meen*
antinuclear *antinükleer* an·tee·newk·le·*er*
antique n *antika* an·tee·*ka*
antiseptic n *antiseptik* an·te·sep·*teek*
any *herhangi bir* her·*han*·gee beer
apartment *apartman dairesi*
  a·part·*man* da·ee·re·*see*
appendix (body) *apandis* a·pan·*dees*
apple *elma* el·*ma*
appointment *randevu* ran·de·*voo*
apricot *kayısı* ka·yuh·*suh*
April *Nisan* nee·*san*
Arabic (language) *Arapça* a·*rap*·cha
archaeological *arkeolojik* ar·ke·o·lo·*zheek*
architect *mimar* mee·*mar*
architecture (art) *mimari yapı*
  mee·ma·ree ya·*puh*
architecture (profession) *mimarlık*
  mee·mar·*luhk*
argue *tartışmak* tar·tuhsh·*mak*
arm (body) *kol* kol
aromatherapy *aromaterapi*
  a·ro·ma·te·ra·*pee*
arrest v *tutuklamak* too·took·la·*mak*
arrivals *gelen yolcu* ge·len yol·*joo*
arrive *varmak* var·*mak*
art *sanat* sa·*nat*
art gallery *sanat galerisi* sa·nat ga·le·ree·*see*
artist *sanatçı* sa·nat·*chuh*
ashtray *kül tablası* kewl tab·la·*suh*
Asia *Asya* as·*ya*
ask (a question) v *sormak* sor·*mak*
ask (for something) v *istemek* ees·te·*mek*
asparagus *kuşkonmaz* koosh·kon·*maz*
aspirin *aspirin* as·pee·*reen*
asthma *astım* as·*tuhm*
at -*da*/-*de*/-*ta*/-*te* ·da/·de/·ta/·te
athletics *atletizm* at·le·*teezm*
atmosphere *atmosfer* at·mos·*fer*
aubergine *patlıcan* pat·luh·*jan*
August *Ağustos* a·oos·*tos*
aunt (maternal) *teyze* tay·*ze*
aunt (paternal) *hala* ha·*la*
Australia *Avustralya* a·voos·*tral*·ya
Australian Rules Football *Avustralya*
  futbolu a·voos·*tral*·ya foot·bo·*loo*
Austria *Avusturya* a·voos·*toor*·ya
automated teller machine (ATM)
  bankamatik ban·ka·ma·*teek*

autumn *sonbahar* son·ba·*har*
avenue *cadde* jad·*de*
avocado *avokado* a·vo·ka·*do*
awful *korkunç* kor·*koonch*
Azerbaijan *Azerbaycan* a·zer·bai·*jan*

B

B&W film *siyah beyaz film*
  see·*yah* be·*yaz* feelm
baby n *bebek* be·*bek*
baby food *bebek maması*
  be·bek ma·ma·*suh*
baby powder *bebek pudrası*
  be·bek pood·ra·*suh*
babysitter *dadı* da·*duh*
back (body) *sırt* suhrt
back (position) *arka* ar·*ka*
backgammon *tavla* tav·*la*
backpack *sırt çantası* suhrt chan·ta·*suh*
bacon *domuz eti* do·mooz e·*tee*
bad *kötü* ker·*tew*
bag *çanta* chan·*ta*
baggage *bagaj* ba·*gazh*
baggage allowance *bagaj hakkı*
  ba·*gazh* hak·*kuh*
baggage claim *bagaj konveyörü*
  ba·*gazh* kon·ve·yer·*rew*
bait *yem* yem
bakery *fırın* fuh·*ruhn*
balance (account) *hesap bakiyesi*
  he·*sap* ba·kee·ye·*see*
balcony *balkon* bal·*kon*
ball (sport) n *top* top
ballet *bale* ba·*le*
banana *muz* mooz
band (music) *müzik gurubu*
  mew·*zeek* goo·roo·*boo*
bandage *bandaj* ban·*dazh*
Band-Aid *yara bandı* ya·ra ban·*duh*
bank n *banka* ban·*ka*
bank account *banka hesabı*
  ban·ka he·sa·*buh*
banknote *kağıt para* ka·*uht* pa·*ra*
baptism *vaftiz* vaf·*teez*
bar *bar* bar
bar work *bar işi* bar ee·*shee*
barber *berber* ber·*ber*
baseball *beysbol* bays·*bol*
basilica *büyük kilise* bew·*yewk* kee·lee·*se*
basket *sepet* se·*pet*
basketball *basketbol* bas·ket·*bol*
bath n *banyo* ban·*yo*

bathing suit *mayo* ma·*yo*
bathroom *banyo* ban·*yo*
battery (dry) *pil* peel
battery (car) *akü* a·*kew*
bazaar *pazar* pa·*zar*
be *olmak* ol·*mak*
beach *plaj* plazh
beach volleyball *plaj voleybolu*
   plazh vo·lay·bo·*loo*
bean *fasulye* fa·*sool*·ye
bean sprout *fasulye filizi*
   fa·*sool*·ye fee·lee·zee
beautiful *güzel* gew·*zel*
beauty salon *güzellik salonu*
   gew·zel·leek sa·lo·noo
because *çünkü* chewn·*kew*
bed *yatak* ya·*tak*
bed linen *çarşaf* char·*shaf*
bedding *yatak takımı* ya·*tak* ta·kuh·*muh*
bedroom *yatak odası* ya·*tak* o·da·*suh*
bee *arı* a·*ruh*
beef *sığır eti* suh·*uhr* e·*tee*
beer *bira* bee·*ra*
beerhall *birahane* bee·ra·ha·ne
beetroot *pancar* pan·*jar*
before *önce* ern·*je*
beggar *dilenci* dee·len·*jee*
behind *arkasında* ar·ka·suhn·*da*
Belgium *Belçika* bel·chee·ka
below *aşağısında* a·sha·uh·suhn·*da*
beside *yanında* ya·nuhn·*da*
best a *en iyi* en ee·*yee*
bet n *bahis* ba·*hees*
better *daha iyi* da·*ha* ee·*yee*
between *arasında* a·ra·suhn·*da*
Bible *incil* een·*jeel*
bicycle *bisiklet* bee·seek·*let*
big *büyük* bew·*yewk*
bigger *daha büyük* da·*ha* bew·*yewk*
biggest *en büyük* en bew·*yewk*
bike *bisiklet* bee·seek·*let*
bike chain *bisiklet zinciri*
   bee·seek·*let* zeen·jee·*ree*
bike lock *bisiklet kilidi*
   bee·seek·*let* kee·lee·*dee*
bike path *bisiklet yolu* bee·seek·*let* yo·*loo*
bike shop *bisikletçi* bee·seek·*let·chee*
bill (restaurant) n *hesap* he·*sap*
binoculars *dürbün* dewr·*bewn*
bird *kuş* koosh
birth certificate *doğum belgesi*
   do·*oom* bel·ge·*see*
birthday *doğum günü* do·*oom* gew·*new*

biscuit *bisküvi* bees·kew·*vee*
bite (dog) n *köpek ısırması*
   ker·*pek* uh·suhr·ma·*suh*
bite (insect) n *böcek ısırması*
   ber·*jek* uh·suhr·ma·*suh*
bitter *acı* a·*juh*
black *siyah* see·*yah*
Black Sea *Karadeniz* ka·ra·de·neez
bladder *mesane* me·*sa*·ne
blanket *battaniye* bat·*ta*·nee·ye
blind a *kör* ker
blister *kabarcık* ka·bar·*juhk*
blocked *tıkalı* tuh·ka·*luh*
blood *kan* kan
blood group *kan gurubu* kan goo·roo·*boo*
blood pressure *tansiyon* tan·see·*yon*
blood test *kan tahlili* kan tah·lee·*lee*
blue *mavi* ma·vee
board v *binmek* been·*mek*
boarding house *pansiyon* pan·see·*yon*
boarding pass *biniş kartı* bee·*neesh* kar·*tuh*
boat *vapur* va·*poor*
body *vücut* vew·*joot*
boiled *kaynamış* kai·na·*muhsh*
bone *kemik* ke·*meek*
book n *kitap* kee·*tap*
book (reserve) v *yer ayırtmak*
   yer a·yuhrt·*mak*
booked out (full) *dolu* do·*loo*
bookshop *kitapçı* kee·tap·*chuh*
boots *botlar* bot·*lar*
border *sınır* suh·*nuhr*
bored *canı sıkkın* ja·nuh suhk·*kuhn*
boring *sıkıcı* suh·kuh·*juh*
borrow *ödünç almak* er·*dewnch* al·*mak*
botanic garden *botanik bahçe*
   bo·ta·neek bah·*che*
both *her ikisi* her e·kee·*see*
bottle n *şişe* shee·*she*
bottle opener *şişe açacağı*
   shee·*she* a·cha·ja·*uh*
bottle shop *tekel bayii* te·*kel* ba·yee·*ee*
bottom (body) *popo* po·*po*
bottom (position) *dipte* deep·*te*
bowl n *kase* ka·*se*
box n *kutu* koo·*too*
boxer shorts *bokser şort* bok·*ser* short
boxing *boks* boks
boy *oğlan* o·*lan*
boyfriend *erkek arkadaş* er·kek ar·ka·*dash*
bra *sütyen* sewt·*yen*
brakes *fren* fren
brandy *konyak* kon·*yak*

brave *cesur* je·*soor*
bread *ekmek* ek·*mek*
bread rolls *somun ekmek* so·*moon* ek·*mek*
break v *kırmak* kuhr·*mak*
break down v *bozulmak* bo·zool·*mak*
breakfast *kahvaltı* kah·val·*tuh*
breast *göğüs* ger·*ews*
breathe *nefes almak* ne·fes al·*mak*
bribe n *rüşvet* rewsh·*vet*
bridge (structure) *köprü* kerp·*rew*
briefcase *evrak çantası* ev·*rak* chan·ta·*suh*
bring *getirmek* ge·teer·*mek*
broccoli *brokoli* bro·ko·lee
brochure *broşür* bro·*shewr*
broken *kırık* kuh·*ruhk*
broken down *bozuk* bo·*zook*
bronchitis *bronşit* bron·*sheet*
brother *kardeş* kar·*desh*
brown *kahverengi* kah·ve·ren·gee
bruise n *çürük* chew·*rewk*
brush n *fırça* fuhr·cha
bucket *kova* ko·va
Buddhist *Budist* boo·*deest*
budget n *bütçe* bewt·*che*
buddy (dive) *dalış ortağı* da·luhsh or·ta·uh
buffet *büfe* bew·fe
bug n *böcek* ber·*jek*
build *inşa etmek* een·sha et·*mek*
builder *inşaatçı* een·sha·at·*chuh*
building *bina* bee·*na*
Bulgaria *Bulgaristan* bool·ga·rees·*tan*
bumbag *bel çantası* bel chan·ta·*suh*
burley *yem* yem
burn n *yanma* yan·ma
burnt *yanık* ya·*nuhk*
bus (city) *şehir otobüsü*
  she·*heer* o·to·bew·sew
bus (intercity) *şehirlerarası otobüs*
  she·heer·*ler·a·ra·suh* o·to·*bews*
bus station *otobüs terminali*
  o·to·*bews* ter·mee·na·*lee*
bus stop *otobüs durağı* o·to·*bews* doo·ra·uh
business n *iş* eesh
business class *business class* beez·nuhs klas
businessman *iş adamı* eesh a·da·muh
business trip *iş gezisi* eesh ge·zee·*see*
businesswoman *iş kadını* eesh ka·duh·*nuh*
busker *sokak çalgıcısı*
  so·*kak* chal·guh·juh·*suh*
busy *meşgul* mesh·*gool*
but *ama* a·ma
butcher *kasap* ka·*sap*
butter *tereyağ* te·re·ya

butterfly *kelebek* ke·le·*bek*
button *düğme* dew·me
buy v *satın almak* sa·*tuhn* al·*mak*

C

cabbage *lahana* la·ha·na
cable car *teleferik* te·le·fe·*reek*
café *kafe* ka·fe
cake *kek* kek
cake shop *pastane* pas·*ta*·ne
calculator *hesap makinesi*
  he·*sap* ma·kee·ne·*see*
calendar *takvim* tak·*veem*
call (telephone) v *aramak* a·ra·*mak*
call (shout) v *çağırmak* cha·uhr·*mak*
camera *kamera* ka·me·ra
camera shop *fotoğrafçı* fo·to·raf·*chuh*
camp v *kamp yapmak* kamp yap·*mak*
camping ground *kamp alanı* kamp a·la·nuh
camping store *kamp malzemeleri dükkanı*
  kamp mal·ze·me·le·*ree* dewk·ka·*nuh*
camp site *kamp yeri* kamp ye·*ree*
can (be able/have permission) v –*ebilmek/*
  –*abilmek* ·e·beel·mek/·a·beel·mek
can n *teneke kutu* te·ne·ke koo·too
can opener *konserve açacağı*
  kon·ser·ve a·cha·ja·uh
Canada *Kanada* ka·na·da
cancel *iptal etmek* eep·*tal* et·*mek*
cancer *kanser* kan·*ser*
candle *mum* moom
candy *şeker* she·ker
cantaloupe *kavun* ka·voon
capsicum *biber* bee·*ber*
car *araba* a·ra·ba
car hire *araba kiralama* a·ra·ba kee·ra·la·ma
car owner's title *araba yarışında birincilik*
  a·ra·ba ya·ruh·shuhn·da bee·reen·jee·*leek*
car park *otopark* o·to·*park*
car registration *plaka* pla·ka
caravan *karavan* ka·ra·van
caravanserai *kervansaray* ker·van·sa·rai
cardiac arrest *kalp krizi* kalp kree·*zee*
cards (playing) *oyun kağıdı*
  o·yoon ka·uh·duh
care (for someone) v *bakmak* bak·*mak*
caretaker *bakıcı* ba·kuh·*juh*
carpenter *marangoz* ma·ran·*goz*
carrot *havuç* ha·*vooch*
carry *taşımak* ta·shuh·*mak*
carton *karton* kar·ton
cash n *nakit* na·*keet*

cash (a cheque) *(çek) bozdurmak*
(chek) boz·door·mat
cash register *yazar kasa* ya·zar ka·sa
cashew *Hint fıstığı* heent fuhs·tuh·uh
cashier *kasiyer* ka·see·yer
casino *gazino* ga·zee·no
cassette *kaset* ka·set
castle *kale* ka·le
casual work *geçici iş* ge·chee·jee eesh
cat *kedi* ke·dee
catamaran *katamaran* ka·ta·ma·ran
cathedral *katedral* ka·ted·ral
Catholic *Katolik* ka·to·leek
cauliflower *karnabahar* kar·na·ba·har
cave n *mağara* ma·a·ra
CD *CD* see·dee
celebration *kutlama* koot·la·ma
cell phone *cep telefonu* jep te·le·fo·noo
cemetery *mezarlık* me·zar·luhk
cent *sent* sent
centimetre *santimetre* san·tee·met·re
centre n *merkez* mer·kez
ceramics *seramik* se·ra·meek
cereal *tahıl ürünleri* ta·huhl ew·rewn·le·ree
certificate *sertifika* ser·tee·fee·ka
chain n *zincir* zeen·jeer
chair *sandalye* san·dal·ye
chairlift (skiing) *telesiyej* te·le·see·yezh
champagne *şampanya* sham·pan·ya
championships *şampiyona* sham·pee·yo·na
chance *şans* shans
change n *değişiklik* de·ee·sheek·leek
change (coins) n *bozuk para* bo·zook pa·ra
change (money) v *(para) bozdurmak*
(pa·ra) boz·door·mak
changing room *soyunma kabini*
so·yoon·ma ka·bee·nee
charming *çekici* che·kee·jee
chat up v *sohbet etmek* soh·bet et·mek
cheap *ucuz* oo·jooz
cheat n *aldatma* al·dat·ma
check v *kontrol etmek* kon·trol et·mek
check (banking) n *çek* chek
check (bill) n *fatura* fa·too·ra
check-in desk *giriş* gee·reesh
checkpoint *kontrol noktası*
kon·trol nok·ta·suh
cheese *peynir* pay·neer
cheese shop *peynirci* pay·neer·jee
chef *aşçıbaşı* ash·chuh·ba·shuh
cheque (banking) *çek* chek
cherry *kiraz* kee·raz
chess *satranç* sat·ranch

chess board *satranç tahtası*
sat·ranch tah·ta·suh
chest (body) *göğüs* ger·ews
chestnut *kestane* kes·ta·ne
chewing gum *sakız* sa·kuhz
chicken *tavuk* ta·vook
chicken pox *su çiçeği* soo chee·che·ee
chickpea *nohut* no·hoot
child *çocuk* cho·jook
childminding *çocuk bakımı*
cho·jook ba·kuh·muh
child seat *çocuk koltuğu* cho·jook kol·too·oo
children *çocuklar* cho·jook·lar
chilli *acı (biber)* a·juh (bee·ber)
chilli sauce *acı sos* a·juh sos
China *Çin* cheen
chiropractor *çıkıkçı* chuh·kuhk·chuh
chocolate *çikolata* chee·ko·la·ta
choose *seçmek* sech·mek
chopping board *kesme tahtası*
kes·me tah·ta·suh
Christian n *Hıristiyan* huh·rees·tee·yan
Christian name *İlk ad* eelk ad
Christmas *Noel* no·el
Christmas Day *Noel yortusu*
no·el yor·too·soo
Christmas Eve *Noel yortusu arifesi*
no·el yor·too·soo a·ree·fe·see
church *kilise* kee·lee·se
cider *elma şarabı* el·ma sha·ra·buh
cigar *puro* poo·ro
cigarette *sigara* see·ga·ra
cigarette lighter *çakmak* chak·mak
cinema *sinema* see·ne·ma
circus *sirk* seerk
citadel *kale içi* ka·le ee·chee
citizenship *vatandaşlık* va·tan·dash·luhk
city *şehir* she·heer
city centre *şehir merkezi*
she·heer mer·ke·zee
civil rights *medeni haklar* me·de·nee hak·lar
class (category) *kategori* ka·te·go·ree
class system *sınıf sistemi*
suh·nuhf sees·te·mee
classical *klasik* kla·seek
clean a *temiz* te·meez
clean v *temizlemek* te·meez·le·mek
cleaning *temizlik* te·meez·leek
client *müşteri* mewsh·te·ree
cliff *uçurum* oo·choo·room
climb v *tırmanmak* tuhr·man·mak
cloakroom *vestiyer* ves·tee·yer
clock *saat* sa·at

close a *yakın* ya·kuhn
close v *kapatmak* ka·pat·mak
closed *kapalı* ka·pa·luh
clothesline *çamaşır ipi* cha·ma·shuhr ee·pee
clothing *giyim* gee·yeem
clothing store *giyim mağazası*
  gee·yeem ma·a·za·suh
cloud n *bulut* boo·loot
cloudy *bulutlu* boo·loot·loo
clutch (car) *debriyaj* deb·ree·yazh
coach (bus) *otobüs* o·to·bews
coach (trainer) *antrenör* an·tre·ner
coat *palto* pal·to
cocaine *kokain* ko·ka·een
cockroach *hamamböceği* ha·mam·ber·je·ee
cocktail *kokteyl* kok·tayl
cocoa *kakao* ka·ka·o
coconut *Hindistan cevizi*
  heen·dees·tan je·vee·zee
coffee *kahve* kah·ve
coins *madeni para* ma·de·nee pa·ra
cold n & a *soğuk* so·ook
colleague *iş arkadaşı* eesh ar·ka·da·shuh
collect call *ödemeli telefon*
  er·de·me·lee te·le·fon
college *kolej* ko·lezh
colour n *renk* renk
comb n *tarak* ta·rak
come *gelmek* gel·mek
comedy *komedi* ko·me·dee
comfortable *rahat* ra·hat
commission n *komisyon* ko·mees·yon
communications (profession)
  halkla ilişkiler halk·la ee·leesh·kee·ler
communion *komünyon* ko·mewn·yon
communist n *komünist* ko·mew·neest
companion *arkadaş* ar·ka·dash
company (firm) *şirket* sheer·ket
compass *pusula* poo·soo·la
complain *şikayet etmek* shee·ka·yet et·mek
complaint *şikayet* shee·ka·yet
complimentary (free) *ikram* eek·ram
computer *bilgisayar* beel·gee·sa·yar
computer game *bilgisayar oyunu*
  beel·gee·sa·yar o·yoo·noo
concert *konser* kon·ser
concussion *beyin sarsıntısı*
  be·yeen sar·suhn·tuh·suh
conditioner (hair) *balsam* bal·sam
condom *prezervatif* pre·zer·va·teef
conference (big) *konferans* kon·fe·rans
conference (small) *görüşme* ger·rewsh·me

confession (religious) *günah çıkarma*
  gew·nah chuh·kar·ma
confirm (a booking) v *teyit etmek*
  te·yeet et·mek
congratulations *tebrikler* teb·reek·ler
conjunctivitis *konjonktivit iltihabı*
  kon·jonk·tee·veet eel·tee·ha·buh
connection (link) *bağlantı* ba·lan·tuh
connection (trip) *aktarma* ak·tar·ma
conservative n *tutucu* too·too·joo
constipation *kabızlık* ka·buhz·luhk
consulate *konsolosluk* kon·so·los·look
contact lens solution *kontak lens*
  solüsyonu kon·tak lens so·lews·yo·noo
contact lenses *kontak lens* kon·tak lens
contraceptives *doğum kontrol hapı*
  do·oom kon·trol ha·puh
contract n *kontrat* kon·trat
convenience store *bakkal* bak·kal
convent *manastır* ma·nas·tuhr
cook n *aşçı* ash·chuh
cook v *pişirmek* pee·sheer·mek
cookie *kurabiye* koo·ra·bee·ye
cooking *yemek pişirme*
  ye·mek pee·sheer·me
cool (cold) a *serin* se·reen
cool (exciting) a *hoş* hosh
corkscrew *tirbüşon* teer·bew·shon
corn *mısır* muh·suhr
corner *köşe* ker·she
cornflakes *mısır gevreği* muh·suhr gev·re·ee
corrupt a *bozuk* bo·zook
cost v *mal olmak* mal ol·mak
cotton *pamuk* pa·mook
cotton balls *pamuk yumağı*
  pa·mook yoo·ma·uh
cotton buds *kulak temizleme çubuğu*
  koo·lak te·meez·le·me choo·boo·oo
cough v *öksürmek* erk·sewr·mek
cough medicine *öksürük ilacı*
  erk·sew·rewk ee·la·juh
count v *saymak* sai·mak
counter (at bar) *bar* bar
country (nation) *ülke* ewl·ke
countryside *şehir dışı* she·heer duh·shuh
coupon *kupon* koo·pon
courgette *kabak* ka·bak
court (legal) *mahkeme* mah·ke·me
court (sport) *kort* kort
couscous *kuskus* koos·koos
cover charge *fiks ücret* feeks ewj·ret
cow *inek* ee·nek
crafts *sanat* sa·nat

crash n çarpışma char·puhsh·ma
crazy deli de·lee
cream (food) krema kre·ma
cream (lotion) krem krem
credit n kredi kre·dee
credit card kredi kartı kre·dee kar·tuh
cricket (sport) kriket kree·ket
crop (food) n ürün ew·rewn
cross (religious) n haç hach
crowded kalabalık ka·la·ba·luhk
cucumber salatalık sa·la·ta·luhk
cup fincan feen·jan
cupboard dolap do·lap
currency exchange döviz kuru
    der·veez koo·roo
current (electricity) akım a·kuhm
current affairs gündem gewn·dem
curry kari ka·ree
custom gelenek ge·le·nek
customs gümrük gewm·rewk
cut v kesmek kes·mek
cutlery çatal bıçak takımı
    cha·tal buh·chak ta·kuh·muh
CV özgeçmiş erz·gech·meesh
cycle v bisiklete binmek
    bee·seek·le·te been·mek
cycling bisiklet sporu bee·seek·let spo·roo
cyclist bisikletçi bee·seek·let·chee
Cyprus Kıbrıs kuhb·ruhs
cystitis sistit sees·teet

D

dad babacığım ba·ba·juh·uhm
daily günlük gewn·lewk
dance v dans etmek dans et·mek
dancing dans dans
dangerous tehlikeli teh·lee·ke·lee
dark (colour) koyu ko·yoo
dark (night) karanlık ka·ran·luhk
date (a person) v çıkmak chuhk·mak
date (appointment) n randevu ran·de·voo
date (day) n tarih ta·reeh
date (fruit) n hurma hoor·ma
date of birth doğum tarihi
    do·oom ta·ree·hee
daughter kız kuhz
dawn n şafak sha·fak
day gün gewn
day after tomorrow öbür gün er·bewr gewn
day before yesterday önceki gün
    ern·je·kee gewn
dead ölü er·lew

deaf sağır sa·uhr
deal (cards) v karmak kar·mak
December Aralık a·ra·luhk
decide karar vermek ka·rar ver·mek
deep derin de·reen
deforestation ormansızlaştırma
    or·man·suhz·lash·tuhr·ma
degrees (temperature) derece de·re·je
delay n gecikme ge·jeek·me
delicatessen şarküteri shar·kew·te·ree
deliver teslim etmek tes·leem et·mek
democracy demokrasi de·mok·ra·see
demonstration (protest) gösteri gers·te·ree
Denmark Danimarka da·nee·mar·ka
dental dam oral seks kondomu
    o·ral seks kon·do·moo
dental floss diş ipi deesh ee·pee
dentist dişçi deesh·chee
deodorant deodorant de·o·do·rant
depart ayrılmak ai·ruhl·mak
department store büyük mağaza
    bew·yewk ma·a·za
departure gidiş gee·deesh
departure gate gidiş kapısı
    gee·deesh ka·puh·suh
deposit (bank) depozito de·po·zee·to
derailleur bisiklet vites mekaniği
    bee·seek·let vee·tes me·ka·nee·ee
dervish derviş der·veesh
dervish ceremony derviş seramonisi
    der·veesh se·ra·mo·nee·see
descendent soy soy
desert n çöl cherl
design n desen de·sen
dessert tatlı tat·luh
destination gidilecek yer gee·dee·le·jek yer
details ayrıntı ai·ruhn·tuh
diabetes şeker hastalığı
    she·ker has·ta·luh·uh
dial tone çevir sesi che·veer se·see
diaper bebek bezi be·bek be·zee
diaphragm diyafram dee·yaf·ram
diarrhoea ishal ees·hal
diary günlük gewn·lewk
dice n zar zar
dictionary sözlük serz·lewk
die v ölmek erl·mek
diet diyet dee·yet
different farklı fark·luh
difficult zor zor
digital a dijital dee·zhee·tal
dining car yemekli vagon ye·mek·lee va·gon
dinner akşam yemeği ak·sham ye·me·ee

direct a *direk* dee-rek
direct-dial *direk arama* dee-rek a-ra-ma
direction *yön* yern
director *yönetmen* yer-net-men
dirty a *kirli* keer-lee
disabled *özürlü* er-zewr-lew
disco *disko* dees-ko
discount n *indirim* een-dee-reem
discrimination *ayrım* ai-ruhm
disease *hastalık* has-ta-luhk
dish n *yemek* ye-mek
disk (CD-ROM) *disk* deesk
disk (floppy) *disket* dees-ket
dive n *dalış* da-luhsh
dive v *dalmak* dal-mak
diving *dalış* da-luhsh
diving boat *dalış teknesi* da-luhsh tek-ne-see
diving course *dalış kursu* da-luhsh koor-soo
diving equipment *dalış malzemeleri*
da-luhsh mal-ze-me-le-ree
divorced *boşanmış* bo-shan-muhsh
dizzy *başı dönen* ba-shuh der-nen
do *yapmak* yap-mak
doctor *doktor* dok-tor
documentary *belgesel* bel-ge-sel
dog *köpek* ker-pek
dole *sadaka* sa-da-ka
doll *oyuncak bebek* o-yoon-jak be-bek
dollar *dolar* do-lar
dome *kubbe* koob-be
door *kapı* ka-puh
dope (drugs) *haşhaş* hash-hash
double *çift* cheeft
double bed *iki kişilik yatak*
ee-kee kee-shee-leek ya-tak
double room *iki kişilik oda*
ee-kee kee-shee-leek o-da
down *aşağı* a-sha-uh
downhill *yokuş aşağı* yo-koosh a-sha-uh
dozen *düzine* dew-zee-ne
drama *dram* dram
drawing *çizim* chee-zeem
dream n *rüya* rew-ya
dress n *elbise* el-bee-se
dried *kuru* koo-roo
dried fruit *kuru meyve* koo-roo may-ve
drink (alcoholic) n *alkollü içecek*
al-kol-lew ee-che-jek
drink (general) n *içecek* ee-che-jek
drink v *içmek* eech-mek
drive v *sürmek* sewr-mek
drivers licence *ehliyet* eh-lee-yet

drug (illegal) n *uyuşturucu*
oo-yoosh-too-roo-joo
drug (medication) n *ilaç* ee-lach
drug addiction *uyuşturucu bağımlılığı*
oo-yoosh-too-roo-joo ba-uhm-luh-luh-uh
drug dealer *uyuşturucu satıcısı*
oo-yoosh-too-roo-joo sa-tuh-juh-suh
drug trafficking *uyuşturucu alış-verişi*
oo-yoosh-too-roo-joo a-luhsh-ve-ree-shee
drug user *uyuşturucu bağımlısı*
oo-yoosh-too-roo-joo ba-uhm-luh-suh
drum (music) n *davul* da-vool
drunk a *sarhoş* sar-hosh
dry a *kuru* koo-roo
dry v *kurulamak* koo-roo-la-mak
dry (clothes) v *kurutmak* koo-root-mak
duck *ördek* er-dek
dummy (pacifier) *emzik* em-zeek
Dutch (language) *Hollandaca*
hol-lan-da-ja
duty-free *gümrüksüz satış*
gewm-rewk-sewz sa-tuhsh
DVD *DVD* dee-vee-dee

E

each *her bir* her beer
ear *kulak* koo-lak
early *erken* er-ken
earn *kazanmak* ka-zan-mak
earplugs *kulak tıkacı* koo-lak tuh-ka-juh
earrings *küpe* kew-pe
Earth *yeryüzü* yer-yew-zew
earthquake *deprem* dep-rem
east *doğu* do-oo
Easter *Paskalya* pas-kal-ya
easy *kolay* ko-lai
eat *yemek yemek* ye-mek ye-mek
economy class *ekonomi sınıfı*
e-ko-no-mee suh-nuh-fuh
ecstasy (drug) *ekstasi* eks-ta-see
eczema *egzama* eg-za-ma
editor *yazı işleri müdürü*
ya-zuh eesh-le-ree mew-dew-rew
education *eğitim* e-ee-teem
egg *yumurta* yoo-moor-ta
eggplant *patlıcan* pat-luh-jan
election *seçim* se-cheem
electrical store *seçim bürosu*
se-cheem bew-ro-soo
electricity *elektrik* e-lek-treek
elevator *asansör* a-san-ser
email n *e-posta* e-pos-ta

embarrassed *mahcup* mah-*joop*
embassy *elçilik* el-chee-*leek*
emergency *acil durum* a-*jeel* doo-*room*
emotional *duygusal* dooy-goo-*sal*
employee *çalışan* cha-luh-*shan*
employer *işveren* eesh-ve-*ren*
empty a *boş* bosh
end n *son* son
endangered species
   nesli tükenmekte olan hayvanlar
   nes-*lee* tew-ken-mek-*te* o-*lan* hai-van-*lar*
engaged (busy) *meşgul* mesh-*gool*
engaged (to marry) *nişanlı* nee-shan-*luh*
engagement (to marry) *nişan* nee-*shan*
engine *motor* mo-*tor*
engineer n *mühendis* mew-hen-*dees*
engineering *mühendislik*
   mew-hen-dees-*leek*
England *İngiltere* een-geel-*te*-re
English (language) *İngilizce* een-gee-*leez*-je
English (nationality) *İngiliz* een-gee-*leez*
enjoy (oneself) *eğlenmek* e-len-*mek*
enough *yeterli* ye-ter-*lee*
enter *girmek* geer-*mek*
entertainment guide *eğlence rehberi*
   e-len-*je* reh-be-*ree*
entry *giriş* gee-*reesh*
envelope *zarf* zarf
environment *çevre* chev-*re*
epilepsy *sara* sa-*ra*
equal opportunity *fırsat eşitliği*
   fuhr-*sat* e-sheet-lee-*ee*
equality *eşitlik* e-sheet-*leek*
equipment *teçhizat* tech-hee-*zat*
escalator *yürüyen merdiven*
   yew-rew-*yen* mer-dee-*ven*
estate agency *emlakçı* em-lak-*chuh*
euro *euro* yoo-*ro*
Europe *Avrupa* av-*roo*-pa
euthanasia *ötenazi* er-te-na-*zee*
evening *akşam* ak-*sham*
every *her* her
everyone *herkes* her-*kes*
everything *herşey* her-*shay*
exactly *tam olarak* tam o-la-*rak*
example *örnek* er-*nek*
excellent *mükemmel* mew-kem-*mel*
excess baggage *fazla yük* faz-*la* yewk
exchange n *değiş-tokuş* de-eesh-to-*koosh*
exchange (money) v *(para) bozdurmak*
   (pa-*ra*) boz-door-*mak*
exchange (general) v *değiştirmek*
   de-eesh-teer-*mek*

exchange rate *döviz kuru* der-veez koo-*roo*
excluded *hariç* ha-*reech*
exhaust (car) *egzoz* eg-*zoz*
exhibition *sergi* ser-*gee*
exit n *çıkış* chuh-*kuhsh*
expensive *pahalı* pa-ha-*luh*
experience n *deneyim* de-ne-*yeem*
expiry date *son kullanma tarihi*
   son kool-lan-*ma* ta-ree-*hee*
exploitation *sömürü* ser-mew-*rew*
express a *ekspres* eks-*pres*
express mail *ekspres posta* eks-*pres* pos-*ta*
extension (visa) *uzatma* oo-zat-*ma*
eye drops *göz damlası* gerz dam-la-*suh*
eyes *gözler* gerz-*ler*

F

fabric *kumaş* koo-*mash*
face *yüz* yewz
face cloth *yüz havlusu* yewz hav-loo-*soo*
factory *fabrika* fab-ree-*ka*
factory worker *fabrika işçisi*
   fab-ree-*ka* eesh-chee-*see*
fall (autumn) *sonbahar* son-ba-*har*
fall v *düşmek* dewsh-*mek*
family *aile* a-ee-*le*
family name *soyad* soy-*ad*
family room (home) *oturma odası*
   o-toor-*ma* o-da-*suh*
family room (restaurant) *aile bölümü*
   a-ee-*le* ber-lew-*mew*
family quarters *aile için kalacak yer*
   a-ee-*le* ee-*cheen* ka-la-*jak* yer
famous *ünlü* ewn-*lew*
fan (machine) *vantilatör* van-tee-la-*ter*
fan (sport, etc) *taraftar* ta-raf-*tar*
fanbelt *kayış* ka-*yuhsh*
far *uzak* oo-*zak*
fare *yol parası* yol pa-ra-*suh*
farm n *çiftlik* cheeft-*leek*
farmer *çiftçi* cheeft-*chee*
Farsi (Persian) *İranlı* ee-ran-*luh*
fashion n *moda* mo-*da*
fast a *hızlı* huhz-*luh*
fat a *şişman* sheesh-*man*
father *baba* ba-*ba*
father-in-law *kayınpeder* ka-yuhn-pe-*der*
faucet *musluk* moos-*look*
fault (someone's) *hata* ha-*ta*
faulty *bozuk* bo-*zook*
fax (document/machine) *faks* faks
February *Şubat* shoo-*bat*

feed v *beslemek* bes·le·mek
feel (touch) v *hissetmek* hees·set·mek
feeling (physical) *dokunma* do·koon·ma
feelings *duygular* dooy·goo·lar
female (animal) a *dişi* dee·shee
female (human) a *bayan* ba·yan
fence n *çit* cheet
fencing (sport) *eskrim* es·kreem
ferry n *feribot* fe·ree·bot
festival *festival* fes·tee·val
fever *ateş* a·tesh
few *birkaç* beer·kach
fiancé(e) *nişanlı* nee·shan·luh
fiction *roman* ro·man
fig *incir* een·jeer
fight n *kavga* kav·ga
fill v *doldurmak* dol·door·mak
fillet *fileto* fee·le·to
film (camera/cinema) n *film* feelm
film speed *film hızı* feelm huh·zuh
filtered *filtre edilmiş* feelt·re e·deel·meesh
find v *bulmak* bool·mak
fine n *para cezası* pa·ra je·za·suh
fine a *iyi* ee·yee
finger *parmak* par·mak
finish n *bitiş* bee·teesh
finish v *bitirmek* bee·teer·mek
Finland *Finlandiya* feen·lan·dee·ya
fire (small fire under control) *ateş* a·tesh
fire (out of control) *yangın* yan·guhn
firewood *yakacak odun* ya·ka·jak o·doon
first a *ilk* eelk
first-aid kit *ilk yardım çantası*
    eelk yar·duhm chan·ta·suh
first class *birinci sınıf* bee·reen·jee suh·nuhf
first name *ilk ad* eelk ad
fish n *balık* ba·luhk
fishmonger *balıkçı* ba·luhk·chuh
fishing *balık avlama* ba·luhk av·la·ma
fishing line *misina* mee·see·na
fishing rod *olta* ol·ta
fish shop *balıkçı* ba·luhk·chuh
flag *bayrak* bai·rak
flannel (cloth for washing) *sabunluk*
    sa·boon·look
flare (fishing) *ışıltı* uh·shuhl·tuh
flash (camera) n *flaş* flash
flashlight (small torch) *cep feneri*
    jep fe·ne·ree
flat (apartment) n *apartman dairesi*
    a·part·man da·ee·re·see
flat a *düz* dewz
flea *pire* pee·re

fleamarket *bit pazarı* beet pa·za·ruh
flight *uçuş* oo·choosh
float (fishing) n *yüzmek* yewz·mek
flood n *sel* sel
floor (storey) *kat* kat
floor (surface) *yer* yer
florist *çiçekçi* chee·chek·chee
flour *un* oon
flower *çiçek* chee·chek
flu *grip* greep
fly v *uçmak* ooch·mak
foggy *sisli* sees·lee
follow *takip etmek* ta·keep et·mek
food *yiyecek* yee·ye·jek
food supplies *erzak* er·zak
foot *ayak* a·yak
football (soccer) *futbol* foot·bol
footpath *patika* pa·tee·ka
foreign *yabancı* ya·ban·juh
forest *orman* or·man
forever *sonsuza dek* son·soo·za dek
forget *unutmak* oo·noot·mak
forgive *affetmek* af·fet·mek
fork n *çatal* cha·tal
fortnight *iki hafta* ee·kee haf·ta
fortune teller *falcı* fal·juh
foul (football) n *faul* fa·ool
fountain (natural) *pınar* puh·nar
fortress *kale* ka·le
foyer (hotel entry) *lobi* lo·bee
fragile *kırılabilir* kuh·ruh·la·bee·leer
France *Fransa* fran·sa
free (available) *boş* bosh
free (gratis) *ücretsiz* ewj·ret·seez
free (not bound) *serbest* ser·best
free kick *frikik* free·keek
freeze (to get cold) *donmak* don·mak
freeze (to make cold) *dondurmak*
    don·door·mak
French (language) *Fransızca* fran·suhz·ja
fresh *taze* ta·ze
Friday *Cuma* joo·ma
fridge *buzdolabı* booz·do·la·buh
fried *kızarmış* kuh·zar·muhsh
friend *arkadaş* ar·ka·dash
from *-dan/-den/-tan/-ten* dan/·den/·tan/·ten
frost n *don* don
frozen *donmuş* don·moosh
fruit *meyve* may·ve
fruit picking *meyve toplama*
    may·ve top·la·ma
fry v *kızartmak* kuh·zart·mak

frying pan *kızartma tavası* kuh·zart·*ma* ta·va·*suh*
full (not empty) *dolu* do·*loo*
full (not hungry) *doymuş* doy·*moosh*
full-time *tam mesai* tam me·*sa*·ee
fun *eğlence* e·len·*je*
funeral *cenaze töreni* je·na·*ze* ter·re·*nee*
funny *komik* ko·*meek*
furniture *mobilya* mo·*beel*·ya
future n *gelecek* ge·le·*jek*

G

game (football) *maç* mach
game (sport) *oyun* o·*yoon*
garage *garaj* ga·*razh*
garbage *çöp* cherp
garbage can *çöp tenekesi* cherp te·ne·ke·*see*
garden n *bahçe* bah·*che*
gardener *bahçıvan* bah·chuh·*van*
gardening *bahçe işleri* bah·*che* eesh·le·*ree*
garlic *sarmısak* sar·muh·*sak*
gas (for cooking) *doğal gaz* do·*al* gaz
gas (petrol) *benzin* ben·*zeen*
gas cartridge *gaz tüpü* gaz tew·*pew*
gastroenteritis *mide ve bağırsak enfeksiyonu* mee·*de* ve ba·uhr·*sak* en·fek·see·yo·*noo*
gate (airport) *kapı* ka·*puh*
gauze *gazlı bez* gaz·*luh* bez
gay (homosexual) *eşcinsel* esh·jeen·*sel*
gearbox *vites kutusu* vee·*tes* koo·too·*soo*
gendarme *jandarma* zhan·dar·*ma*
Georgia *Gürcistan* gewr·jees·*tan*
German (language) *Almanca* al·man·*ja*
Germany *Almanya* al·man·*ya*
get *almak* al·*mak*
gift (present) *hediye* he·dee·*ye*
gift (talent) *yetenek* ye·te·*nek*
gig *eğlence* e·len·*je*
gin *cin* jeen
girl *kız* kuhz
girlfriend *kız arkadaş* kuhz ar·ka·*dash*
give *vermek* ver·*mek*
given name *İlk ad* eelk ad
glandular fever *glandüler ateş* glan·dew·*ler* a·*tesh*
glass (drinking) *bardak* bar·*dak*
glass (window) *cam* jam
glasses (spectacles) *gözlük* gerz·*lewk*
gloves (medical) *lateks eldiven* la·*teks* el·dee·*ven*

gloves (warm) *eldivenler* el·dee·ven·*ler*
glue n *tutkal* toot·*kal*
go *gitmek* geet·*mek*
go out *dışarıya çıkmak* duh·sha·ruh·ya chuhk·*mak*
go out with *ile çıkmak* ee·*le* chuhk·*mak*
go shopping *alış-verişe gitmek* a·luhsh·ve·ree·*she* geet·*mek*
goal (football) n *gol* gol
goalkeeper *kaleci* ka·le·*jee*
goat *keçi* ke·*chee*
god (general) *tanrı* tan·*ruh*
goggles (skiing) *kayak gözlüğü* ka·*yak* gerz·lew·*ew*
goggles (swimming) *deniz gözlüğü* de·*neez* gerz·lew·*ew*
gold n *altın* al·*tuhn*
golf ball *golf topu* golf to·*poo*
golf course *golf sahası* golf sa·ha·*suh*
good *iyi* ee·*yee*
government *devlet* dev·*let*
gram *gram* gram
grandchild *torun* to·*roon*
grandfather *büyükbaba* bew·*yewk*·ba·ba
grandmother *büyükanne* bew·*yewk*·an·ne
grandma *nine* nee·*ne*
grandpa *dede* de·*de*
grapefruit *greyfurt* gray·*foort*
grape(s) *üzüm* ew·*zewm*
grass (lawn) n *çim* cheem
grateful *müteşekkir* mew·te·shek·*keer*
grave n *mezar* me·*zar*
great (fantastic) *harika* ha·ree·*ka*
Greece *Yunanistan* yoo·na·nees·*tan*
green *yeşil* ye·*sheel*
greengrocer *manav* ma·*nav*
grey *gri* gree
grill n *ızgara* uhz·*ga*·ra
grocery *bakkal* bak·*kal*
grow *büyümek* bew·yew·*mek*
guaranteed *garantili* ga·ran·tee·*lee*
guess v *tahmin etmek* tah·*meen* et·*mek*
guesthouse *misafirhane* mee·sa·feer·ha·*ne*
guide (audio) *elektronik rehber* e·lek·tro·neek reh·*ber*
guide (person) n *rehber* reh·*ber*
guidebook *rehber kitap* reh·*ber* kee·*tap*
guide dog *rehber köpek* reh·*ber* ker·*pek*
guided tour *rehberli tur* reh·ber·*lee* toor
guilty *suçlu* sooch·*loo*
guitar *gitar* gee·*tar*
gum (chewing) *sakız* sa·*kuhz*
gun *silah* see·*lah*

gym (place) *jimnastik salonu*
zheem-nas-*teek* sa-lo-*noo*
gymnastics *jimnastik* zheem-nas-*teek*
gynaecologist *jinekolog* zhee-ne-ko-*log*

H

hair *saç* sach
hairbrush *saç fırçası* sach fuhr-cha-*suh*
haircut *saç kestirme* sach kes-teer-me
hairdresser *kuaför* koo-a-*fer*
halal *helal* he-*lal*
half *yarım* ya-*ruhm*
hallucination *halüsinasyon*
ha-lew-see-nas-*yon*
ham *jambon* zham-*bon*
hammer n *çekiç* che-*keech*
hammock *hamak* ha-*mak*
hand (body) *el* el
handbag *el çantası* el chan-ta-*suh*
handball *hentbol* hent-*bol*
handicrafts *el sanatları* el sa-nat-la-*ruh*
handkerchief *mendil* men-*deel*
handlebars *kulp* koolp
handmade *el işi* el ee-*shee*
handsome *yakışıklı* ya-kuh-shuhk-*luh*
happy *mutlu* moot-*loo*
harassment *taciz* ta-*jeez*
harbour n *liman* lee-*man*
hard (difficult) *zor* zor
hard (not soft) *sert* sert
hard-boiled *haşlanmış-katı*
hash-lan-*muhsh*-ka-tuh
hardware store *hırdavatçı dükkanı*
huhr-da-vat-*chuh* dewk-ka-*nuh*
hash (drug) *esrar* es-*rar*
hat *şapka* shap-*ka*
have *sahip olmak* sa-heep ol-*mak*
have a cold *üşütmek* ew-shewt-*mek*
have fun *eğlenmek* e-len-*mek*
hay fever *saman nezlesi* sa-*man* nez-le-*see*
hazelnut *fındık* fuhn-*duhk*
he *o* o
head n *baş* bash
headache *baş ağrısı* bash a-ruh-*suh*
headlights *farlar* far-*lar*
health *sağlık* sa-*luhk*
hear *duymak* dooy-*mak*
hearing aid *işitme cihazı*
ee-sheet-*me* jee-ha-*zuh*
heart (body) *kalp* kalp
heart attack *kalp krizi* kalp kree-*zee*

heart condition *kalp rahatsızlığı*
kalp ra-hat-suhz-luh-*uh*
heat n *ısı* uh-*suh*
heated *ısıtılmış* uh-suh-tuhl-*muhsh*
heater *ısıtıcı* uh-suh-tuh-*juh*
heating *ısıtma* uh-suht-*ma*
heavy *ağır* a-*uhr*
helmet *kask* kask
help n *yardım* yar-*duhm*
help v *yardım etmek* yar-*duhm* et-*mek*
hepatitis (common term) *sarılık* sa-ruh-*luhk*
hepatitis (medical term) *hepatit* he-pa-*teet*
her (object) *onu* o-*noo*
her (possessive) *onun* o-*noon*
herb *bitki* beet-*kee*
herbalist *aktar* ak-*tar*
here *burada* boo-ra-*da*
heroin *eroin* e-ro-*een*
herring *ringa balığı* reen-ga ba-luh-*uh*
high a *yüksek* yewk-*sek*
high school *lise* lee-*se*
highchair *mama sandalyesi*
ma-*ma* san-dal-ye-*see*
highway *otoyol* o-to-*yol*
hike v *uzun yürüyüşe çıkmak*
oo-*zoon* yew-rew-yew-*she* chuhk-*mak*
hiking *kırda uzun yürüyüş*
kuhr-*da* oo-*zoon* yew-rew-*yewsh*
hiking boots *yürüyüş ayakkabısı*
yew-rew-*yewsh* a-yak-ka-buh-*suh*
hiking route *yürüyüş güzergahı*
yew-rew-*yewsh* gew-zer-ga-*huh*
hill *tepe* te-*pe*
him *onu* o-*noo*
Hindu *Hindu* heen-*doo*
hire v *kiralamak* kee-ra-la-*mak*
his *onun* o-*noon*
historical *tarihi* ta-ree-*hee*
history *tarih* ta-*reeh*
hitchhike *otostop yapmak*
o-tos-*top* yap-*mak*
HIV *HIV* heev
hockey *hokey* ho-*kay*
holiday(s) *tatil* ta-*teel*
home *ev* ev
homeless *evsiz* ev-*seez*
homemaker *ev hanımı* ev ha-nuh-*muh*
homeopathy *homeopati* ho-me-o-pa-*tee*
homosexual *homoseksüel* ho-mo-sek-sew-*el*
honey *bal* bal
honeymoon *balayı* ba-la-*yuh*
hook(s) *olta iğnesi* ol-*ta* ee-ne-*see*
horoscope *yıldız falı* yuhl-*duhz* fa-*luh*

horse *at* at
horse riding *binicilik* bee·nee·jee·leek
hospital *hastane* has·ta·ne
hospitality *misafirperverlik*
mee·sa·feer·per·ver·leek
hot *sıcak* suh·jak
hot water *sıcak su* suh·jak soo
hotel *otel* o·tel
hour *saat* sa·at
house n *ev* ev
housework *ev işi* ev ee·shee
how *nasıl* na·suhl
hug v *sarılmak* sa·ruhl·mak
huge *kocaman* ko·ja·man
human resources *personel servisi*
per·so·nel ser·vee·see
human rights *insan hakları*
een·san hak·la·ruh
humanities *uygarlık tarihi*
ooy·gar·luhk ta·ree·hee
hundred *yüz* yewz
hungry *aç* ach
hunting *avlanma* av·lan·ma
hurt v *canı acımak* ja·nuh a·juh·mak
husband *koca* ko·ja
hydrofoil *deniz otobüsü*
de·neez o·to·bew·sew

I

I *ben* ben
ice *buz* booz
ice axe *buz kıracağı* booz kuh·ra·ja·uh
ice cream *dondurma* don·door·ma
ice-cream parlour *dondurmacı*
don·door·ma·juh
ice hockey *buz hokeyi* booz ho·ke·yee
identification *kimlik* keem·leek
identification card (ID) *kimlik kartı*
keem·leek kar·tuh
idiot *aptal* ap·tal
if *eğer* e·er
ill *hasta* has·ta
immigration *göç* gerch
important *önemli* er·nem·lee
impossible *imkansız* eem·kan·suhz
in *içinde* ee·cheen·de
in a hurry *acele ile* a·je·le ee·le
in front of *önünde* er·newn·de
included *dahil* da·heel
income tax *gelir vergisi* ge·leer ver·gee·see
India *Hindistan* heen·dees·tan
indicator (car) *gösterge* gers·ter·ge

indigestion *hazımsızlık*
ha·zuhm·suhz·luhk
indoor *içeride yapılan*
ee·che·ree·de ya·puh·lan
industry *endüstri* en·dews·tree
infection *enfeksiyon* en·fek·see·yon
inflammation *iltihap* eel·tee·hap
influenza *grip* greep
information *bilgi* beel·gee
ingredient *malzeme* mal·ze·me
inhaler *rahatlatıcı* ra·hat·la·tuh·juh
inject *iğne yapmak* ee·ne yap·mak
injection *iğne* ee·ne
injured *yaralı* ya·ra·luh
injury *yara* ya·ra
inner tube *iç lastik* eech las·teek
innocent *masum* ma·soom
inside *içeride* ee·che·ree·de
instructor *öğretmen* er·ret·men
insurance *sigorta* see·gor·ta
interesting *ilginç* eel·geench
intermission *ara* a·ra
international *uluslararası*
oo·loos·lar·a·ra·suh
Internet *internet* een·ter·net
Internet café *internet kafe* een·ter·net ka·fe
interpreter *tercüman* ter·jew·man
interview n *mülakat* mew·la·kat
invite v *davet etmek* da·vet et·mek
Iran *İran* ee·ran
Iraq *Irak* uh·rak
Ireland *İrlanda* eer·lan·da
iron (clothes) n *ütü* ew·tew
island *ada* a·da
Israel *İsrail* ees·ra·eel
it *o* o
IT *ET (enformasyon teknolojisi)*
e·te (en·for·mas·yon tek·no·lo·jee·see)
Italian (language) *İtalyanca* ee·tal·yan·ja
Italy *İtalya* ee·tal·ya
itch n *kaşıntı* ka·shuhn·tuh
itemised *ayrıntılı yazılmış*
ay·ruhn·tuh·luh ya·zuhl·muhsh
itinerary *yolculukta izlenecek yol*
yol·joo·look·ta eez·le·ne·jek yol
IUD *rahim içi araç* ra·heem ee·chee a·rach

J

jacket *ceket* je·ket
jail n *hapishane* ha·pees·ha·ne
jam n *marmelat* mar·me·lat
January *Ocak* o·jak

english–turkish

Japan *Japonya* zha·pon·ya
Japanese (language) *Japonca* zha·pon·ja
jar *kavanoz* ka·va·noz
jaw *çene* che·ne
jealous *kıskanç* kuhs·kanch
jeans *kot pantolon* kot pan·to·lon
jeep *cip* jeep
jet lag *yol yorgunluğu* yol·goon·loo·oo
jewellery *mücevherler* mew·jev·her·ler
Jewish *Yahudi* ya·hoo·dee
job *meslek* mes·lek
jogging *yavaş koşu* ya·vash ko·shoo
joke n *şaka* sha·ka
journalist *gazeteci* ga·ze·te·jee
journey n *yolculuk* yol·joo·look
judge n *yargıç* yar·guhch
juice *suyu* soo·yoo
July *Temmuz* tem·mooz
jump v *atlamak* at·la·mak
jumper (sweater) *kazak* ka·zak
jumper leads *akü takviye kablosu*
a·kew tak·vee·ye kab·lo·soo
June *Haziran* ha·zee·ran

K

kayaking *kayak yapmak* ka·yak yap·mak
ketchup *ketçap* ket·chap
key n *anahtar* a·nah·tar
keyboard *klavye* klav·ye
kick v *tekmelemek* tek·me·le·mek
kidney *böbrek* berb·rek
kilogram *kilogram* kee·log·ram
kilometre *kilometre* kee·lo·met·re
kind (nice) *kibar* kee·bar
kindergarten *ana okulu* a·na o·koo·loo
king *kral* kral
kiosk *satış kulübesi* sa·tuhsh koo·lew·be·see
kiss n *öpücük* er·pew·jewk
kiss v *öpmek* erp·mek
kitchen *mutfak* moot·fak
kiwifruit *kivi* kee·vee
knee *diz* deez
knife n *bıçak* buh·chak
know *bilmek* beel·mek
kosher *koşer* ko·sher

L

labourer *işçi* eesh·chee
lace *dantel* dan·tel
lake *göl* gerl
lamb *kuzu* koo·zoo

land n *toprak parçası* top·rak par·cha·suh
landlady/lord *mülk sahibi* mewlk sa·hee·bee
language *lisan* lee·san
laptop *diz üstü bilgisayar*
deez ews·tew beel·gee·sa·yar
large *iri* ee·ree
last (final) *son* son
last (previous) *önceki* ern·je·kee
last (week) *geçen (hafta)* ge·chen (haf·ta)
late *geç* gech
later *sonra* son·ra
laugh v *gülmek* gewl·mek
launderette *çamaşırhane*
cha·ma·shuhr·ha·ne
laundry (clothes) *çamaşır* cha·ma·shuhr
laundry (room) *çamaşırlık*
cha·ma·shuhr·luhk
law *kanun* ka·noon
law (study, profession) *hukuk* hoo·kook
lawyer *avukat* a·voo·kat
laxative *müsil ilacı* mew·seel ee·la·juh
lazy *tembel* tem·bel
leader *lider* lee·der
leaf n *yaprak* yap·rak
learn *öğrenmek* er·ren·mek
leather *deri* de·ree
Lebanon *Lübnan* lewb·nan
lecturer *okutman* o·koot·man
ledge *çıkıntı* chuh·kuhn·tuh
leek *pırasa* puh·ra·sa
Lefkosia *Lefkoşa* lef·ko·sha
left (direction) *sol* sol
left luggage *emanet* e·ma·net
left-luggage office *emanet bürosu*
e·ma·net bew·ro·soo
left-wing *sol·kanat* sol·ka·nat
leg (body) *bacak* ba·jak
legal *yasal* ya·sal
legislation *yasama* ya·sa·ma
legume *bakliyat* bak·lee·yat
lemon *limon* lee·mon
lemonade *limonata* lee·mo·na·ta
lens *lens* lens
lentil *mercimek* mer·jee·mek
lesbian n *lezbiyen* lez·bee·yen
less *daha az* da·ha az
letter (mail) *mektup* mek·toop
lettuce *marul* ma·rool
liar *yalancı* ya·lan·juh
library *kütüphane* kew·tewp·ha·ne
lice *bit* beet
licence n *ehliyet* eh·lee·yet
license plate number *plaka* pla·ka

lie (not stand) v *uzanmak* oo·zan·mak
lie (not tell the truth) v *yalan söylemek*
  ya·lan say·le·mek
life n *hayat* ha·yat
life jacket *can yeleği* jan ye·le·ee
lift (elevator) *asansör* a·san·ser
light n *ışık* uh·shuhk
light (colour) a *açık* a·chuhk
light (weight) a *hafif* ha·feef
light bulb *ampül* am·pewl
light meter *ışık ölçer* uh·shuhk erl·cher
lighter (cigarette) *çakmak* chak·mak
like v *sevmek* sev·mek
lime n *misket limonu* mees·ket lee·mo·noo
linen (material) *yatak takımı*
  ya·tak ta·kuh·muh
linen (sheets etc) *çarşaf* char·shaf
lip balm *nemlendirici ruj*
  nem·len·dee·ree·jee roozh
lips *dudaklar* doo·dak·lar
lipstick *ruj* roozh
liquor store *tekel bayii* te·kel ba·yee·ee
listen to *dinlemek* deen·le·mek
little a *küçük* kew·chewk
little n *az* az
live (somewhere) v *oturmak* o·toor·mak
liver *karaciğer* ka·ra·jee·er
lizard *kertenkele* ker·ten·ke·le
local a *yerel* ye·rel
lock n *kilit* kee·leet
lock v *kilitlemek* kee·leet·le·mek
locked *kilitli* kee·leet·lee
lollies *şeker* she·ker
long a *uzun* oo·zoon
look v *bakmak* bak·mak
look after *bakımını yapmak*
  ba·kuh·muh·nuh yap·mak
look for *aramak* a·ra·mak
lookout *gözlem yeri* gerz·lem ye·ree
loose *serbest* ser·best
loose change *bozuk para* bo·zook pa·ra
lose *kaybetmek* kai·bet·mek
lost *kayıp* ka·yuhp
lost-property office *kayıp eşya bürosu*
  ka·yuhp esh·ya bew·ro·soo
(a) lot *çok* chok
loud *yüksek ses* yewk·sek ses
love n *aşk* ashk
love (fall in) v *aşık olmak* a·shuhk ol·mak
lover *sevgili* sev·gee·lee
low *alçak* al·chak
lubricant *yağlayıcı madde*
  ya·la·yuh·juh mad·de

luck *şans* shans
lucky *şanslı* shans·luh
luggage *bagaj* ba·gazh
luggage lockers *kilitli eşya dolabı*
  kee·leet·lee esh·ya do·la·buh
luggage tag *bagaj etiketi*
  ba·gazh e·tee·ke·tee
lump *yumru* yoom·roo
lunch *öğle yemeği* er·le ye·me·ee
lung *akciğer* ak·jee·er
lure (fishing) n *yem* yem
luxury a *lüks* lewks

M

machine *makine* ma·kee·ne
magazine *dergi* der·gee
mail (letters) n *mektup* mek·toop
mail (postal system) n *posta* pos·ta
mailbox *posta kutusu* pos·ta koo·too·soo
main a *esas* e·sas
main road *anayol* a·na·yol
make *yapmak* yap·mak
make-up *makyaj* mak·yazh
male a *erkek* er·kek
mammogram *meme röntgeni*
  me·me rernt·ge·nee
man *adam* a·dam
manager (business) *müdür* mew·dewr
manager (sport) *menejer* me·ne·zher
Mandarin (language) *Çince* cheen·je
mandarin *mandalina* man·da·lee·na
mango *mango* man·go
mansion *konak* ko·nak
manual worker *amele* a·me·le
many *çok* chok
map (of country) *ülke haritası*
  ewl·ke ha·ree·ta·suh
map (of town) *kasaba haritası*
  ka·sa·ba ha·ree·ta·suh
March *Mart* mart
margarine *margarin* mar·ga·reen
marijuana *marihuana* ma·ree·hoo·a·na
marital status *medeni hal* me·de·nee hal
market n *pazar* pa·zar
marmalade *marmelat* mar·me·lat
marriage *evlilik* ev·lee·leek
married *evli* ev·lee
marry v *evlenmek* ev·len·mek
martial arts *savunma sporları*
  sa·voon·ma spor·la·ruh
mass (Catholic) *ekmek ve şarap ayini*
  ek·mek ve sha·rap a·yee·nee

massage n *masaj* ma·*sazh*
masseur *masör* ma·*ser*
masseuse *masöz* ma·*serz*
mat *paspas* pas·*pas*
match (sports) *maç* mach
matches (for lighting) *kibrit* keeb·*reet*
mattress *şilte* sheel·*te*
May *Mayıs* ma·*yuhs*
maybe *belki* bel·*kee*
mayonnaise *mayonez* ma·yo·*nez*
mayor *belediye başkanı*
 be·le·dee·ye bash·ka·nuh
me *beni* be·*nee*
me (obj) *bana* ba·*na*
meal *yemek* ye·*mek*
measles *kızamık* kuh·za·*muhk*
meat *et* et
mechanic (car) *araba tamircisi*
 a·ra·*ba* ta·meer·jee·*see*
media *basın* ba·*suhn*
medicine (medication) *ilaç* ee·*lach*
medicine (study, profession) *tıp* tuhp
meditation *meditasyon* me·dee·tas·*yon*
Mediterranean Sea *Akdeniz* ak·de·*neez*
meet (first time) v *tanışmak* ta·nuhsh·*mak*
meet (get together) v *buluşmak*
 boo·loosh·*mak*
melon *kavun* ka·*voon*
member *üye* ew·*ye*
men's quarters *erkekler bölümü*
 er·kek·ler ber·lew·*mew*
menstruation *adet* a·*det*
menu *yemek listesi* ye·mek lees·te·*see*
message n *mesaj* me·*sazh*
metal n *metal* me·*tal*
metre *metre* met·*re*
metro (train) *metro* met·*ro*
metro station *metro istasyonu*
 met·ro ees·tas·yo·*noo*
microwave oven *mikrodalga*
 meek·ro·dal·*ga*
midday *gün ortası* gewn or·ta·*suh*
midnight *gece yarısı* ge·je ya·ruh·*suh*
migraine *migren* meeg·*ren*
military n *askeriye* as·ke·ree·*ye*
military service *askerlik hizmeti*
 as·ker·*leek* heez·me·*tee*
milk *süt* sewt
millimetre *milimetre* mee·lee·met·*re*
million *milyon* meel·*yon*
minaret *minare* mee·na·*re*
mince n *kıyma* kuhy·*ma*
mineral water *maden suyu* ma·den soo·*yoo*

minute *dakika* da·kee·*ka*
mirror *ayna* ai·*na*
miscarriage *düşük* dew·*shewk*
miss (feel absence of) *özlemek* erz·le·*mek*
mistake n *hata* ha·*ta*
mix v *karıştırmak* ka·ruhsh·tuhr·*mak*
mobile phone *cep telefonu* jep te·le·fo·*noo*
modem *modem* mo·*dem*
modern *modern* mo·*dern*
moisturiser *nemlendirici*
 nem·len·dee·ree·*jee*
monastery *manastır* ma·nas·*tuhr*
Monday *Pazartesi* pa·zar·te·see
money *para* pa·*ra*
monk *keşiş* ke·*sheesh*
month *ay* ai
monument *anıt* a·*nuht*
moon *ay* ai
more *daha fazla* da·ha faz·*la*
morning *sabah* sa·*bah*
morning sickness *sabah bulantıları*
 sa·*bah* boo·lan·tuh·la·*ruh*
mosque *cami* ja·*mee*
mosquito *sivrisinek* seev·ree·see·*nek*
mosquito coil *spiral sinek kovar*
 spee·ral see·nek ko·*var*
mosquito net *cibinlik* jee·been·*leek*
motel *motel* mo·*tel*
mother *anne* an·*ne*
mother-in-law *kayınvalide*
 ka·yuhn·va·lee·de
motorbike *motosiklet* mo·to·seek·*let*
motorboat *motorbot* mo·tor·bot
motorway (tollway) *paralı yol* pa·ra·luh yol
mountain *dağ* da
mountain bike *dağ bisikleti*
 da bee·seek·le·tee
mountain path *dağ yolu* da yo·loo
mountain range *sıra dağlar* suh·ra da·*lar*
mountaineering *dağcılık* da·juh·*luhk*
mouse (animal) *fare* fa·*re*
mouth *ağız* a·*uhz*
movie *film* feelm
Mr *Bay* bai
Mrs/Ms/Miss *Bayan* ba·yan
mud *çamur* cha·*moor*
muesli *musli* moos·lee
mum *anneciğim* an·ne·jee·*eem*
mumps *kabakulak* ka·ba·koo·*lak*
murder n *cinayet* jee·na·yet
murder v *cinayet işlemek*
 jee·na·yet eesh·le·*mek*
muscle *kas* kas

museum *müze* mew-*ze*
mushroom *mantar* man-*tar*
music *müzik* mew-*zeek*
music shop *müzik mağazası*
   mew-*zeek* ma-a-za-*suh*
musician *müzisyen* mew-*zees*-yen
Muslim *Müslüman* mews-lew-*man*
Muslim cleric *Müslüman din adamı*
   mews-lew-*man* deen a-da-*muh*
mussel *midye* meed-ye
mustard *hardal* har-*dal*
mute (person) *dilsiz* deel-*seez*
my *benim* be-*neem*

N

nail clippers *tırnak makası*
   tuhr-*nak* ma-ka-*suh*
name n *ad* ad
napkin *peçete* pe-*che*-te
nappy *bebek bezi* be-*bek* be-*zee*
nappy rash *pişik* pee-*sheek*
national park *milli park* meel-*lee* park
nationality *milliyet* meel-lee-*yet*
nature *doğa* do-*a*
naturopathy *naturapati* na-too-ra-pa-*tee*
nausea *bulantı* boo-lan-*tuh*
near *yakında* ya-kuhn-*da*
nearby *yakın* ya-*kuhn*
nearest *en yakın* en ya-*kuhn*
necessary *gerekli* ge-rek-*lee*
neck *boyun* bo-*yoon*
necklace *kolye* kol-ye
nectarine *nektarin* nek-ta-*reen*
need v *ihtiyacı olmak*
   eeh-tee-ya-juh ol-*mak*
needle (sewing) *dikiş iğnesi*
   dee-*keesh* ee-ne-*see*
needle (syringe) *şırınga* shuh-ruhn-*ga*
negative a *olumsuz* o-loom-*sooz*
neighbourhood *mahalle* ma-hal-*le*
neither *hiçbiri* heech-bee-ree
net n *ağ* a
Netherlands *Hollanda* hol-*lan*-da
never *asla* as-*la*
new *yeni* ye-nee
New Year's Day *Yeni Yıl* ye-*nee* yuhl
New Year's Eve *Yeni Yıl arifesi*
   ye-*nee* yuhl a-ree-fe-*see*
New Zealand *Yeni Zelanda* ye-nee ze-*lan*-da
news *haberler* ha-ber-*ler*
newsstand *gazete satış kulübesi*
   ga-ze-te sa-*tuhsh* koo-lew-be-*see*

newsagency *gazete bayii* ga-ze-te ba-yee-*ee*
newspaper *gazete* ga-ze-te
next (month) *gelecek (ay)* ge-le-*jek* (ai)
next to *yanında* ya-nuhn-*da*
nice *hoş* hosh
nickname n *lakap* la-*kap*
night *gece* ge-je
night dive n *gece dalışı* ge-je da-luh-*shuh*
night out *akşam gezmesi*
   ak-*sham* gez-me-see
nightclub *gece kulübü* ge-je koo-lew-*bew*
Nikosia (Lefkosia) *Lefkoşa* lef-*ko*-sha
no *hayır* ha-yuhr
noisy *gürültülü* gew-rewl-tew-*lew*
none *hiçbiri* heech-bee-ree
nonsmoking *sigara içilmeyen*
   see-ga-ra ee-*cheel*-me-yen
noodles *erişte* e-reesh-te
noon *öğle* er-le
north *kuzey* koo-zay
Norway *Norveç* nor-vech
nose *burun* boo-*roon*
not *değil* de-*eel*
notebook *not defteri* not def-te-ree
nothing *hiç birşey* heech beer-*shay*
November *Kasım* ka-*suhm*
now *şimdi* sheem-dee
nuclear energy *nükleer enerji*
   newk-le-er e-ner-*jee*
nuclear testing *nükleer deneme*
   newk-le-er de-ne-me
nuclear waste *nükleer atık* newk-le-er a-tuhk
number (general) *sayı* sa-*yuh*
number (house/street) *numara* noo-ma-ra
numberplate *plaka* pla-ka
nun *rahibe* ra-hee-be
nurse *hemşire* hem-shee-re
nut *çerez* che-rez

O

oar(s) *kürek* kew-*rek*
oats *yulaf* yoo-*laf*
ocean *okyanus* ok-ya-*noos*
October *Ekim* e-keem
off (spoiled) *bozuk* bo-*zook*
office *ofis* o-fees
office worker *memur* me-*moor*
often *sık sık* suhk suhk
oil (food) *yağ* ya
oil (petrol) *benzin* ben-*zeen*
old (object) *eski* es-kee
old (person) *yaşlı* yash-*luh*

olive n *zeytin* zay·*teen*
olive oil *zeytinyağı* zay·*teen*·ya·uh
Olympic Games *Olimpiyat Oyunları*
o·leem·pee·*yat* o·yoon·la·*ruh*
omelette *omlet* om·*let*
on *-da/-de/-ta/-te* da/de/ta/·te
on time *zamanında* za·ma·nuhn·da
once *bir kez* beer kez
one *bir* beer
one-way *a gidiş* gee·*deesh*
onion *soğan* so·*an*
only *sadece* sa·de·*je*
open a *açık* a·*chuhk*
open v *açmak* ach·*mak*
opening hours *açılış saatleri*
a·chuh·*luhsh* sa·at·le·*ree*
opera *opera* o·pe·*ra*
opera house *opera binası*
o·pe·*ra* bee·na·*suh*
operation (medical) *ameliyat* a·me·lee·*yat*
operator *operatör* o·pe·ra·*ter*
opinion *fikir* fee·*keer*
opposite *karşısında* kar·shuh·suhn·*da*
optometrist *gözlükçü* gerz·lewk·*chew*
or *veya* ve·*ya*
orange n *portakal* por·ta·*kal*
orange (colour) *turuncu* too·roon·*joo*
orange juice *portakal suyu*
por·ta·*kal* soo·*joo*
orchestra *orkestra* or·*kes*·tra
order n *sipariş* see·pa·*reesh*
order v *sipariş vermek* see·pa·*reesh* ver·*mek*
ordinary *sıradan* suh·ra·*dan*
orgasm *orgazm* or·*gazm*
original *orijinal* o·ree·zhee·*nal*
other *diğer* dee·*er*
our *bizim* bee·*zeem*
out of order *bozuk* bo·*zook*
outside *dışarıda* duh·sha·ruh·*da*
ovarian cyst *yumurtalık tümörü*
yoo·moor·ta·*luhk* tew·mer·*rew*
ovary *yumurtalık* yoo·moor·ta·*luhk*
oven *fırın* fuh·*ruhn*
overcoat *palto* pal·*to*
overdose n *aşırı doz* a·shuh·ruh· doz
overnight *bir gecelik* beer ge·je·*leek*
overseas *yurt dışı* yoort duh·*shuh*
owe *borcu olmak* bor·joo ol·*mak*
owner *sahip* sa·*heep*
oxygen *oksijen* ok·see·*zhen*
oyster *istiridye* ees·tee·reed·*ye*
ozone layer *ozon tabakası*
o·*zon* ta·ba·ka·*suh*

P

pacemaker *kalp pili* kalp pee·*lee*
pacifier (dummy) *emzik* em·*zeek*
package *ambalaj* am·ba·*lazh*
packet *paket* pa·*ket*
padlock *asma kilit* as·ma kee·*leet*
page n *sayfa* sai·*fa*
pain n *ağrı* a·ruh
painful *ağrılı* a·ruh·*luh*
painkiller *ağrı kesici* a·ruh ke·see·*jee*
painter (artist) *ressam* res·*sam*
painter (occupation) *boyacı* bo·ya·*juh*
painting (a work) *tablo* tab·*lo*
painting (the art) *ressamlık* res·sam·*luhk*
pair (two) *çift* cheeft
Pakistan *Pakistan* pa·kees·*tan*
palace *saray* sa·*rai*
pan *tava* ta·*va*
pants (trousers) *pantolon* pan·to·*lon*
panty liners *kadın bağı* ka·duhn ba·uh
pantyhose *külotlu çorap*
kew·lot·loo cho·*rap*
pap smear *rahim ağzı kanser tarama testi*
ra·heem a·zuh kan·ser ta·ra·ma tes·tee
paper *kağıt* ka·uht
paperwork *kağıt işlemleri*
ka·uht eesh·lem·le·*ree*
paraplegic *felçli* felch·*lee*
parcel *paket* pa·*ket*
parents *ana baba* a·na ba·ba
park n *park* park
park (a car) v *park etmek* park et·*mek*
parliament *parlamento* par·la·men·*to*
part (component) *parça* par·*cha*
part-time *a yarım gün* ya·ruhm gewn
party (night out/politics) *parti* par·*tee*
pass v *geçmek* gech·*mek*
passenger *yolcu* yol·*joo*
passport *pasaport* pa·sa·*port*
passport number *pasaport numarası*
pa·sa·port noo·ma·ra·*suh*
past n *geçmiş* gech·*meesh*
pasta *makarna* ma·*kar*·na
pastry *hamur işi* ha·moor ee·*shee*
pastry shop *börekçi* ber·rek·*chee*
path *patika* pa·tee·*ka*
pavillion *büyük çadır* bew·*yewk* cha·*duhr*
pay v *ödemek* er·de·*mek*
payment *ödeme* er·de·*me*
pea *bezelye* be·zel·*ye*
peace *barış* ba·*ruhsh*
peach *şeftali* shef·ta·*lee*

peak (mountain) *zirve* zeer·ve

peanut *fıstık* fuhs·*tuhk*

pear *armut* ar·*moot*

pedal n *pedal* pe·*dal*

pedestrian *yaya* ya·ya

pedestrian crossing *yaya geçidi*
ya·ya ge·chee·dee

pen (ballpoint) *tükenmez kalem*
tew·ken·mez ka·*lem*

penalty (football) *penaltı* pe·nal·tuh

pencil *kurşun kalem* koor·shoon ka·*lem*

penicillin *penisilin* pe·nee·see·*leen*

penis *penis* pe·*nees*

penknife *çakı* cha·*kuh*

pensioner *emekli* e·mek·*lee*

people *kişi(ler)* kee·shee·(ler)

pepper (bell) *biber* bee·*ber*

pepper (black) *kara biber* ka·*ra* bee·*ber*

per (day) (gün) *başına* (gewn) ba·shuh·na

per cent *yüzde* yewz·de

perfect a *mükemmel* mew·kem·*mel*

performance *gösteri* gers·te·ree

perfume n *parfüm* par·*fewm*

period pain *adet ağrısı* a·det a·ruh·suh

permission *izin* ee·zeen

permit n *ruhsat* rooh·*sat*

person *kişi* kee·shee

petrol *benzin* ben·*zeen*

petrol station *benzin istasyonu*
ben·*zeen* ees·tas·yo·*noo*

pharmacist *eczacı* ej·za·*juh*

pharmacy *eczane* ej·za·ne

phone book *telefon rehberi*
te·le·fon reh·be·ree

phone box *telefon kulübesi*
te·le·fon koo·lew·be·see

phone call *telefon konuşması*
te·le·fon ko·noosh·ma·suh

phone card *telefon kartı* te·le·fon kar·*tuh*

phone number *telefon numarası*
te·le·fon noo·ma·ra·suh

photo *fotoğraf* fo·to·raf

photographer *fotoğrafçı* fo·to·raf·*chuh*

photography *fotoğrafçılık*
fo·to·raf·chuh·*luhk*

phrasebook *pratik konuşma kılavuzu*
pra·*teek* ko·noosh·ma kuh·la·voo·zoo

pickaxe *kazma* kaz·ma

pickles *turşu* toor·*shoo*

picnic n *piknik* peek·*neek*

piece n *parça* par·*cha*

pig *domuz* do·mooz

pill *hap* hap

the pill *doğum kontrol hapı*
do·oom kon·*trol* ha·*puh*

pillow *yastık* yas·*tuhk*

pillowcase *yastık kılıfı* yas·*tuhk* kuh·luh·*fuh*

pineapple *ananas* a·na·*nas*

pink *pembe* pem·be

pistachio *şamfıstığı* sham·fuhs·tuh·*uh*

place n *yer* yer

place of birth *doğum yeri* do·oom ye·ree

plane *uçak* oo·*chak*

planet *gezegen* ge·ze·gen

plant n *bitki* beet·kee

plastic a *plastik* plas·*teek*

plate *tabak* ta·*bak*

plateau *plato* pla·*to*

platform (train) *peron* pe·*ron*

play cards v *kağıt oynamak*
ka·*uht* oy·na·*mak*

play guitar v *gitar çalmak* gee·*tar* chal·*mak*

play (theatre) n *oyun* o·*yoon*

player *oyuncu* o·yoon·joo

plug (bath) n *tapa* ta·*pa*

plug (electricity) n *fiş* feesh

plum *erik* e·*reek*

poached *suda pişmiş* soo·*da* peesh·*meesh*

pocket *cep* jep

pocketknife *çakı* cha·*kuh*

poetry *şiir* shee·*eer*

point (decimal/dot) n *nokta* nok·*ta*

point (score) n *puan* poo·*an*

point v *göstermek* gers·ter·*mek*

poisonous *zehirli* ze·heer·*lee*

police *polis* po·lees

police officer *polis memuru*
po·lees me·moo·roo

police station *polis karakolu*
po·lees ka·ra·ko·loo

policy *politika* po·lee·tee·ka

politician *politikacı* po·lee·tee·ka·*juh*

politics *politika* po·lee·tee·*ka*

pollen *polen* po·*len*

pollution *kirlilik* keer·lee·*leek*

pool (game) *bilardo* bee·*lar*·do

pool (swimming) *yüzme havuzu*
yewz·me ha·voo·zoo

poor *fakir* fa·*keer*

popular *popüler* po·pew·*ler*

pork *domuz eti* do·mooz e·*tee*

port (sea) *liman* lee·*man*

Portugal *Portekiz* por·te·*keez*

positive a *olumlu* o·loom·loo

possible *muhtemel* mooh·te·*mel*

postage *posta ücreti* pos·*ta* ewj·re·*tee*

postcard *kartpostal* kart·pos·*tal*
post code *posta kodu* pos·ta ko·doo
post office *postane* pos·ta·ne
poster *poster* pos·ter
pot (ceramics) *toprak kap* top·rak kap
potato *patates* pa·ta·tes
pottery *çömlekçilik* cherm·lek·chee·*leek*
pound (money) *sterlin* ster·*leen*
pound (weight) *libre* leeb·re
poverty *yoksulluk* yok·sool·look
powder n *pudra* pood·ra
power n *güç* gewch
prawn *karides* ka·ree·des
prayer *dua* doo·a
prayer book *dua kitabı* doo·a kee·ta·buh
prefer *tercih etmek* ter·jeeh et·mek
pregnancy test kit *gebelik test çubuğu* ge·be·*leek* test choo·boo·oo
pregnant *hamile* ha·mee·le
premenstrual tension *adet öncesi gerginlik* a·det ern·je·see ger·geen·leek
prepare *hazırlamak* ha·zuhr·la·mak
prescription *reçete* re·che·te
present (gift) *hediye* he·dee·ye
present (time) *şimdiki zaman* sheem·dee·kee za·man
president *başkan* bash·kan
pressure n *basınç* ba·suhnch
pretty *hoş* hosh
previous *önceki* ern·je·kee
price n *fiyat* fee·yat
priest *papaz* pa·paz
prime minister *başbakan* bash·ba·kan
printer (computer) *printer* preen·ter
prison *cezaevi* je·za·e·vee
prisoner *mahkum* mah·koom
private a *özel* er·zel
produce v *üretmek* ew·ret·mek
profit n *kar* kar
program n *program* prog·ram
projector *projektör* pro·zhek·ter
promise v *söz vermek* serz ver·mek
prostitute n *fahişe* fa·hee·she
protect *korumak* ko·roo·mak
protected (species) *koruma altına alınmış* ko·roo·ma al·tuh·na a·luhn·muhsh
protest n *protesto* pro·tes·to
protest v *protesto etmek* pro·tes·to et·mek
provisions *erzak* er·zak
prune n *kuru erik* koo·roo e·reek
pub (bar) *bar* bar
public baths *hamam* ha·mam
public gardens *park* park

public relations *halkla ilişkiler* halk·la ee·leesh·kee·ler
public telephone *umumi telefon* oo·moo·mee te·le·fon
public toilet *umumi tuvalet* oo·moo·mee too·va·let
pull v *çekmek* chek·mek
pump n *pompa* pom·pa
pumpkin *bal kabağı* bal ka·ba·uh
puncture n *patlak* pat·lak
pure *saf* saf
purple *mor* mor
purse n *cüzdan* jewz·dan
push v *itmek* eet·mek
put *koymak* koy·mak

Q

quadriplegic *her iki kolu ve bacağı felçli* her ee·*kee* ko·loo ve ba·ja·uh felch·lee
qualifications *nitelikler* nee·te·leek·ler
quality *kalite* ka·lee·te
quarantine *karantina* ka·ran·tee·na
quarter *çeyrek* chay·rek
quay *rıhtım* ruh·tuhm
queen *kraliçe* kra·lee·che
question n *soru* so·roo
queue n *sıra* suh·ra
quick a *çabuk* cha·book
quiet a *sakin* sa·keen
quit *bırakmak* buh·rak·mak

R

rabbit *tavşan* tav·shan
race (sport) n *yarış* ya·ruhsh
racetrack *yarış pisti* ya·ruhsh pees·tee
racing bike *yarış bisikleti* ya·ruhsh bee·seek·le·tee
racism *ırkçılık* uhrk·chuh·luhk
racquet *raket* ra·ket
radiator *radyatör* rad·ya·ter
radio n *radyo* rad·yo
radish *kırmızı turp* kuhr·muh·zuh toorp
railway station *tren istasyonu* tren ees·tas·yo·noo
rain n *yağmur* ya·moor
raincoat *yağmurluk* ya·moor·look
raisin *kuru üzüm* koo·roo ew·zewm
Ramadan *Ramazan* ra·ma·zan
rape n *tecavüz* te·ja·vewz
rare (food) *az pişmiş* az peesh·meesh

rare (uncommon) *az bulunur*
az boo·loo·noor
rash *isilik* ee·see·leek
raspberry *ahududu* a·hoo·doo·doo
rat *sıçan* suh·chan
rave n *rave parti* rayv par·tee
raw *çiğ* chee
razor *traş makinesi* trash ma·kee·ne·see
razor blade *jilet* jee·let
read v *okumak* o·koo·mak
reading *okuma* o·koo·ma
ready *hazır* ha·zuhr
real estate agent *emlakçı* em·lak·chuh
realistic *gerçekçi* ger·chek·chee
rear (location) *geri* ge·ree
reason *sebep* se·bep
receipt *makbuz* mak·booz
recently *yakın zamanda* ya·kuhn za·man·da
recommend *tavsiye etmek* tav·see·ye et·mek
record v *kaydetmek* kai·det·mek
recording *kayıt* ka·yuht
recyclable *yeniden kazanılabilir*
ye·nee·den ka·za·nuh·la·bee·leer
recycle *yeniden kazanmak*
ye·nee·den ka·zan·mak
red *kırmızı* kuhr·muh·zuh
referee *hakem* ha·kem
reference n *referans* re·fe·rans
reflexology *refleksoloji* ref·lek·so·lo·zhee
refrigerator *buzdolabı* booz·do·la·buh
refugee *mülteci* mewl·te·jee
refund n *para iadesi* pa·ra ee·a·de·see
refuse v *reddetmek* red·det·mek
regional *bölgesel* berl·ge·sel
registered mail/post *taahhütlü posta*
ta·ah·hewt·lew pos·ta
rehydration salts *rehidrasyon tuzu*
re·heed·ras·yon too·zoo
reiki *reiki* re·ee·kee
relationship (family) *akrabalık* ak·ra·ba·luhk
relationship (general) *ilişki* ee·leesh·kee
relax v *dinlenmek* deen·len·mek
relic *eski eser* es·kee e·ser
religion *din* deen
religious *dini* dee·nee
remote a *uzak* oo·zak
remote control *uzaktan kumanda*
oo·zak·tan koo·man·da
rent v *kiralamak* kee·ra·la·mak
repair v *tamir etmek* ta·meer et·mek
republic *cumhuriyet* joom·hoo·ree·yet
reservation n *rezervasyon* re·zer·vas·yon
rest v *dinlenmek* deen·len·mek

restaurant *restoran* res·to·ran
résumé *özgeçmiş* erz·gech·meesh
retired *emekli* e·mek·lee
return (come back) v *geri dönmek*
ge·ree dern·mek
return a *gidiş-dönüş* gee·deesh·der·newsh
review n *yeniden gözden geçirme*
ye·nee·den gerz·den ge·cheer·me
rhythm *ritim* ree·teem
rib *kaburga* ka·boor·ga
rice (cooked) *pilav* pee·lav
rice (uncooked) *pirinç* pee·reench
rich (wealthy) *zengin* zen·geen
ride n *binmek* been·mek
ride (horse) v *ata binmek* a·ta been·mek
right (correct) a *doğru* do·roo
right (direction) a *doğru yön* do·roo yern
right-wing *sağ-kanat* sa·ka·nat
ring (on finger) *yüzük* yew·zewk
ring (phone) v *çalmak* chal·mak
rip-off n *kazıklama* ka·zuhk·la·ma
risk n *risk* reesk
river *nehir* ne·heer
road *yol* yol
road map *yol haritası* yol ha·ree·ta·suh
rob *soymak* soy·mak
rock n *kaya* ka·ya
rock (music) *rok* rok
rock climbing *kaya tırmanışı*
ka·ya tuhr·ma·nuh·shuh
rock group *rok gurubu* rok goo·roo·boo
rockmelon *kavun* ka·voon
roll (bread) *hamburger ekmeği*
ham·boor·ger ek·me·ee
rollerblading *paten* pa·ten
Romania *Romanya* ro·man·ya
romantic *romantik* ro·man·teek
room *oda* o·da
room number *oda numarası*
o·da noo·ma·ra·suh
rope *ip* eep
round a *yuvarlak* yoo·var·lak
roundabout *trafik adası* tra·feek a·da·suh
route n *rota* ro·ta
rowing *kürek çekme* kew·rek chek·me
rubbish n *çöp* cherp
rubella *kızamıkçık* kuh·za·muhk·chuhk
rug *kilim* kee·leem
rugby *ragbi* rag·bee
ruins *harabeler* ha·ra·be·ler
rule n *kural* koo·ral
rum *rom* rom
run v *koşmak* kosh·mak

running *koşu* ko-*shoo*
runny nose *burun akıntısı*
  boo-*roon* a-kuhn-tuh-*suh*
Russia *Rusya* roos-ya
Russian (language) *Rusça* roos-cha

S

sad *üzgün* ewz-*gewn*
saddle n *eyer* e-*yer*
safe n *kasa* ka-sa
safe a *emniyetli* em-nee-yet-*lee*
safe sex *güvenli seks* gew-ven-*lee* seks
sailing boat *yelkenli tekne* yel-ken-*lee* tek-ne
saint *aziz* a-*zeez*
salad *salata* sa-la-ta
salami *salam* sa-*lam*
salary *maaş* ma-*ash*
sale n *indirimli satış*
  een-dee-reem-*lee* sa-*tuhsh*
sales tax *satış vergisi* sa-*tuhsh* ver-gee-*see*
salmon *som balığı* som ba-luh-*uh*
salt *tuz* tooz
same *aynı* ai-*nuh*
sand n *kum* koom
sandal *sandalet* san-da-*let*
sanitary napkin *hijyenik kadın bağı*
  heezh-ye-neek ka-*duhn* ba-*uh*
Saturday *Cumartesi* joo-mar-te-see
sauce n *sos* sos
saucepan *sos tenceresi* sos ten-je-re-*see*
sauna *sauna* sa-oo-na
sausage *sosis* so-*sees*
say v *söylemek* say-le-*mek*
scalp n *kafa derisi* ka-fa de-ree-*see*
scarf *atkı* at-*kuh*
school *okul* o-*kool*
science *bilim* bee-*leem*
scientist *bilim adamı* bee-*leem* a-da-*muh*
scissors *makas* ma-*kas*
score v *puan* poo-*an*
scoreboard *puan tahtası* poo-*an* tah-ta-*suh*
Scotland *İskoçya* ees-*koch*-ya
scrambled *karıştırılmış*
  ka-ruhsh-tuh-ruhl-*muhsh*
scuba diving *aletli dalış* a-let-*lee* da-*luhsh*
sculpture *heykel* hay-*kel*
sea *deniz* de-*neez*
seasick *deniz tutmuş* de-*neez* toot-*moosh*
seaside n *deniz kenarı* de-*neez* ke-na-*ruh*
season *mevsim* mev-*seem*
seat (place) *yer* yer

seatbelt *emniyet kemeri*
  em-nee-yet ke-me-*ree*
second (time) n *saniye* sa-nee-ye
second a *ikinci* ee-keen-*jee*
second class n *ikinci sınıf*
  ee-keen-*jee* suh-*nuhf*
second-hand a *ikinci el* ee-keen-*jee* el
second-hand shop *eskici* es-kee-*jee*
secretary *sekreter* sek-re-ter
see *görmek* ger-*mek*
self service *self-servis* self-ser-vees
self-employed *serbest çalışan*
  ser-best cha-luh-*shan*
selfish *bencil* ben-*jeel*
sell *satmak* sat-*mak*
send *göndermek* gern-der-*mek*
sensible *makul* ma-*kool*
sensual *erotik* e-ro-*teek*
separate a *ayrı* ai-*ruh*
September *Eylül* ay-*lewl*
serious *ciddi* jeed-dee
service n *servis* ser-vees
service charge *hizmet ücreti*
  heez-met ewj-re-tee
service station *benzin istasyonu*
  ben-zeen ees-tas-yo-noo
serviette *peçete* pe-che-te
several *birkaç* beer-*kach*
sew *dikiş dikmek* dee-keesh deek-*mek*
sex (gender) *cinsiyet* jeen-see-*yet*
sex (intercourse) *seks* seks
sexism *cinsiyet ayrımı*
  jeen-see-*yet* ai-ruh-*muh*
sexy *seksi* sek-see
shade n *gölge* gerl-ge
shadow n *gölge* gerl-ge
shadow-puppet theatre *gölge oyunu*
  gerl-ge o-yoo-noo
shampoo *şampuan* sham-poo-*an*
shape n *biçim* bee-*cheem*
share v *paylaşmak* pai-lash-*mak*
share with v *ile paylaşmak*
  ee-le pai-lash-*mak*
shave v *tıraş olmak* tuh-*rash* ol-*mak*
shaving cream *tıraş kremi* tuh-*rash* kre-mee
she o o
sheep *koyun* ko-*yoon*
sheet (bed) *çarşaf* char-*shaf*
shelf *raf* raf
shiatsu *akupresyon* a-koo-pres-yon
shingles (illness) *zona* zo-na
ship n *gemi* ge-mee
shirt *gömlek* germ-*lek*

shoe shop *ayakkabıcı* a·yak·ka·buh·*juh*
shoes *ayakkabılar* a·yak·ka·buh·*lar*
shoot v *ateş etmek* a·*tesh* et·*mek*
shop n *dükkan* dewk·*kan*
shop v *alış-veriş yapmak*
   a·*luhsh*·ve·*reesh* yap·*mak*
shopping *alış-veriş* a·*luhsh*·ve·*reesh*
shopping centre *alış-veriş merkezi*
   a·*luhsh*·ve·*reesh* mer·ke·*zee*
short (height) *kısa* kuh·*sa*
shortage *eksiklik* ek·seek·*leek*
shorts *şort* short
shoulder *omuz* o·*mooz*
shout v *bağırmak* ba·uhr·*mak*
show n *gösteri* gers·te·*ree*
show v *göstermek* gers·ter·*mek*
shower n *duş* doosh
shrine *tapınak* ta·puh·*nak*
shut a *kapalı* ka·pa·*luh*
shy *utangaç* oo·tan·*gach*
sick *hasta* has·*ta*
side n *kenar* ke·*nar*
sign n *işaret* ee·sha·*ret*
sign v *imzalamak* eem·za·la·*mak*
signature *imza* eem·*za*
silk *ipek* ee·*pek*
silver n *gümüş* gew·*mewsh*
SIM card *SİM kart* seem kart
similar *benzer* ben·*zer*
simple *basit* ba·*seet*
since (May) *(Mayıs)tan beri*
   (ma·*yuhs*)·*tan* be·*ree*
sing *şarkı söylemek* shar·*kuh* say·le·*mek*
Singapore *Singapur* seen·ga·*poor*
singer *şarkıcı* shar·kuh·*juh*
single (not married) *bekar* be·*kar*
single room *tek kişilik oda*
   tek kee·shee·*leek* o·*da*
singlet *atlet* at·*let*
sinker (fishing) *olta kurşunu*
   ol·*ta* koor·shoo·*noo*
sister (kız) *kardeş* kar·*desh*
sit *oturmak* o·toor·*mak*
size n *beden* be·*den*
skate v *patenle kaymak* pa·ten·*le* kai·*mak*
skateboarding *kay-kay* kai·*kai*
ski v *kayak yapmak* ka·*yak* yap·*mak*
skiing *kayak* ka·*yak*
skim milk *az yağlı süt* az ya·*luh* sewt
skin n *cilt* jeelt
skirt *etek* e·*tek*
skull *kafatası* ka·fa·ta·*suh*
sky *gökyüzü* gerk·yew·*zew*

sled n *kızak* kuh·*zak*
sleep v *uyumak* oo·yoo·*mak*
sleeping bag *uyku tulumu*
   ooy·*koo* too·loo·*moo*
sleeping berth *yatak* ya·*tak*
sleeping car *yataklı vagon* ya·tak·*luh* va·*gon*
sleeping pills *uyku hapı* ooy·*koo* ha·*puh*
sleepy *uykulu* ooy·koo·*loo*
slice n *dilim* dee·*leem*
slide (film) *slayt* slait
slow a *yavaş* ya·*vash*
slowly *yavaşça* ya·vash·*cha*
small *küçük* kew·*chewk*
smaller *daha küçük* da·*ha* kew·*chewk*
smallest *en küçük* en kew·*chewk*
smell n *koku* ko·*koo*
smile v *gülümsemek* gew·lewm·se·*mek*
smoke v *sigara içmek* see·ga·*ra* eech·*mek*
snack n *hafif yemek* ha·*feef* ye·*mek*
snack bar *büfe* bew·*fe*
snail *salyangoz* sal·yan·*goz*
snake *yılan* yuh·*lan*
snorkelling *şnorkelli dalış*
   shnor·kel·*lee* da·*luhsh*
snow n *kar* kar
snowboarding *board kayağı* bord ka·ya·*uh*
snow pea *taze bezelye* ta·ze be·zel·*ye*
soap *sabun* sa·*boon*
soap opera *pembe dizi* pem·be dee·*zee*
soccer *futbol* foot·*bol*
social welfare *toplum refahı*
   top·*loom* re·fa·*huh*
socialist a *sosyalist* sos·ya·*leest*
socks *çoraplar* cho·rap·*lar*
soft-boiled *az haşlanmış* az hash·lan·*muhsh*
soft drink *meşrubat* mesh·roo·*bat*
soldier n *asker* as·*ker*
some *biraz* bee·*raz*
someone *birisi* bee·ree·*see*
something *birşey* beer·*shay*
sometimes *bazen* ba·*zen*
son *oğul* o·*ool*
song *şarkı* shar·*kuh*
soon *yakında* ya·kuhn·*da*
sore a *ağrılı* a·ruh·*luh*
soup *çorba* chor·*ba*
sour cream *kaymak* kai·*mak*
south *güney* gew·*nay*
souvenir *hediyelik eşya*
   he·dee·ye·*leek* esh·*ya*
souvenir shop *hediyelik eşya dükkanı*
   he·dee·ye·*leek* esh·ya dewk·ka·*nuh*
soy milk *soya sütü* so·ya sew·*tew*

soy sauce *soya sosu* so·ya so·soo
space (place) *yer* yer
space (universe) *uzay* oo·zai
Spain *İspanya* ees·pan·ya
Spanish (language) *İspanyolca* ees·pan·yol·ja
sparkling wine *köpüklü şarap* ker·pewk·lew sha·rap
speak *konuşmak* ko·noosh·mak
special a *özel* er·zel
specialist *uzman* ooz·man
speed (velocity) n *hız* huhz
speed limit *hız sınırı* huhz suh·nuh·ruh
speedometer *hız göstergesi* huhz gers·ter·ge·see
spider *örümcek* er·rewm·jek
spinach *ıspanak* uhs·pa·nak
spoilt (person) *şımarık* shuh·ma·ruhk
spoke n *tekerlek parmaklığı* te·ker·lek par·mak·luh·uh
spoon n *kaşık* ka·shuhk
sport n *spor* spor
sports store *spor malzemeleri mağazası* spor mal·ze·me·le·ree ma·a·za·suh
sportsperson *sporcu* spor·joo
sprain n *burkulma* boor·kool·ma
spring (coil) n *yay* yai
spring (season) *ilkbahar* eelk·ba·har
spring water *memba suyu* mem·ba soo·yoo
square (town) *meydan* may·dan
stadium *stadyum* stad·yoom
stairway *merdiven* mer·dee·ven
stale *bayat* ba·yat
stamp (postage) *pul* pool
stand-by a *açık* a·chuhk
star *yıldız* yuhl·duhz
(four-)star (dört) yıldızlı (dert) yuhl·duhz·luh
start n *başlangıç* bash·lan·guhch
start v *başlamak* bash·la·mak
station *istasyon* ees·tas·yon
stationer's *kırtasiyeci* kuhr·ta·see·ye·jee
statue *heykel* hay·kel
stay (at a hotel) v (otelde) kalmak (o·tel·de) kal·mak
stay (in one place) v *durmak* door·mak
steak (beef) *biftek* beef·tek
steal v *çalmak* chal·mak
steep a *sarp* sarp
step n *adım* a·duhm
stereo n *stereo* ster·yo
still water *durgun su* door·goon soo
stock (food) *stok* stok

stockings *çorap* cho·rap
stolen *çalıntı* cha·luhn·tuh
stomach *mide* mee·de
stomachache *mide ağrısı* mee·de a·ruh·suh
stone n *taş* tash
stoned (drugged) *uyuşturucu etkisi altında* oo·yoosh·too·roo·joo et·kee·see al·tuhn·da
stop (bus etc) n ... *durağı* ... doo·ra·uh
stop (cease) v *durmak* door·mak
stop (prevent) v *durdurmak* door·door·mak
storm *fırtına* fuhr·tuh·na
story *hikaye* hee·ka·ye
stove *ocak* o·jak
straight a *düz* dewz
strange *acayip* a·ja·yeep
stranger *yabancı* ya·ban·juh
strawberry *çilek* chee·lek
stream *akıntı* a·kuhn·tuh
street *sokak* so·kak
street market *semt pazarı* semt pa·za·ruh
strike (stop work) n *grev* grev
striker (football) *golcü* gol·jew
string *ip* eep
stroke (health) *felç* felch
stroller *puset* poo·set
strong *güçlü* gewch·lew
stubborn *inatçı* ee·nat·chuh
student *öğrenci* er·ren·jee
studio *stüdyo* stewd·yo
stupid *aptal* ap·tal
style *tarz* tarz
subtitles *altyazı* alt·ya·zuh
suburb *bölge* berl·ge
subway (pedestrian) *alt geçit* alt ge·cheet
subway (train) *metro* met·ro
sugar *şeker* she·ker
suitcase *bavul* ba·vool
sultana *kuru üzüm* koo·roo ew·zewm
summer *yaz* yaz
sun *güneş* gew·nesh
sunblock *güneşten koruma kremi* gew·nesh·ten ko·roo·ma kre·mee
sunburn *güneş yanığı* gew·nesh ya·nuh·uh
Sunday *Pazar* pa·zar
sunglasses *güneş gözlüğü* gew·nesh gerz·lew·ew
sunny *güneşli* gew·nesh·lee
sunrise *gün doğumu* gewn do·oo·moo
sunset *gün batımı* gewn ba·tuh·muh
sunstroke *güneş çarpması* gew·nesh charp·ma·suh
supermarket *süpermarket* sew·per·mar·ket

superstition *batıl inanç* ba·*tuhl* ee·*nanch*
supporter (politics/sport) *taraftar* ta·raf·*tar*
surf v *sörf yapmak* serf yap·*mak*
surface mail (land) *kara yoluyla gönderi*
ka·*ra* yo·*looy*·la gern·de·*ree*
surface mail (sea) *deniz yoluyla gönderi*
de·*neez* yo·*looy*·la gern·de·*ree*
surfboard *sörf tahtası* serf tah·ta·*suh*
surfing *sörf* serf
surname *soyad* soy·ad
surprise n *sürpriz* sewrp·*reez*
sweater *kazak* ka·*zak*
Sweden *İsveç* ees·*vech*
sweet a *tatlı* tat·*luh*
sweets *şeker* she·ker
swelling *şişlik* sheesh·*leek*
swim v *yüzmek* yewz·*mek*
swimming (sport) *yüzme* yewz·*me*
swimming pool *yüzme havuzu*
yewz·*me* ha·voo·*zoo*
swimsuit *mayo* ma·*yo*
Switzerland *İsviçre* ees·*veech*·re
synagogue *havra* hav·ra
synthetic *sentetik* sen·te·*teek*
Syria *Suriye* soo·ree·*ye*
syringe *şırınga* shuh·ruhn·*ga*

T

table n *masa* ma·*sa*
table tennis *masa tenisi* ma·*sa* te·nee·*see*
tablecloth *masa örtüsü* ma·*sa* er·tew·*sew*
tail n *kuyruk* kooy·*rook*
tailor *terzi* ter·*zee*
take v *almak* al·*mak*
take a photo *fotoğraf çekmek*
fo·to·*raf* chek·*mek*
talk v *konuşmak* ko·noosh·*mak*
tall (person) *uzun boylu* oo·*zoon* boy·*loo*
tampon *tampon* tam·*pon*
tanning lotion *güneş yağı* gew·*nesh* ya·*uh*
tap *musluk* moos·*look*
tap water *çeşme suyu* chesh·*me* soo·*yoo*
tasty *lezzetli* lez·zet·*lee*
tax n *vergi* ver·*gee*
taxi *taksi* tak·*see*
taxi rank *taksi durağı* tak·*see* doo·ra·*uh*
tea *çay* chai
tea garden *çay bahçesi* chai bah·che·*see*
tea glass *çay bardağı* chai bar·da·*uh*
teapot *çaydanlık* chai·dan·*luhk*
teaspoon *çay kaşığı* chai ka·shuh·*uh*
tea urn *semaver* se·ma·*ver*

teacher *öğretmen* er·ret·*men*
team *takım* ta·*kuhm*
technique *teknik* tek·*neek*
teeth *dişler* deesh·*ler*
telegram n *telgraf* tel·*graf*
telephone n *telefon* te·le·*fon*
telephone v *telefon etmek* te·le·*fon* et·*mek*
telephone box *telefon kulübesi*
te·le·*fon* koo·lew·be·*see*
telephone centre *telefon santralı*
te·le·*fon* san·tra·*luh*
telescope *teleskop* te·les·*kop*
television *televizyon* te·le·veez·*yon*
tell *anlatmak* an·lat·*mak*
temperature (fever) *ateş* a·*tesh*
temperature (weather) *derece* de·re·*je*
temple *tapınak* ta·puh·*nak*
tennis *tenis* te·*nees*
tennis court *tenis kortu* te·*nees* kor·*too*
tent *çadır* cha·*duhr*
tent peg *çadır kazığı* cha·*duhr* ka·zuh·*uh*
terrible *korkunç* kor·*koonch*
test n *test* test
thank v *teşekkür etmek* te·shek·*kewr* et·*mek*
that (one) *şunu/onu* shoo·*noo*/o·*noo*
theatre *tiyatro* tee·yat·ro
their *onların* on·la·*ruhn*
them *onları* on·la·*ruh*
there *orada* o·ra·da
thermal bath *kaplıca hamamı*
kap·*luh*·ja ha·ma·*muh*
thermal spring *kaplıca* kap·*luh*·ja
they *onlar* on·*lar*
thick *kalın* ka·*luhn*
thief *hırsız* huhr·*suhz*
thin a *ince* een·*je*
think v *düşünmek* dew·shewn·*mek*
third a *üçüncü* ew·chewn·*jew*
thirsty *susamış* soo·sa·*muhsh*
this (month) *bu (ay)* bu (ai)
this (one) *bunu* boo·*noo*
thread *iplik* eep·*leek*
throat *boğaz* bo·*az*
thrush (health) *pamukçuk* pa·mook·*chook*
thunderstorm *fırtına* fuhr·tuh·*na*
Thursday *Perşembe* per·shem·*be*
ticket *bilet* bee·*let*
ticket booth *bilet gişesi* bee·*let* gee·she·*see*
ticket collector *biletçi* bee·let·*chee*
ticket machine *bilet makinesi*
bee·*let* ma·kee·ne·*see*
ticket office *bilet gişesi* bee·*let* gee·she·*see*
tide *dalga* dal·*ga*

tight *sıkı* suh-*kuh*
time n *zaman* za-*man*
time difference *zaman farkı* za-*man* far-*kuh*
timetable *tarife* ta-ree-*fe*
tin (can) *teneke kutu* te-ne-*ke* koo-*too*
tin opener *konserve açacağı*
    kon-*ser*-ve a-cha-ja-*uh*
tiny *küçücük* kew-chew-*jewk*
tip (gratuity) *bahşiş* bah-*sheesh*
tire *lastik* las-*teek*
tired *yorgun* yor-*goon*
tissues *kağıt mendil* ka-*uht* men-*deel*
to -*a*/-*e*/-*ya*/-*ye* -*a*/-*e*/-*ya*/-*ye*
toast n *kızarmış ekmek*
    kuh-*zar*-muhsh ek-*mek*
toaster *ekmek kızartma makinesi*
    ek-*mek* kuh-*zart*-ma ma-ke-ne-*see*
tobacco *tütün* tew-*tewn*
tobacconist *tütüncü* tew-tewn-*jew*
today *bugün* boo-*gewn*
toe *ayak parmağı* a-*yak* par-ma-*uh*
tofu *soya peyniri* so-*ya* pay-nee-*ree*
together *birlikte* beer-leek-*te*
toilet *tuvalet* too-va-*let*
toilet paper *tuvalet kağıdı*
    too-va-*let* ka-uh-*duh*
tomato *domates* do-*ma*-tes
tomato sauce *domates sosu*
    do-*ma*-tes so-*soo*
tomb *mezar* me-*zar*
tomorrow *yarın* ya-*ruhn*
tomorrow afternoon *yarın öğleden sonra*
    ya-*ruhn* er-le-*den* son-ra
tomorrow evening *yarın akşam*
    ya-*ruhn* ak-*sham*
tomorrow morning *yarın sabah*
    ya-*ruhn* sa-*bah*
tonight *bu gece* boo ge-*je*
too (expensive etc) *çok* chok
tooth *diş* deesh
toothache *diş ağrısı* deesh a-ruh-*suh*
toothbrush *diş fırçası* deesh fuhr-cha-*suh*
toothpaste *diş macunu* deesh ma-joo-*noo*
toothpick *kürdan* kewr-*dan*
torch (flashlight) n *el feneri* el fe-ne-*ree*
touch v *dokunmak* do-koon-*mak*
tour n *tur* toor
tourist *turist* too-*reest*
tourist office *turizm bürosu*
    too-*reezm* bew-ro-*soo*
towel *havlu* hav-*loo*

toxic waste *zararlı atık* za-rar-*luh* a-*tuhk*
toy shop *oyuncakçı* o-yoon-jak-*chuh*
track (path) *patika* pa-tee-*ka*
track (sport) *yarış pisti* ya-*ruhsh* pees-*tee*
trade n *ticaret* tee-ja-*ret*
tradesperson *tüccar* tewj-*jar*
traffic n *trafik* tra-*feek*
traffic light *trafik ışığı* tra-*feek* uh-shuh-*uh*
trail n *patika* pa-tee-*ka*
train n *tren* tren
train station *tren istasyonu*
    \tren ees-tas-yo-*noo*
tram *tramvay* tram-*vai*
transit lounge *transit yolcu salonu*
    tran-*seet* yol-joo sa-lo-*noo*
translate *çevirmek* che-veer-*mek*
transport n *ulaşım* oo-la-*shuhm*
travel v *seyahat* se-ya-*hat*
travel agency *seyahat acentesi*
    seya-*hat* a-jen-te-*see*
travel sickness *araç tutması*
    a-*rach* toot-ma-*suh*
travellers cheque *seyahat çeki*
    se-ya-*hat* che-*kee*
tree *ağaç* a-*ach*
trip (journey) *gezi* ge-*zee*
trolley *trolli* trol-*lee*
trousers *pantolon* pan-to-*lon*
truck *kamyon* kam-*yon*
trust v *güvenmek* gew-ven-*mek*
try (attempt) v *teşebbüs etmek*
    te-sheb-*bews* et-*mek*
try on v *denemek* de-ne-*mek*
T-shirt *tişört* tee-*shert*
tube (tyre) *iç lastik* eech las-*teek*
Tuesday *Salı* sa-*luh*
tumour *tümör* tew-*mer*
tuna *ton balığı* ton ba-luh-*uh*
tune n *melodi* me-lo-*dee*
turkey *hindi* heen-*dee*
Turkey *Türkiye* tewr-kee-*ye*
Turkish (language) *Türkçe* tewrk-*che*
Turkish bath *hamam* ha-*mam*
Turkish delight *lokum* lo-*koom*
Turkish Republic of
    Northern Cyprus (TRNC)
    Kuzey Kıbrıs Türk Cumhuriyeti (KKTC)
    koo-*zay* kuhb-*ruhs* tewrk
    joom-hoo-ree-ye-*tee* (ka-ka-te-*je*)
turn v *çevirmek* che-veer-*mek*
TV *TV* te-*ve*
tweezers *cımbız* juhm-*buhz*
twice *iki kez* ee-*kee* kez

twin beds *çift yatak* cheeft ya·*tak*
twins *ikiz* ee·*keez*
two *iki* ee·*kee*
type n *çeşit* che·*sheet*
typical *tipik* tee·*peek*
tyre *lastik* las·*teek*

U

ultrasound *ultrason* ool·tra·*son*
umbrella *şemsiye* shem·see·*ye*
uncomfortable *rahatsız* ra·hat·*suhz*
understand *anlamak* an·la·*mak*
underwear *iç çamaşırı*
   eech cha·ma·shuh·*ruh*
unemployed *işsiz* eesh·*seez*
unfair *haksız* hak·*suhz*
uniform n *üniforma* ew·nee·*for*·ma
universe *kainat* ka·ee·*nat*
university *üniversite* ew·nee·ver·see·te
unleaded *kurşunsuz* koor·shoon·*sooz*
unsafe *tehlikeli* teh·lee·ke·*lee*
until (Friday) *(Cuma)ya kadar*
   (joo·ma)·ya ka·*dar*
unusual *alışılmadık* a·luh·shuhl·ma·*duhk*
up *yukarı* yoo·ka·*ruh*
uphill *yokuş yukarı* yo·koosh yoo·ka·*ruh*
urgent *acil* a·*jeel*
urinary infection *idrar yolları enfeksiyonu*
   eed·*rar* yol·la·*ruh* en·fek·see·yo·*noo*
USA *ABD (Amerika Birleşik Devletleri)* a·be·de
   (a·me·ree·ka beer·le·sheek dev·let·le·*ree*)
useful *yararlı* ya·rar·*luh*

V

vacancy *yer* yer
vacant *boş* bosh
vacation *tatil* ta·*teel*
vaccination *aşı* a·*shuh*
vagina *vajina* va·zhee·na
validate *geçerli kılmak* ge·cher·*lee* kuhl·*mak*
valley *vadi* va·dee
valuable *değerli* de·er·*lee*
value n *değer* de·*er*
van *van* van
veal *dana eti* da·na e·tee
vegetable n *sebze* seb·ze
vegetarian n & a *vejeteryan* ve·zhe·ter·*yan*
vein *damar* da·*mar*
venereal disease *zührevi hastalık*
   zewh·re·vee has·ta·*luhk*

venue *toplantı yeri* top·lan·*tuh* ye·*ree*
very *çok* chok
video camera *video kamera*
   vee·de·o ka·me·*ra*
video recorder *video kayıt cihazı*
   vee·de·o ka·*yuht* jee·ha·*zuh*
video tape *video kaset* vee·de·o ka·*set*
view n *manzara* man·za·*ra*
villa *villa* veel·la
village *köy* kay
vine *asma* as·ma
vinegar *sirke* seer·ke
vineyard *bağ* ba
virus *virüs* vee·*rews*
visa *vize* vee·ze
visit v *ziyaret etmek* zee·ya·*ret* et·*mek*
vitamins *vitaminler* vee·ta·meen·*ler*
voice *ses* ses
volleyball (sport) *voleybol* vo·lay·bol
volume *ses* ses
vote v *oy vermek* oy ver·*mek*

W

wage n *maaş* ma·*ash*
wait for *beklemek* bek·le·*mek*
waiter *garson* gar·son
waiting room *bekleme odası*
   bek·le·me o·da·*suh*
wake up v *uyandırmak* oo·yan·duhr·*mak*
Wales *Galler* gal·*ler*
walk v *yürümek* yew·rew·*mek*
wall *duvar* doo·var
want v *istemek* ees·te·*mek*
war n *savaş* sa·*vash*
wardrobe *gardırop* gar·duh·*rop*
warm a *ılık* uh·*luhk*
warn *uyarmak* oo·yar·*mak*
wash (oneself) *yıkanmak* yuh·kan·*mak*
wash (something) *yıkamak* yuh·ka·*mak*
wash cloth (flannel) *sabunluk* sa·boon·*look*
washing machine *çamaşır makinesi*
   cha·ma·*shuhr* ma·kee·ne·*see*
watch n *saat* sa·*at*
watch v *izlemek* eez·le·*mek*
water n *su* soo
water bottle *su şişesi* soo shee·she·*see*
water bottle (hot) *termofor* ter·mo·*for*
waterfall *şelale* she·la·le
watermelon *karpuz* kar·*pooz*
water-pipe (Turkish) *nargile* nar·gee·le
waterproof *su geçirmez* soo ge·cheer·*mez*

water-skiing *su kayağı* soo ka·ya·*uh*
wave (sea) *dalga* dal·*ga*
way *yol* yol
we *biz* beez
weak *zayıf* za·*yuhf*
wealthy *zengin* zen·*geen*
wear v *giymek* geey·*mek*
weather *hava* ha·*va*
wedding *düğün* dew·*ewn*
wedding cake *düğün pastası*
   dew·*ewn* pas·ta·suh
wedding present *düğün hediyesi*
   dew·*ewn* he·dee·ye·*see*
Wednesday *Çarşamba* char·sham·*ba*
(this) week *(bu) hafta* (boo) haf·*ta*
weekend *hafta sonu* haf·ta so·*noo*
weigh *tartmak* tart·*mak*
weight(s) *ağırlık* a·uhr·*luhk*
welcome v *hoş geldiniz* hosh gel·dee·neez
welfare *refah* re·*fah*
well a *iyi* ee·*yee*
west *batı* ba·*tuh*
wet a *ıslak* uhs·*lak*
what *ne* ne
wheel *tekerlek* te·ker·*lek*
wheelchair *tekerlekli sandalye*
   te·ker·lek·*lee* san·dal·ye
when *ne zaman* ne za·*man*
where *nerede* ne·*re*·de
which *hangi* han·ge
white *beyaz* be·*yaz*
who *kim* keem
wholemeal bread *kepekli ekmek*
   ke·pek·*lee* ek·mek
why *neden* ne·*den*
wide *geniş* ge·*neesh*
wife *karı* ka·*ruh*
win v *kazanmak* ka·zan·*mak*
wind n *rüzgar* rewz·*gar*
window *pencere* pen·je·re
windscreen *oto ön camı* o·to ern ja·muh
windsurfing *rüzgar sörfü* rewz·gar ser·*few*
wine *şarap* sha·*rap*
winehall *meyhane* may·ha·ne
wine shop *şarap dükkanı*
   sha·rap dewk·ka·nuh
winner *galip* ga·*leep*
winter *kış* kuhsh
wish v *dilemek* dee·le·*mek*
with *ile* ee·le
within (an hour) *(bir saat) içinde*
   (beer sa·*at*) ee·cheen·de

without *-sız/-siz/-suz/-süz*
   ·suhz/·seez/·sooz/·sewz
wok *çin tavası* cheen ta·va·*suh*
woman *kadın* ka·*duhn*
women's quarters *kadınlar bölümü*
   ka·duhn·*lar* ber·lew·*mew*
wonderful *şahane* sha·ha·ne
wood *odun* o·doon
wool *yün* yewn
word n *kelime* ke·lee·me
work n *iş* eesh
work v *çalışmak* cha·luhsh·*mak*
work experience *deneyim* de·ne·*yeem*
workout n *egzersiz* eg·zer·*seez*
work permit *çalışma izni*
   cha·luhsh·ma eez·nee
workshop *atölye* a·terl·ye
world *dünya* dewn·ya
World Cup *Dünya Kupası*
   dewn·ya koo·pa·*suh*
worms *solucanlar* so·loo·jan·*lar*
worried *endişeli* en·dee·she·*lee*
worship v *ibadet etmek* ee·ba·det et·*mek*
wreck n *batık* ba·*tuhk*
wrist *bilek* bee·*lek*
write *yazı yazmak* ya·zuh yaz·*mak*
writer *yazar* ya·*zar*
wrong *yanlış* yan·*luhsh*

Y

yacht (general) *yat* yat
yacht (traditional Turkish) *gulet* goo·*let*
(this) year *(bu) yıl* (boo) yuhl
yellow *sarı* sa·*ruh*
yes *evet* e·*vet*
yesterday *dün* dewn
yoga *yoga* yo·ga
yogurt *yoğurt* yo·oort
you sg inf *sen* sen
you sg pol & pl inf/pol *siz* seez
young *genç* gench
your *senin* se·*neen*
youth hostel *gençlik hosteli* gench·*leek*
   hos·te·lee

Z

zip(per) *fermuar* fer·moo·*ar*
zodiac *burçlar* boorch·*lar*
zoo *hayvanat bahçesi*
   hai·va·nat bah·che·see
zucchini *kabak* ka·*bak*

You'll find the English words marked as adjective a, noun n, verb v, singular sg, plural pl, informal inf and polite pol where necessary. All verbs are provided in the infinitive, and all nouns are in the nominative case. For any food items, refer to the **culinary reader**.

A

ABD (Amerika Birleşik Devletleri) a·be·*de* (a·me·ree·ka beer·le·*sheek* dev·let·le·*ree*) USA

acayip a·ja·*yeep* strange

acele ile a·je·*le* ee·*le* in a hurry

acı a·*juh* bitter

acil a·*jeel* urgent
— **durum** doo·*room* emergency

aç ach hungry

açık a·*chuhk* light (colour) a • open a
— **bilet** bee·*let* stand-by ticket

açılış saatleri a·chuh·*luhsh* sa·at·le·*ree* opening hours

açmak ach·*mak* open v

ad ad name n

ada a·*da* island

adam a·*dam* man

adaptör a·dap·*ter* adaptor

adet a·*det* menstruation
— **ağrısı** a·ruh·*suh* period pain
— **öncesi gerginlik** ern·je·*see* ger·geen·*leek* premenstrual tension

adım a·*duhm* step n

adres ad·*res* address n

affetmek af·fet·*mek* forgive

ağ a net n

ağaç a·*ach* tree

ağır a·*uhr* heavy

ağırlık a·uhr·*luhk* weight(s)

ağız a·*uhz* mouth

ağrı a·*ruh* pain n
— **kesici** ke·see·*jee* painkiller

ağrılı a·ruh·*luh* painful • sore a

aile a·ee·*le* family
— **bölümü** ber·lew·*mew* family room (restaurant)
— **için kalacak yer** ee·*cheen* ka·la·*jak* yer family quarters

akciğer ak·jee·*er* lung

Akdeniz ak·de·*neez* Mediterranean Sea

akım a·*kuhm* current (electricity)

akıntı a·kuhn·*tuh* stream

akrabalık a·kra·ba·*luhk* relationship (family)

akşam ak·*sham* evening
— **gezmesi** gez·me·*see* night out
— **yemeği** ye·me·*ee* dinner

aktar ak·*tar* herbalist

aktarma ak·tar·*ma* connection (trip)

akupresyon a·koo·pres·*yon* shiatsu

akü a·*kew* battery (car)
— **takviye kablosu** tak·vee·*ye* kab·lo·*soo* jumper leads

alçak al·*chak* low

aldatma al·dat·*ma* cheat n

alışılmadık a·luh·*shuhl*·ma·duhk unusual

alış-veriş a·luhsh·ve·*reesh* shopping
— **merkezi** mer·ke·*zee* shopping centre

alış-verişe gitmek a·luhsh·ve·ree·*she* geet·*mek* go shopping

almak al·*mak* get • take

Almanca al·man·*ja* German (language)

Almanya al·man·*ya* Germany

alt geçit alt ge·*cheet* subway

altın al·*tuhn* gold n

altyazı alt·ya·*zuh* subtitles

ama a·*ma* but

ambalaj am·ba·*lazh* package

amele a·me·*le* manual worker

ameliyat a·me·lee·*yat* operation (medical)

ampül am·*pewl* light bulb

ana baba a·*na* ba·*ba* parents

ana cadde a·*na* jad·*de* main road

anahtar a·nah·*tar* key n

anayol a·*na*·yol main road

anıt a·*nuht* monument

anlamak an·la·*mak* understand

anlatmak an·lat·*mak* tell

anne an·*ne* mother

anneciğim an·ne·jee·*eem* mum

apandis a·pan·*dees* appendix (body)

apartman dairesi a·part·man da·ee·re·*see apartment* • *flat* n
aptal ap·*tal idiot*
ara a·*ra intermission*
araba a·ra·ba *car*
— **kiralama** kee·ra·la·*ma car hire*
— **tamircisi** ta·meer·jee·*see mechanic*
— **yarışında birincilik** ya·ruh·shuhn·*da* bee·reen·jee·*leek car owner's title*
araç tutması a·*rach* toot·ma·*suh travel sickness*
Aralık a·ra·*luhk December*
aramak a·ra·*mak call (telephone)* v • *look for*
Arapça a·*rap·cha Arabic (language)*
arasında a·ra·suhn·*da between*
arı a·*ruh bee*
arka ar·ka *back (position)*
arkadaş ar·ka·*dash companion* • *friend*
arkasında ar·ka·suhn·*da behind*
asansör a·san·*ser elevator* • *lift*
asker as·ker *soldier* n
askeriye as·ke·ree·ye *military* n
askerlik hizmeti as·ker·*leek* heez·me·te·*tee military service*
asla as·la *never*
asma as·ma *vine*
asma kilit as·ma kee·*leet padlock*
astım as·*tuhm asthma*
aşağı a·sha·*uh down*
aşağısında a·sha·uh·suhn·*da below*
aşçı ash·*chuh cook* n
aşçıbaşı ash·chuh·ba·shuh *chef*
aşı a·*shuh vaccination*
aşık olmak a·*shuhk* ol·*mak fall in love* v
aşırı doz a·shuh·ruh *doz overdose* n
aşk ashk *love* n
at at *horse*
ata binmek a·*ta* been·*mek ride a horse* v
ateş a·*tesh fever* • *small fire under control*
— **etmek** et·*mek shoot* v
atkı at·*kuh scarf*
atlamak at·la·*mak jump* v
atlet at·*let singlet*
atölye a·terl·ye *workshop*
avlanma av·lan·ma *hunting*
Avrupa av·roo·pa *Europe*
avukat a·voo·*kat lawyer*
ay ai *month* • *moon*
ayak a·*yak foot*
— **bileği** bee·le·ee *ankle*
— **parmağı** par·ma·uh *toe*
ayakkabıcı a·yak·ka·buh·*juh shoe shop*
ayakkabılar a·yak·ka·buh·*lar shoes*

ayna ai·na *mirror*
aynı ai·nuh *same*
— **fikirde olmak** fee·keer·de ol·mak *agree*
ayrı ai·ruh *separate* a
ayrılmak ai·ruhl·*mak depart*
ayrım ai·ruhm *discrimination*
ayrıntı ai·ruhn·*tuh details*
ayrıntılı yazılmış ay·ruhn·tuh·*luh* ya·zuhl·*muhsh itemised*
az az *little* n • *least* a
— **bulunur** boo·loo·*noor rare*
aziz a·*zeez saint*

B

baba ba·ba *father*
babacığım ba·ba·juh·*uhm dad*
bacak ba·*jak leg (body)*
bağ ba *vineyard*
bagaj ba·*gazh baggage* • *luggage*
— **etiketi** e·tee·ke·*tee luggage tag*
— **hakkı** hak·*kuh baggage allowance*
— **konveyörü** kon·ve·yer·*rew baggage claim*
bağımlılık ba·uhm·luh·*luhk addiction*
bağırmak ba·uhr·*mak shout* v
bağlantı ba·lan·*tuh connection (link)*
bahçe bah·*che garden* n
— **işleri** eesh·le·*ree gardening*
bahçıvan bah·chuh·*van gardener*
bahis ba·*hees bet* n
bakıcı ba·kuh·*juh caretaker*
bakımını yapmak ba·kuh·muh·*nuh* yap·*mak look after*
bakkal bak·*kal convenience store* • *grocery*
bakliyat bak·lee·*yat legume*
bakmak bak·*mak care (for someone)* v • *look* v
balayı ba·la·*yuh honeymoon*
bale ba·le *ballet*
balık ba·*luhk fish* n
— **avlama** av·la·*ma fishing*
balıkçı ba·luhk·*chuh fishmonger* • *fish shop*
balsam bal·*sam hair conditioner*
bana ba·na *me*
bandaj ban·*dazh bandage*
banka hesabı ban·ka he·sa·*buh bank account*
bankamatik ban·ka·ma·*teek ATM*
banyo ban·yo *bath* • *bathroom*
bardak bar·*dak drinking glass*
bar işi bar ee·*shee bar work*

barış ba-*ruhsh peace*
basın ba-*suhn media*
basınç ba-*suhnch pressure* n
basit ba-*seet simple*
baş bash *head* n
— **ağrısı** a-ruh-*suh headache*
başbakan bash-ba-kan *prime minister*
başı dönen ba-*shuh* der-nen *dizzy*
(gün) başına (gewn) ba-shuh-*na per (day)*
başkan bash-*kan president*
başlamak bash-la-*mak start* v
başlangıç bash-lan-*guhch start* n
batı ba-*tuh west*
batıl inanç ba-*tuhl* ee-*nanch superstition*
battaniye bat-ta-nee-ye *blanket*
bavul ba-*vool suitcase*
Bay bai *Mr/Sir*
Bayan ba-yan *Mrs/Ms/Miss/Madam*
bayan ba-yan *female (human)* a
bayrak bai-*rak flag*
bazen ba-zen *sometimes*
bebek be-*bek baby* n
— **bezi** be-zee *diaper • nappy*
— **maması** ma-ma-*suh baby food*
— **pudrası** pood-ra-*suh baby powder*
beden be-*den size* n
bekar be-*kar single (not married)*
bekleme odası bek-le-me o-da-*suh*
waiting room
beklemek bek-le-*mek wait for*
bel çantası bel chan-ta-*suh*
bumbag • fanny sack
belediye başkanı be-le-dee-ye
bash-ka-*nuh mayor*
belgesel bel-ge-*sel documentary*
belki bel-*kee maybe*
ben ben *I*
bencil ben-*jeel selfish*
beni be-*nee me*
benim be-*neem my*
benzer ben-*zer similar*
benzin ben-zeen *gas • oil • petrol*
— **istasyonu** ees-tas-yo-*noo*
petrol station • service station
beri be-*ree since*
beslemek bes-le-*mek feed* v
beyaz be-*yaz white*
beyin sarsıntısı be-yeen sar-suhn-tuh-*suh*
concussion
bıçak buh-*chak knife* n
bırakmak buh-rak-*mak quit*
biçim bee-*cheem shape* n
bilardo bee-*lar-*do *pool (game)*

bilet bee-*let ticket*
— **gişesi** gee-she-*see*
ticket booth • ticket office
biletçi bee-let-*chee ticket collector*
bilgi beel-*gee information*
bilgisayar beel-gee-sa-yar *computer*
bilgisayar oyunu beel-gee-sa-yar
o-yoo-noo *computer game*
bilim bee-*leem science*
— **adamı** a-da-*muh scientist*
bilmek beel-*mek know*
bina bee-*na building*
binicilik bee-nee-jee-*leek horse riding*
biniş kartı bee-neesh kar-*tuh boarding pass*
binmek been-*mek board* v • *ride* n
bir beer *one*
— **de** de *also*
— **gecelik** ge-je-*leek overnight*
bira bee-*ra beer*
birahane bee-ra-ha-*ne beerhall*
biraz bee-*raz some*
birinci sınıf bee-reen-jee suh-*nuhf first class*
birisi bee-ree-*see someone*
birkaç beer-*kach few • several*
bir kez beer kez *once*
birlikte beer-leek-*te together*
birşey beer-*shay something*
bisiklet bee-seek-*let bicycle*
— **kilidi** kee-lee-*dee bike lock*
— **sporu** spo-*roo cycling*
— **yolu** yo-*loo bike path*
— **zinciri** zeen-jee-*ree bike chain*
bisikletçi bee-seek-let-*chee*
bike shop • cyclist
bisiklete binmek bee-seek-le-*te*
been-*mek cycle* v
bit beet *lice*
— **pazarı** pa-za-*ruh fleamarket*
bitirmek bee-teer-*mek finish* v
bitiş bee-*teesh finish* n
bitki beet-*kee herb • plant*
biz beez *we*
bizim bee-*zeem our*
board kayağı bord ka-ya-*uh snowboarding*
boğaz bo-*az throat*
borcu olmak bor-*joo* ol-*mak owe*
boş bosh *available • empty • vacant*
boşanmış bo-shan-*muhsh divorced*
botlar bot-*lar boots*
boyacı bo-ya-*juh painter (occupation)*
boyun bo-*yoon neck (body)*

bozuk bo-*zook* broken down • corrupt • faulty • off (spoiled) • out of order
— **para** pa-*ra* change (coins) • loose change
bozulmak bo-zool-*mak* break down v
böbrek berb-*rek* kidney
böcek ber-*jek* bug n
— **ısırması** uh-suhr-ma-*suh* bite (insect) n
bölge berl-*ge* suburb
bölgesel berl-ge-*sel* regional
börekçi ber-rek-*chee* pastry shop
bronşit bron-*sheet* bronchitis
bu boo this
— **gece** ge-*je* tonight
bugün boo-*gewn* today
bulantı boo-lan-*tuh* nausea
Bulgaristan bool-ga-rees-*tan* Bulgaria
bulmak bool-*mak* find v
buluşmak boo-loosh-*mak* meet (get together) v
bulut boo-*loot* cloud n
bulutlu boo-loot-*loo* cloudy
bunu boo-*noo* this one
burada boo-ra-*da* here
burçlar boorch-*lar* zodiac
burkulma boor-kool-*ma* sprain n
burun boo-*roon* nose
— **akıntısı** a-kuhn-tuh-*suh* runny nose
buz booz ice
— **kıracağı** kuh-ra-ja-*uh* ice axe
buzdolabı booz-do-la-*buh* refrigerator
bütçe bewt-*che* budget n
büyük bew-*yewk* big
— **çadır** cha-*duhr* pavillion
— **kilise** kee-lee-*se* basilica
— **mağaza** ma-a-*za* department store
— **meydan** may-*dan* agora (open ground, town square)
büyükanne bew-*yewk*-an-ne grandmother
büyükbaba bew-*yewk*-ba-ba grandfather
büyükelçi bew-*yewk*-el-chee ambassador
büyümek bew-yew-*mek* grow

C

cadde jad-*de* avenue
cam jam glass (window)
cami ja-*mee* mosque
canı acımak ja-*nuh* a-juh-*mak* hurt v
canı sıkkın ja-*nuh* suhk-*kuhn* bored
can yeleği jan ye-le-*ee* life jacket
ceket je-*ket* jacket

cenaze töreni je-na-*ze* ter-re-*nee* funeral
cep jep pocket
— **feneri** fe-ne-*ree* flashlight • torch
— **telefonu** te-le-fo-*noo* cell phone • mobile phone
cesur je-*soor* brave
cevap je-*vap* answer n
cezaevi je-za-e-*vee* prison
cımbız juhm-*buhz* tweezers
cibinlik jee-been-*leek* mosquito net
ciddi jeed-*dee* serious
cilt jeelt skin n
cin jeen gin
cinayet jee-na-*yet* murder n
— **işlemek** eesh-le-*mek* murder v
cinsiyet jeen-see-*yet* sex (gender)
— **ayrımı** ai-ruh-*muh* sexism
cip jeep jeep
Cuma joo-*ma* Friday
Cumartesi joo-mar-te-*see* Saturday
cumhuriyet joom-hoo-ree-*yet* republic
cüzdan jewz-*dan* purse

Ç

çabuk cha-*book* quick a
çadır cha-*duhr* tent
— **kazığı** ka-zuh-*uh* tent peg
çağırmak cha-uhr-*mak* call (shout) v
çakı cha-*kuh* pocketknife
çakmak chak-*mak* cigarette lighter
çalar saat cha-*lar* sa-*at* alarm clock
çalıntı cha-luhn-*tuh* stolen
çalışan cha-luh-*shan* employee
çalışma izni cha-luhsh-*ma* eez-*nee* work permit
çalışmak cha-luhsh-*mak* work v
çalmak chal-*mak* play (an instrument) v • ring (phone) v • steal v
çamaşır cha-ma-*shuhr* laundry (clothes)
— **ipi** ee-*pee* clothesline
— **makinesi** ma-kee-ne-*see* washing machine
çamaşırhane cha-ma-shuhr-*ha*-ne launderette
çamaşırlık cha-ma-shuhr-*luhk* laundry (room)
çamur cha-*moor* mud
çanta chan-*ta* bag
çarpışma char-puhsh-*ma* crash n
çarşaf char-*shaf* sheet (bed)
Çarşamba char-sham-*ba* Wednesday

çatal cha·*tal* fork n
— **bıçak takımı** buh·*chak* ta·kuh·*muh* cutlery
çay chai tea n
— **bahçesi** bah·che·*see* tea garden
— **bardağı** chai bar·*da·uh* tea glass
— **kaşığı** ka·shuh·*uh* teaspoon
çaydanlık chai·dan·*luhk* teapot
çek bozdurmak chek boz·*door·mak* cash a cheque
çekici che·kee·*jee* charming
çekiç che·*keech* hammer n
çekmek chek·*mek* pull v
çene che·*ne* jaw
çerez che·*rez* nut
çeşit che·*sheet* type n
çeşme suyu chesh·me soo·*yoo* tap water
çevirmek che·veer·*mek* translate • turn v
çevir sesi che·veer se·*see* dial tone
çevre chev·*re* environment
çeyrek chay·*rek* quarter n
çıkıkçı chuh·kuhk·*chuh* chiropractor
çıkıntı chuh·kuhn·*tuh* ledge
çıkış chuh·*kuhsh* exit n
çıkmak chuhk·*mak* date (a person) v
çiçek chee·*chek* flower n
çiçekçi chee·chek·*chee* florist
çift cheeft double a • pair a
— **yatak** ya·*tak* twin beds
çiftçi cheeft·*chee* farmer
çiftlik cheeft·*leek* farm n
çiğ chee raw
çim cheem grass (lawn) n
Çin cheen China
Çince cheen·*jee* Mandarin (language) n
çit cheet fence n
çizim chee·*zeem* drawing
çocuk cho·*jook* child
— **aldırma** al·duhr·*ma* abortion
— **bakımı** ba·kuh·*muh* childminding
— **koltuğu** kol·too·oo child seat
çocuklar cho·jook·*lar* children
çok chok a lot • many • too • very
çorap cho·*rap* stockings
çoraplar cho·rap·*lar* socks
çöl cherl desert n
çömlekçilik cherm·lek·chee·*leek* pottery
çöp cherp garbage • rubbish n
— **tenekesi** te·ne·ke·*see* garbage can
çünkü chewn·*kew* because
çürük chew·*rewk* bruise n

D

dadı da·*duh* babysitter
dağ da mountain
— **bisikleti** bee·seek·le·*tee* mountain bike
— **yolu** yo·*loo* mountain path
dağcılık da·juh·*luhk* mountaineering
daha az da·ha az less
daha büyük da·ha bew·*yewk* bigger
daha fazla da·ha faz·*la* more
daha iyi da·ha ee·*yee* better
daha küçük da·ha kew·*chewk* smaller
dahil da·*heel* included
dakika da·kee·*ka* minute
dalga dal·*ga* tide • wave (sea)
dalış da·*luhsh* dive n • diving
— **kursu** koor·*soo* diving course
— **malzemeleri** mal·ze·me·le·*ree* diving equipment
— **ortağı** or·ta·*uh* dive buddy
— **teknesi** tek·ne·*see* diving boat
dalmak dal·*mak* dive v
damar da·*mar* vein
dantel dan·*tel* lace
davet etmek da·vet et·*mek* invite v
davul da·*vool* drum (music) n
debriyaj deb·ree·*yazh* clutch (car)
değer de·*er* value n
değerli de·er·*lee* valuable a
değil de·*eel* not
değişiklik de·ee·sheek·*leek* change n
değiştirmek de·eesh·teer·*mek* exchange v
değiş-tokuş de·eesh·to·*koosh* exchange n
deli de·*lee* crazy
denemek de·ne·*mek* try on v
deneyim de·ne·*yeem* experience • work experience
deniz de·*neez* sea
— **gözlüğü** gerz·lew·*ew* swimming goggles
— **kenarı** ke·na·*ruh* seaside n
— **otobüsü** o·to·bew·*sew* hydrofoil
— **tutmuş** toot·*moosh* seasick
— **yoluyla gönderi** yo·*luh*·la gern·de·*ree* surface mail (sea)
deprem dep·*rem* earthquake
derece de·re·*je* degrees • temperature (weather)
dergi der·*gee* magazine
deri de·*ree* leather
derin de·*reen* deep
devlet dev·*let* government
dışarıda duh·sha·ruh·*da* outside

dışarıya çıkmak duh·sha·ruh·*ya* chuhk·*mak* go out
diğer dee·*er* another • other
dikiş dikmek dee·*keesh* deek·*mek* sew
dikiş iğnesi dee·*keesh* ee·ne·*see* needle (sewing)
dilekçe dee·lek·*che* petition n
dilemek dee·le·*mek* wish v
dilenci dee·len·*jee* beggar
dilim dee·*leem* slice n
dilsiz deel·*seez* mute (person)
din deen religion
dini dee·*nee* religious
dinlemek deen·le·*mek* listen to
dinlenmek deen·len·*mek* relax v • rest v
dipte deep·*te* bottom (position)
direk dee·*rek* direct a
diş deesh tooth
— ağrısı a·ruh·*suh* toothache
— fırçası fuhr·cha·*suh* toothbrush
— ipi ee·*pee* dental floss
— macunu ma·joo·*noo* toothpaste
dişçi deesh·*chee* dentist
dişi dee·*shee* female (animal) a
diz deez knee
— üstü bilgisayar ews·*tew* beel·gee·sa·*yar* laptop
doğa do·*a* nature
doğal gaz do·*al* gaz gas (for cooking)
doğru do·*roo* right (correct) a
— yön yern right (direction) a
doğu do·*oo* east
doğum belgesi do·*oom* bel·ge·*see* birth certificate
doğum günü do·*oom* gew·*new* birthday
doğum kontrol hapı do·*oom* kon·*trol* ha·*puh* contraceptives • the pill
doğum tarihi do·*oom* ta·ree·*hee* date of birth
doğum yeri do·*oom* ye·*ree* place of birth
dokunma do·koon·*ma* feeling (physical)
dokunmak do·koon·*mak* touch v
dolap do·*lap* cupboard
doldurmak dol·door·*mak* fill v
dolu do·*loo* full • booked out
domuz do·*mooz* pig
don don frost n
dondurmacı don·door·ma·*juh* ice-cream parlour
donmuş don·*moosh* frozen
doymuş doy·*moosh* full (not hungry)
döviz kuru der·*veez* koo·*roo* currency exchange • exchange rate

dua doo·*a* prayer
— kitabı kee·ta·*buh* prayer book
dudaklar doo·dak·*lar* lips
durak doo·*rak* stop (bus etc) n
durdurmak door·door·*mak* stop (prevent) v
durgun su door·*goon* soo still water
durmak door·*mak* stay (in one place) v • stop (cease) v
duş doosh shower n
duvar doo·*var* wall
duygular dooy·goo·*lar* feelings
duygusal dooy·goo·*sal* emotional
duymak dooy·*mak* hear
düğme dew·*me* button
düğün dew·*ewn* wedding
— hediyesi he·dee·ye·*see* wedding present
— pastası pas·ta·*suh* wedding cake
dükkan dewk·*kan* shop n
dün dewn yesterday
dünya dewn·*ya* world
dürbün dewr·*bewn* binoculars
düşmek dewsh·*mek* fall v
düşük dew·*shewk* miscarriage
düşünmek dew·shewn·*mek* think v
düz dewz flat a • straight
düzine dew·zee·*ne* dozen

E

eczacı ej·za·*juh* pharmacist
eczane ej·za·*ne* pharmacy
Ege Denizi e·ge de·nee·*zee* Aegean Sea
egzoz eg·*zoz* exhaust (car)
eğer e·*er* if
eğitim e·ee·*teem* education
eğlence e·len·*je* fun a • gig n
— rehberi reh·be·*ree* entertainment guide
eğlenmek e·len·*mek* enjoy (oneself) • have fun
ehliyet eh·lee·*yet* drivers licence • licence
Ekim e·*keem* October
ekmek ek·*mek* bread
— ve şarap ayini ve sha·*rap* a·yee·*nee* mass (Catholic)
eksiklik ek·seek·*leek* shortage
el el hand (body)
— bileği bee·le·*ee* wrist
— çantası chan·ta·*suh* handbag
— feneri fe·ne·*ree* torch n
— işi ee·*shee* handmade
— sanatları sa·nat·la·*ruh* handicrafts

elbise el-bee-se *dress* n
elçilik el-chee-leek *embassy*
eldivenler el-dee-ven-ler *gloves (warm)*
emanet e-ma-net *left luggage*
— bürosu bew-ro-soo *left-luggage office*
emekli e-mek-lee *pensioner* n • *retired* a
emlakçı em-lak-chuh
estate agency • *real estate agent*
emniyet kemeri em-nee-yet ke-me-ree
seatbelt
emniyetli em-nee-yet-lee *safe* a
emzik em-zeek *dummy* • *pacifier*
en en *most*
— büyük bew-yewk *biggest*
— iyi ee-yee *best*
— küçük kew-chewk *smallest*
— yakın ya-kuhn *nearest*
endişeli en-dee-she-lee *worried*
erkek er-kek *male* a
— arkadaş er-ka-dash *boyfriend*
erkekler bölümü er-kek-ler ber-lew-mew
men's quarters
erken er-ken *early*
erzak er-zak *food supplies* • *provisions*
esas e-sas *main* a
eski es-kee *old (object)*
— eser e-ser *relic*
eskici es-kee-jee *second-hand shop*
eskrim es-kreem *fencing (sport)*
esrar es-rar *hash (drug)*
eşcinsel esh-jeen-sel *gay (homosexual)*
eşitlik e-sheet-leek *equality*
et et *meat*
ET (enformasyon teknolojisi)
e-te (en-for-mas-yon tek-no-lo-jee-see) *IT*
etek e-tek *skirt*
etrafında et-ra-fuhn-da *about*
ev ev *home* • *house*
— işi ee-shee *housework*
— hanımı ha-nuh-muh *homemaker*
evlenmek ev-len-mek *marry* v
evli ev-lee *married*
evlilik ev-lee-leek *marriage*
evrak çantası ev-rak chan-ta-suh *briefcase*
evsiz ev-seez *homeless*
eyer e-yer *saddle* n
Eylül ay-lewl *September*

F

fabrika fab-ree-ka *factory*
— işçisi eesh-chee-see *factory worker*
fahişe fa-hee-she *prostitute* n

fakir fa-keer *poor*
falcı fal-juh *fortune teller*
fare fa-re *mouse (animal)*
farklı fark-luh *different*
farlar far-lar *headlights*
fatura fa-too-ra *bill* n • *check* n *(restaurant)*
faul fa-ool *foul (football)* n
fazla yük faz-la yewk *excess baggage*
felçli felch-lee
paraplegic n • *stroke (health)* n
fermuar fer-moo-ar *zip* • *zipper*
fikir fee-keer *opinion*
fiks ücret feeks ewj-ret *cover charge*
film hızı feelm huh-zuh *film speed*
filtre edilmiş feelt-re e-deel-meesh *filtered*
fincan feen-jan *cup (drinking)*
fırça fuhr-cha *brush* n
fırın fuh-ruhn *bakery* • *oven*
fırsat eşitliği fuhr-sat e-sheet-lee-ee
equal opportunity
fırtına fuhr-tuh-na *storm* • *thunderstorm*
fıskiye fuhs-kee-ye *fountain (decorative)*
fiş feesh *plug (electricity)* n
fiyat fee-yat *price* n
fotoğraf fo-to-raf *photo*
— çekmek chek-mek *take a photo*
fotoğrafçı fo-to-raf-chuh
camera shop • *photographer*
fotoğrafçılık fo-to-raf-chuh-luhk
photography
fren fren *brakes*

G

galip ga-leep *winner*
Galler gal-ler *Wales*
garantili ga-ran-tee-lee *guaranteed*
gardırop gar-duh-rop *wardrobe*
gazete ga-ze-te *newspaper*
— bayii ba-yee-ee *newsagency*
gazeteci ga-ze-te-jee *journalist*
gazlı bez gaz-luh bez *gauze*
gaz tüpü gaz tew-pew *gas cartridge*
gebelik test çubuğu ge-be-leek test
choo-boo-oo *pregnancy test kit*
gece ge-je *night*
— kulübü koo-lew-bew *nightclub*
— yarısı ya-ruh-suh *midnight*
gecikme ge-jeek-me *delay* n
geç gech *late*
geçen a ge-chen *last*
geçici iş ge-chee-jee eesh *casual work*
geçmek gech-mek *pass* v

geçmiş gech·*meesh* past n
gelecek ge·le·*jek* future n • *next*
gelenek ge·le·*nek* custom
gelen yolcu ge·*len* yol·*joo* arrivals
gelir vergisi ge·*leer* ver·gee·*see* income tax
gelmek gel·*mek* come
gemi ge·*mee* ship n
genç gench young
gençlik hosteli gench·*leek* hos·te·*lee* youth hostel
geniş ge·*neesh* wide
gerçekçi ger·chek·*chee* realistic
gerekli ge·rek·*lee* necessary
geri ge·*ree* rear (location)
— **dönmek** dern·*mek* return v
getirmek ge·teer·*mek* bring
gezegen ge·ze·*gen* planet
gezi ge·*zee* trip (journey)
gidilecek yer gee·dee·le·*jek* yer destination
gidiş gee·*deesh* departure
— **bileti** bee·le·*tee* one-way a
— **kapısı** ka·puh·*suh* departure gate
gidiş-dönüş ge·deesh·der·*newsh* return a
giriş gee·*reesh* admission price • check-in desk • entry
girmek geer·*mek* enter
gitmek geet·*mek* go
giyim gee·*yeem* clothing
— **mağazası** ma·a·za·suh clothing store
giymek geey·*mek* wear v
glandüler ateş glan·dew·ler a·*tesh* glandular fever
golf sahası golf sa·ha·*suh* golf course
golf topu golf to·*poo* golf ball
göç gerch immigration
göğüs ger·*ews* breast • chest
gökyüzü gerk·yew·*zew* sky
göl gerl lake
gölge gerl·*ge* shade • shadow
— **oyunu** o·yoo·*noo* shadow-puppet theatre
gömlek germ·*lek* shirt
göndermek gern·der·*mek* send
görmek ger·*mek* see
görüşme ger·rewsh·*me* small conference
gösterge gers·ter·*ge* indicator
gösteri gers·te·*ree* demonstration (protest) • performance • show n
göstermek gers·ter·*mek* point v • show v
göz damlası gerz dam·la·*suh* eye drops
gözlem yeri gerz·*lem* ye·*ree* lookout

gözler gerz·*ler* eyes
gözlük gerz·*lewk* glasses (spectacles)
gözlükçü gerz·lewk·*chew* optometrist
grev grev strike (stop work) n
gri gree grey
grip greep influenza
gulet goo·*let* traditional Turkish yacht
güçlü gewch·*lew* strong
gülmek gewl·*mek* laugh v
gülümsemek gew·lewm·se·*mek* smile v
gümrük gewm·*rewk* customs
gümüş gew·*mewsh* silver n
gün gewn day
— **batımı** ba·tuh·*muh* sunset
— **doğumu** do·oo·*moo* sunrise
— **ortası** or·ta·*suh* midday
günah çıkarma gew·*nah* chuh·kar·*ma* confession (religious)
gündem gewn·*dem* current affairs
güneş gew·*nesh* sun
— **çarpması** charp·ma·*suh* sunstroke
— **gözlüğü** gerz·lew·*ew* sunglasses
— **yağı** ya·*uh* tanning lotion
— **yanığı** ya·nuh·*uh* sunburn
güneşli gew·nesh·*lee* sunny
güneşten koruma kremi gew·nesh·*ten* ko·roo·ma kre·mee sunblock
güney gew·*nay* south
günlük gewn·*lewk* daily • diary n
Gürcistan gewr·jees·*tan* Georgia
gürültülü gew·rewl·tew·*lew* noisy
güvenli seks gew·ven·*lee* seks safe sex
güvenmek gew·ven·*mek* trust v
güzel gew·*zel* beautiful
güzellik salonu gew·zel·*leek* sa·lo·*noo* beauty salon

H

haberler ha·ber·*ler* news
haç hach cross (religious) n
hafif ha·*feef* light (weight) a
— **yemek** ye·*mek* snack n
hafta haf·*ta* week
— **sonu** so·*noo* weekend
hakem ha·*kem* referee
haksız hak·*suhz* unfair
hala ha·*la* aunt (paternal)
halkla ilişkiler *halk·la* ee·leesh·kee·*ler* communications (job) • public relations
halüsinasyon ha·lew·see·nas·*yon* hallucination

hamak ha-*mak* hammock
hamam ha-*mam* Turkish bath
hamile ha-mee-*le* pregnant
hangi han-gee which
hap hap pill
hapishane ha-pees-*ha*-ne jail n
harabeler ha-ra-be-*ler* ruins
hariç ha-*reech* excluded
harika ha-ree-*ka* great (fantastic)
hasta has-*ta* ill • sick
hastalık has-ta-*luhk* disease
hastane has-*ta*-ne hospital
haşhaş hash-hash opium (drugs)
hata ha-*ta* someone's fault • mistake
hava ha-*va* air • weather
   — yolları yol-la-*ruh* airline
   — yoluyla yo-*looy*-la airmail
havaalanı ha-*va*-a-la-nuh airport
havlu hav-*loo* towel
havra hav-*ra* synagogue
hayat ha-*yat* life n
hayvan hai-*van* animal
hayvanat bahçesi
  hai-va-*nat* bah-che-*se* zoo
hazımsızlık ha-zuhm-suhz-*luhk* indigestion
hazır ha-*zuhr* ready
hazırlamak ha-zuhr-la-*mak* prepare
Haziran ha-zee-*ran* June
hediye he-dee-*ye* gift • present
hediyelik eşya he-dee-ye-*leek* esh-ya
  souvenir
   — dükkanı dewk-ka-*nuh* souvenir shop
hemen hemen he-*men* he-*men* almost
hemşire hem-shee-*re* nurse
hentbol hent-bol handball
henüz (değil) he-*newz* (de-*eel*) (not) yet
hepsi hep-see all
her her every
   — bir beer each
   — iki kolu ve bacağı felçli ee-*kee* ko-*loo*
   ve ba-ja-*uh* felch-*lee* quadriplegic a
   — ikisi ee-*kee*-see both
   — zaman za-*man* always
herhangi bir her-han-gee beer any
herkes her-kes everyone
herşey her-shay everything
hesap he-*sap* account (bank) • bill
   — bakiyesi ba-kee-ye-*see* balance (bank)
   — makinesi ma-kee-ne-*se* calculator
heykel hay-*kel* sculpture • statue
hırdavatçı dükkanı huhr-da-vat-*chuh*
  dewk-ka-*nuh* hardware store
Hıristiyan huh-rees-tee-*yan* Christian n

hırsız huhr-*suhz* thief
hız huhz speed n
   — göstergesi gers-ter-ge-*see*
  speedometer
   — sınırı suh-nuh-*ruh* speed limit
hızlı huhz-*luh* fast a
hiç birşey heech beer-*shay* nothing
hiçbiri heech-bee-ree neither • none
hijyenik kadın bağı heezh-ye-*neek*
  ka-*duhn* ba-uh sanitary napkin
hikaye hee-ka-*ye* story
Hindistan heen-dees-*tan* India
hissetmek hees-set-*mek* feel (touch) v
hizmet ücreti heez-*met* ewj-re-tee
  service charge
hoş hosh cool (exciting) • nice • pretty
   — geldiniz gel-*dee*-neez welcome v
hukuk hoo-*kook* law (study, profession)

ılık uh-*luhk* warm a
ırkçılık uhrk-chuh-*luhk* racism
ısı uh-*suh* heat n
ısıtıcı uh-suh-tuh-*juh* heater
ısıtılmış uh-suh-tuhl-*muhsh* heated
ısıtma uh-suht-*ma* heating
ıslak uhs-*lak* wet a
ışık uh-*shuhk* light n
   — ölçer erl-*cher* light meter

ibadet etmek ee-*ba*-det et-*mek* worship v
iç çamaşırı eech cha-ma-shuh-*ruh*
  underwear
içecek ee-che-*jek* drink n
içeride ee-che-ree-*de* inside
   — yapılan ya-puh-*lan* indoor
içinde ee-cheen-*de* in • within
iç lastik eech las-*teek* inner tube
içmek eech-*mek* drink v
idrar yolları enfeksiyonu eed-*rar* yol-la-*ruh*
  en-fek-see-yo-*noo* urinary infection
iğne ee-*ne* injection
   — yapmak yap-*mak* inject
ihtiyacı olmak eeh-tee-ya-*juh* ol-*mak* need v
iki ee-*kee* two
   — hafta haf-*ta* fortnight
   — kez kez twice
   — kişilik oda kee-shee-*leek* o-da
  double room
   — kişilik yatak kee-shee-*leek* ya-*tak*
  double bed

ikinci ee·keen·*jee* second a
— **el** el *second-hand* a
— **sınıf** suh·*nuhf* second class n
ikiz ee·*keez* twins
ikram eek·*ram* complimentary (free)
ilaç ee·*lach* medication
ilan ee·*lan* advertisement
ile ee·*le* with
— **çıkmak** chuhk·*mak* go out with
— **paylaşmak** pai·lash·*mak* share with v
ileride ee·lee·ree·*de* ahead
ilginç eel·*geench* interesting
ilişki ee·leesh·*kee* relationship (general)
ilk eelk *first* a
— **yardım çantası** yar·*duhm* chan·ta·*suh*
first-aid kit
ilkbahar eelk·ba·*har* spring (season)
iltihap eel·tee·*hap* inflammation
imkansız eem·kan·*suhz* impossible
imza eem·*za* signature
imzalamak eem·za·la·*mak* sign v
inatçı ee·nat·*chuh* stubborn
ince een·*je* thin a
incil een·*jeel* bible
indirim een·dee·*reem* discount n
indirimli satış een·dee·reem·*lee* sa·*tuhsh*
sale n
inek ee·*nek* cow
inmek een·*mek* get off
insan hakları een·*san* hak·la·*ruh*
human rights
inşa etmek een·*sha* et·*mek* build v
inşaatçı een·sha·at·*chuh* builder
ip eep rope • string
ipek ee·*pek* silk
iplik eep·*leek* thread
iptal etmek eep·*tal* et·*mek* cancel
İranlı ee·ran·*luh* Farsi (language)
iri ee·*ree* large
ishal ees·*hal* diarrhoea
isilik ee·see·*leek* rash
istemek ees·te·*mek*
ask for something • want v
İsveç ees·*vech* Sweden
İsviçre ees·veech·*re* Switzerland
iş eesh business • work n
— **adamı** a·da·*muh* businessman
— **arkadaşı** ar·ka·da·*shuh* colleague
— **gezisi** ge·zee·*see* business trip
— **kadını** ka·duh·*nuh* businesswoman
işaret ee·sha·*ret* sign n
işçi eesh·*chee* labourer

işitme cihazı ee·sheet·*me* jee·ha·*zuh*
hearing aid
işsiz eesh·*seez* unemployed
işveren eesh·ve·*ren* employer
itmek eet·*mek* push v
iyi ee·*yee* fine • good • well
izin ee·*zeen* permission
izlemek eez·le·*mek* watch v

jambon zham·*bon* ham
jandarma zhan·dar·*ma* gendarme
jilet jee·*let* razor blade
jinekolog zhee·ne·ko·*log* gynaecologist

kabakulak ka·ba·koo·*lak* mumps
kabarcık ka·bar·*juhk* blister
kabızlık ka·buhz·*luhk* constipation
kabul etmek ka·*bool* et·*mek* admit
kaburga ka·boor·*ga* rib
kadar ka·*dar* until
kadın ka·*duhn* woman
— **bağı** ba·*uh* panty liners
kadınlar bölümü ka·duhn·*lar* ber·lew·*mew*
women's quarters
kafa derisi ka·*fa* de·ree·*see* scalp n
kafatası ka·fa·ta·*suh* skull
kağıt ka·*uht* paper
— **işlemleri** eesh·lem·le·*ree* paperwork
— **mendil** men·*deel* tissues
— **oynamak** oy·na·*mak* play cards v
— **para** pa·*ra* banknote
kahvaltı kah·val·*tuh* breakfast
kahverengi kah·ve·ren·*gee* brown
kainat ka·ee·*nat* universe
kalabalık ka·la·ba·*luhk* crowded
kalacak yer ka·la·*jak* yer accommodation
kale ka·*le* castle • fortress
— **içi** ee·*chee* citadel
kaleci ka·le·*jee* goalkeeper
kalın ka·*luhn* thick
kalmak kal·*mak* stay (at a hotel) v
kalp kalp heart (body)
— **krizi** kree·*zee*
cardiac arrest • heart attack
— **pili** pee·*lee* pacemaker
— **rahatsızlığı** ra·hat·suhz·luh·*uh*
heart condition
kamp alanı kamp a·la·*nuh* camping ground

kamp malzemeleri dükkanı kamp mal·ze·me·le·ree dewk·ka·nuh *camping store*

kamp yapmak kamp yap·mak *camp* v

kamp yeri kamp ye·ree *camp site*

kamyon kam·yon *truck*

kan kan *blood*

— **gurubu** goo·roo·boo *blood group*

— **tahlili** tah·lee·lee *blood test*

kansızlık kan·suhz·luhk *anaemia*

kanun ka·noon *law*

kapalı ka·pa·luh *closed · shut*

kapatmak ka·pat·mak *close* v

kapı ka·puh *door · gate (airport)*

kaplıca kap·luh·ja *thermal spring*

— **hamamı** ha·ma·muh *thermal bath*

kar kar *profit* n · *snow* n

kara yoluyla gönderi ka·ra yo·looy·la gern·de·ree *surface mail (land)*

karaciğer ka·ra·jee·er *liver*

Karadeniz ka·ra·de·neez *Black Sea*

karanlık ka·ran·luhk *dark (night)*

karar vermek ka·rar ver·mek *decide*

kardeş kar·desh *brother/sister*

karı ka·ruh *wife*

karınca ka·ruhn·ja *ant*

karıştırmak ka·ruhsh·tuhr·mak *mix* v

karmak kar·mak *deal (cards)* v

karşısında kar·shuh·suhn·da *across · opposite*

kas kas *muscle*

kasa ka·sa *safe* n

kasaba haritası ka·sa·ba ha·ree·ta·suh *town map*

kasap ka·sap *butcher*

kase ka·se *bowl* n

Kasım ka·suhm *November*

kasiyer ka·see·yer *cashier*

kask kask *helmet*

kaşık ka·shuhk *spoon* n

kaşıntı ka·shuhn·tuh *itch* n

kat kat *floor (storey)*

kavanoz ka·va·noz *jar*

kavga kav·ga *fight* n

kaya ka·ya *rock* n

kaya tırmanışı ka·ya tuhr·ma·nuh·shuh *rock climbing*

kayak ka·yak *skiing*

— **gözlüğü** gerz·lew·ew *skiing goggles*

— **yapmak** yap·mak *ski* v

kaybetmek kai·bet·mek *lose*

kaydetmek kai·det·mek *record* v

kayınpeder ka·yuhn·pe·der *father-in-law*

kayınvalide ka·yuhn·va·lee·de *mother-in-law*

kayıp ka·yuhp *lost*

— **eşya bürosu** esh·ya bew·ro·soo *lost-property office*

kayış ka·yuhsh *fanbelt*

kayıt ka·yuht *recording*

kay-kay kai·kai *skateboarding*

kaza ka·za *accident*

kazak ka·zak *jumper · sweater*

kazanmak ka·zan·mak *earn · win* v

kazıklama ka·zuhk·la·ma *rip-off* n

KDV (Katma Değer Vergisi) ka·de·ve (kat·ma de·er ver·gee·see) *KDV (Value Added Tax)*

keçi ke·chee *goat*

kedi ke·dee *cat*

kelebek ke·le·bek *butterfly*

kelime ke·lee·me *word* n

kemik ke·meek *bone*

kenar ke·nar *side* n

kertenkele ker·ten·ke·le *lizard*

kesme tahtası kes·me tah·ta·suh *chopping board*

kesmek kes·mek *cut* v

keşiş ke·sheesh *monk*

Kıbrıs kuhb·ruhs *Cyprus*

kırda uzun yürüyüş kuhr·da oo·zoon yew·rew·yewsh *hiking*

kırık kuh·ruhk *broken*

kırılabilir kuh·ruh·la·bee·leer *fragile*

kırmak kuhr·mak *break* v

kırmızı kuhr·muh·zuh *red*

kırtasiyeci kuhr·ta·see·ye·jee *stationer's*

kısa kuh·sa *short (height)*

kıskanç kuhs·kanch *jealous*

kış kuhsh *winter*

kız kuhz *daughter · girl*

— **arkadaş** ar·ka·dash *girlfriend*

— **kardeş** kar·desh *sister*

kızamık kuh·za·muhk *measles*

kızamıkçık kuh·za·muhk·chuhk *rubella*

kızartmak kuh·zart·mak *fry* v

kızartma tavası kuh·zart·ma ta·va·suh *frying pan*

kızgın kuhz·guhn *angry*

kibar kee·bar *kind (nice)*

kibrit keeb·reet *matches (for lighting)*

kilim kee·leem *rug*

kilise kee·lee·se *church*

kilit kee·leet *lock* n

kilitlemek kee·leet·le·mek *lock* v

kilitli kee-leet-lee *locked*
— **eşya dolabı** esh-ya do-la-buh *luggage locker*
kim keem *who*
kimlik keem-leek *identification*
— **kartı** kar-tuh *identification card (ID)*
kiralamak kee-ra-la-mak *hire* v • *rent* v
kirli keer-lee *dirty* a
kirlilik keer-lee-leek *pollution*
kişi kee-shee *person* • *people*
kitap kee-tap *book* n
kitapçı kee-tap-chuh *book shop*
klavye klav-ye *keyboard*
klima klee-ma *air conditioning*
klimalı klee-ma-luh *air-conditioned*
koca ko-ja *husband*
kocaman ko-ja-man *huge*
koku ko-koo *smell* n
kol kol *arm (body)*
kolay ko-lai *easy*
kolye kol-ye *necklace*
konak ko-nak *mansion*
konjonktivit iltihabı kon-jonk-tee-veet eel-tee-ha-buh *conjunctivitis*
konserve açacağı kon-ser-ve a-cha-ja-uh *can opener* • *tin opener*
konsolosluk kon-so-los-look *consulate*
kontrol etmek kon-trol et-mek *check* v
kontrol noktası kon-trol nok-ta-suh *checkpoint*
konuşmak ko-noosh-mak *speak* • *talk*
korkunç kor-koonch *awful* • *terrible*
koruma altına alınmış ko-roo-ma al-tuh-na a-luhn-muhsh *protected species*
korumak ko-roo-mak *protect*
koşmak kosh-mak *run* v
koşu ko-shoo *running*
kot pantolon kot pan-to-lon *jeans*
kova ko-va *bucket*
koymak koy-mak *put*
koyu ko-yoo *dark (colour)*
koyun ko-yoon *sheep*
köpek ker-pek *dog*
— **ısırması** uh-suhr-ma-suh *dog bite* n
köprü kerp-rew *bridge (structure)*
kör ker *blind* a
köşe ker-she *corner* n
kötü ker-tew *bad*
köy kay *village*
kral kral *king*
kraliçe kra-lee-che *queen*
krem krem *cream (lotion)*

krema kre-ma *cream (food)*
kuaför koo-a-fer *hairdresser*
kubbe koob-be *dome*
kulak koo-lak *ear*
— **temizleme çubuğu** te-meez-le-me choo-boo-oo *cotton buds*
— **tıkacı** tuh-ka-juh *earplugs*
kule koo-le *tower* n
kulp koolp *handlebars*
kum koom *sand* n
kumaş koo-mash *fabric*
kurabiye koo-ra-bee-ye *cookie*
kural koo-ral *rule*
kurşun kalem koor-shoon ka-lem *pencil*
kurşunsuz koor-shoon-sooz *unleaded*
kuru koo-roo *dried* • *dry* a
kurulamak koo-roo-la-mak *dry (general)* v
kurutmak koo-root-mak *dry (clothes)* v
kuş koosh *bird*
kutlama koot-la-ma *celebration*
kutu koo-too *box* n
kuyruk kooy-rook *tail* a
kuzey koo-zay *north*
Kuzey Kıbrıs Türk Cumhuriyeti (KKTC) koo-zay kuhb-ruhs tewrk joom-hoo-ree-ye-tee (ka-ka-te-je) *Turkish Republic of Northern Cyprus (TRNC)*
küçücük kew-chew-jewk *tiny*
küçük kew-chewk *little* • *small*
külotlu çorap kew-lot-loo cho-rap *pantyhose*
kül tablası kewl tab-la-suh *ashtray*
küpe kew-pe *earrings*
kürdan kewr-dan *toothpick*
kürek çekme kew-rek chek-me *rowing*
kütüphane kew-tewp-ha-ne *library*

L

lakap la-kap *nickname* n
lastik las-teek *tire* • *tyre*
lateks eldiven la-teks el-dee-ven *gloves (medical)*
Lefkoşa lef-ko-sha *Lefkosia (Nikosia)*
lezzetli lez-zet-lee *tasty*
libre leeb-re *pound (weight)*
liman lee-man *harbour* • *port*
lisan lee-san *language*
lise lee-se *high school*
lokum lo-koom *Turkish delight*
Lübnan lewb-nan *Lebanon*
lüks lewks *luxury* a

M

maaş ma-*ash* salary • wage
maden suyu ma-*den* soo-*yoo* mineral water
madeni para ma-de-*nee* pa-*ra* coins
mağara ma-a-*ra* cave n
mahalle ma-hal-*le* neighbourhood
mahcup mah-*joop* embarrassed
mahkeme mah-ke-*me* court (legal)
mahkum mah-*koom* prisoner
makas ma-*kas* scissors
makbuz mak-*booz* receipt
makul ma-*kool* sensible
makyaj mak-*yazh* make-up
mal olmak mal ol-*mak* cost v
malzeme mal-ze-*me* ingredient
mama sandalyesi ma-*ma* san-dal-ye-*see* highchair
manastır ma-nas-*tuhr* convent • monastery
manav ma-*nav* greengrocer
manzara man-za-*ra* view n
Mart mart March
masa ma-*sa* table n
masum ma-*soom* innocent
mavi ma-vee blue
Mayıs ma-*yuhs* May
mayo ma-*yo* bathing suit • swimsuit
medeni haklar me-de-*nee* hak-*lar* civil rights
medeni hal me-de-*nee* hal marital status
mektup mek-*toop* letter • mail
meme röntgeni me-*me* rernt-ge-*nee* mammogram
memur me-*moor* office worker
mendil men-*deel* handkerchief
merkez mer-*kez* centre n
mesane me-sa-*ne* bladder
meslek mes-*lek* job
meşgul mesh-*gool* busy • engaged (phone)
meşrubat mesh-roo-*bat* soft drink
mevsim mev-*seem* season
meydan may-*dan* town square
meyhane may-ha-*ne* winehall
meyve toplama may-ve top-la-*ma* fruit picking
mezar me-*zar* grave • tomb
mezarlık me-zar-*luhk* cemetery
mide mee-de stomach
— **ağrısı** a-ruh-*suh* stomachache
— **ve bağırsak enfeksiyonu** ve ba-uhr-*sak* en-fek-see-yo-*noo* gastroenteritis
milli park meel-*lee* park national park
milliyet meel-lee-*yet* nationality

mimar mee-*mar* architect
mimarlık mee-mar-*luhk* architecture (profession)
mimari yapı mee-ma-*ree* ya-*puh* architecture (art)
misafirhane mee-sa-feer-ha-*ne* guesthouse
misafirperverlik mee-sa-feer-per-ve-*leek* hospitality
mobilya mo-*beel*ya furniture
mor mor purple
muhtemel mooh-te-*mel* possible
mum moom candle
musluk moos-*look* faucet • tap
mutfak moot-*fak* kitchen
mutlu moot-*loo* happy
mücevherler mew-jev-her-*ler* jewellery
müdür mew-*dewr* manager (business)
mühendis mew-hen-*dees* engineer n
mühendislik mew-hen-dees-*leek* engineering
mükemmel mew-kem-*mel* excellent • perfect
mülakat mew-la-*kat* interview n
mülk sahibi mewlk sa-hee-*bee* landlady • landlord
mülteci mewl-te-*jee* refugee
müsil ilacı mew-*seel* ee-la-*juh* laxative
Müslüman din adamı mews-lew-*man* deen a-da-*muh* Muslim cleric
müşteri mewsh-te-*ree* client
müteşekkir mew-te-shek-*keer* grateful

N

nargile nar-gee-*le* water-pipe
nakit na-*keet* cash n
nasıl na-*suhl* how
ne ne what
neden ne-*den* why
nefes almak ne-*fes* al-*mak* breathe
nehir ne-*heer* river
nemlendirici nem-len-dee-ree-*jee* moisturiser
— **ruj** roozh lip balm
nerede ne-re-de where
nesli tükenmekte olan hayvanlar nes-*lee* tew-ken-mek-*te* o-*lan* hai-van-*lar* endangered species
ne zaman ne za-*man* when
Nisan nee-*san* April
nişan nee-*shan* engagement (to marry)
nişanlı nee-shan-*luh* engaged (to marry) • fiancé • fiancée

nitelikler nee·te·leek·*ler qualifications*
Noel no·*el Christmas*
— **yortusu** yor·too·soo *Christmas Day*
— **yortusu arifesi** yor·too·soo a·ree·fe·*see Christmas Eve*
nokta nok·*ta point (decimal/dot)* n
not defteri not def·te·*ree notebook*
nükleer atık newk·le·er a·*tuhk nuclear waste*
nükleer deneme newk·le·er de·ne·*me nuclear testing*

O

o o *he · she · it · that*
Ocak o·*jak January*
ocak o·*jak stove*
oda o·*da room* n
— **numarası** noo·ma·ra·*suh room number*
odun o·*doon wood*
oğlan o·*lan boy*
oğul o·*ool son*
okul o·*kool school*
okuma o·koo·*ma reading*
okumak o·koo·*mak read* v
okutman o·koot·*man lecturer*
okyanus ok·ya·*noos ocean*
Olimpiyat Oyunları o·leem·pee·yat o·yoon·la·*ruh Olympic Games*
olmak ol·*mak be*
olumlu o·loom·*loo positive* a
olumsuz o·loom·*sooz negative* a
omuz o·*mooz shoulder*
onlar on·*lar they*
onların on·la·*ruhn their*
onu o·*noo that (one)*
onun o·*noon her · his*
opera binası o·pe·*ra bee·na·suh opera house*
orada o·ra·*da there*
oral seks kondomu o·*ral seks kon·do·moo dental dam*
orman or·*man forest*
otobüs o·to·*bews bus · coach*
— **durağı** doo·ra·*uh bus stop*
— **terminali** ter·mee·na·*lee bus station*
oto ön camı o·to ern ja·*muh windscreen*
otoyol o·to·*yol highway*
oturma odası o·toor·ma o·da·*suh family room (home)*
oturmak o·toor·*mak live (somewhere) · sit*

oyun o·*yoon game (sport) · play (theatre)*
— **kağıdı** ka·uh·*duh playing cards*
oyuncak bebek o·yoon·jak be·*bek doll*
oyuncakçı o·yoon·jak·*chuh toy shop*
oyuncu o·yoon·*joo actor · player*
oy vermek oy ver·*mek vote* v
ozon tabakası o·zon ta·ba·ka·*suh ozone layer*

Ö

öbür gün er·bewr *gewn day after tomorrow*
ödeme er·de·*me payment*
ödemek er·de·*mek pay* v
ödemeli telefon er·de·me·*lee te·le·fon collect call*
ödünç almak er·dewnch al·*mak borrow*
öğle er·*le noon*
— **yemeği** ye·me·*ee lunch*
öğleden sonra er·le·den son·ra *afternoon*
öğrenci er·ren·*jee student* n
öğrenmek er·ren·*mek learn*
öğretmen er·ret·*men instructor · teacher*
öksürmek erk·sewr·*mek cough* v
öksürük ilacı erk·sew·rewk ee·la·*juh cough medicine*
ölmek erl·*mek die*
ölü er·*lew dead*
önce ern·*je ago · before*
önceki ern·je·*kee last (previous)*
— **gün** *gewn day before yesterday*
önemli er·nem·*lee important*
önünde er·newn·*de in front of*
öpmek erp·*mek kiss* v
öpücük er·pew·*jewk kiss* n
ördek er·*dek duck*
örnek er·*nek example*
örümcek er·rewm·*jek spider*
özel er·*zel private · special*
özgeçmiş erz·gech·*meesh CV · résumé*
özlemek erz·le·*mek miss (feel absence of)*
özürlü er·zewr·*lew disabled*

P

pahalı pa·ha·*luh expensive*
palto pal·*to coat · overcoat*
pamuk pa·*mook cotton*
— **yumağı** yoo·ma·*uh cotton balls*
pamukçuk pa·mook·*chook thrush (medical)*
pantolon pan·to·*lon pants · trousers*
papaz pa·*paz priest*

para pa·*ra money*
— **bozdurmak** boz·door·*mak exchange (money)* v
— **cezası** je·za·*suh fine* n
— **iadesi** ee·a·de·*see refund* n
paralı yol pa·ra·*luh yol motorway (tollway)* n
parça par·*cha component · part · piece*
park etmek park et·*mek park (a car)* v
parmak par·*mak finger*
parti par·*tee party (night out/politics)* n
Paskalya pas·*kal·ya Easter*
paspas pas·*pas mat*
pastane pas·*ta·ne cake shop*
paten pa·*ten rollerblading* n
patenle kaymak pa·*ten·*le kai·*mak skate* v
patika pa·*tee·ka footpath · path · track · trail*
patlak pat·*lak puncture* n
paylaşmak pai·lash·*mak share* v
pazar pa·*zar bazaar · market*
— **yeri** ye·*ree agora (market place)*
Pazar pa·*zar Sunday*
Pazartesi pa·zar·te·*see Monday*
peçete pe·che·te *napkin · serviette*
pembe pem·*be pink*
— **dizi** dee·*zee soap opera*
pencere pen·je·*re window*
peron pe·*ron platform (train)* n
Perşembe per·shem·*be Thursday*
peynirci pay·neer·*jee cheese shop*
pınar puh·*nar spring (fountain)*
pil peel *battery (dry)*
pire pee·*re flea*
pişik pee·*sheek nappy rash*
pişirmek pee·sheer·*mek cook* v
plaj plazh *beach*
— **voleybolu** vo·lay·bo·*loo beach volleyball*
plaka pla·*ka car registration · license plate number · numberplate*
polis karakolu po·lees ka·ra·ko·*loo police station*
polis memuru po·lees me·moo·*roo police officer*
politika po·lee·tee·*ka policy · politics*
politikacı po·lee·tee·ka·*juh politician*
pompa pom·*pa pump* n
popo po·*po bottom (body)*
posta pos·*ta mail (postal system)*
— **kutusu** koo·too·*soo mailbox*
— **ücreti** ewj·re·*tee postage*
postane pos·*ta·ne post office*

pratik konuşma kılavuzu pra·*teek ko·noosh·ma kuh·la·voo·zoo phrasebook*
prezervatif pre·zer·va·*teef condom*
puan poo·*an point* n · *score* n
— **tahtası** tah·ta·*suh scoreboard*
pul pool *stamp (postage)* n
puro poo·*ro cigar*
puset poo·*set pram · stroller*
pusula poo·soo·*la compass*

R

raf raf *shelf*
rahat ra·*hat comfortable*
rahatlatıcı ra·hat·la·tuh·*juh inhaler*
rahatsız ra·hat·*suhz uncomfortable*
rahibe ra·hee·*be nun*
rahim ağzı kanser tarama testi ra·*heem a·zuh kan·ser ta·ra·ma tes·tee pap smear*
rahim içi araç ra·*heem ee·chee a·rach IUD*
Ramazan ra·ma·*zan Ramadan*
reçete re·che·*te prescription*
reddetmek red·det·*mek refuse* v
refah re·*fah welfare*
rehber reh·*ber guide (person)* n
— **kitap** kee·*tap guidebook*
— **köpek** ker·*pek guide dog*
rehberli tur reh·ber·*lee toor guided tour*
rehidrasyon tuzu re·heed·ras·yon too·*zoo rehydration salts*
renk renk *colour* n
ressam res·*sam painter (artist)*
ressamlık res·sam·*luhk painting (the art)*
rıhtım ruh·*tuhm quay*
rota ro·*ta route* n
ruhsat rooh·*sat permit* n
ruj roozh *lipstick*
Rusça roos·*cha Russian (language)*
rüşvet rewsh·*vet bribe*
rüya rew·*ya dream* n
rüzgar rewz·*gar wind* n
— **sörfü** ser·*few windsurfing*

S

saat sa·*at clock · hour · watch* n
sabah sa·*bah morning*
— **bulantıları** boo·lan·tuh·la·*ruh morning sickness*
sabun sa·*boon soap*
sabunluk sa·boon·*look wash cloth (flannel)*
saç sach *hair*
— **fırçası** fuhr·cha·*suh hairbrush*
— **kestirme** kes·teer·*me haircut*

sadaka sa·da·ka dole
sadece sa·de·je only
saf saf pure
sağ-kanat sa·ka·nat right-wing
sağır sa·uhr deaf
sağlık sa·luhk health
sahip sa·heep owner
— **olmak** ol·mak have
sakız sa·kuhz chewing gum
sakin sa·keen quiet a
Salı sa·luh Tuesday
saman nezlesi sa·man nez·le·see hay fever
sanat sa·nat art • crafts
— **galerisi** ga·le·ree·see art gallery
sanatçı sa·nat·chuh artist
sandalet san·da·let sandal
sandalye san·dal·ye chair
saniye sa·nee·ye second (time) n
sara sa·ra epilepsy
saray sa·rai palace
sarhoş sar·hosh drunk a
sarı sa·ruh yellow
sarılık sa·ruh·luhk hepatitis
sarılmak sa·ruhl·mak hug v
sarp sarp steep
satın almak sa·tuhn al·mak buy v
satış kulübesi sa·tuhsh koo·lew·be·see kiosk
satış vergisi sa·tuhsh ver·gee·see sales tax
satmak sat·mak sell
satranç sat·ranch chess
— **tahtası** tah·ta·suh chess board
savaş sa·vash war n
sayfa sai·fa page n
sayı sa·yuh number
saymak sai·mak count v
sebep se·bep reason n
sebze seb·ze vegetable n
seçim se·cheem election
— **bürosu** bew·ro·soo electrical store
seçmek sech·mek choose
sel sel flood n
semaver se·ma·ver tea urn
semt pazarı semt pa·za·ruh street market
sen sen you sg inf
senin se·neen your
sepet se·pet basket
serbest ser·best free (not bound) • loose
— **çalışan** cha·luh·shan self-employed
sergi ser·gee exhibition
serin se·reen cool (temperature) a
sert sert hard (not soft)
ses ses voice • volume

sevgili sev·gee·lee lover
sevmek sev·mek like v
seyahat se·ya·hat travel v
— **acentesi** a·jen·te·see travel agency
— **çeki** che·kee travellers cheque
sıcak suh·jak hot
— **su** soo hot water
sıçan suh·chan rat
sıkı suh·kuh tight
sıkıcı suh·kuh·juh boring
sık sık suhk suhk often
sınır suh·nuhr border
sıra suh·ra queue n
— **dağlar** da·lar mountain range
sıradan suh·ra·dan ordinary
sırt suhrt back (body)
— **çantası** chan·ta·suh backpack
sigara see·ga·ra cigarette
— **içilmeyen** ee·cheel·me·yen nonsmoking
— **içmek** eech·mek smoke v
sigorta see·gor·ta insurance
silah see·lah gun
sipariş see·pa·reesh order (food/goods) n
— **vermek** ver·mek order (food/goods) v
sisli sees·lee foggy
sistit sees·teet cystitis
sivrisinek seev·ree·see·nek mosquito
siyah see·yah black
— **beyaz film** be·yaz feelm B&W film
siz seez you sg pol & pl inf/pol
slayt slait slide (film)
soğan so·an onion
soğuk so·ook cold n & a
sohbet etmek soh·bet et·mek chat up v
sokak so·kak street
— **çalgıcısı** chal·guh·juh·suh busker
sol sol left (direction)
sol-kanat sol·ka·nat left-wing
solucanlar so·loo·jan·lar worms
son son end v
— **kullanma tarihi** kool·lan·ma ta·ree·hee expiry date
sonbahar son·ba·har autumn • fall
sonra son·ra after • later
sonsuza dek son·soo·za dek forever
sormak sor·mak ask (a question) v
soru so·roo question n
sos tenceresi sos ten·je·re·see saucepan
soy soy descendent
soyad soy·ad family name • surname
soymak soy·mak rob

soyunma kabini so·yoon·*ma* ka·bee·nee changing room

sömürü ser·mew·*rew* exploitation

sörf serf surfing
— **tahtası** tah·ta·*suh* surfboard
— **yapmak** yap·*mak* surf v

söylemek say·le·*mek* say v

söz vermek serz ver·*mek* promise v

sözlük serz·*lewk* dictionary

spiral sinek kovar spee·*ral* see·*nek* ko·*var* mosquito coil

spor malzemeleri mağazası spor mal·ze·me·le·*ree* ma·a·za·*suh* sports store

sporcu spor·*joo* sportsperson

sterlin ster·*leen* pound (money)

su soo water n
— **çiçeği** chee·che·*ee* chicken pox
— **geçirmez** ge·cheer·*mez* waterproof
— **kayağı** ka·ya·*uh* waterskiing
— **şişesi** shee·she·*see* water bottle

suçlu sooch·*loo* guilty

sunak soo·*nak* altar

Suriye soo·ree·*ye* Syria

susamış soo·sa·*muhsh* thirsty

suyu soo·*yoo* juice n

sürmek sewr·*mek* drive v

süt sewt milk

sütyen sewt·*yen* bra

Ş

şafak sha·*fak* dawn n

şahane sha·ha·*ne* wonderful

şaka sha·*ka* joke n

şampiyona sham·pee·yo·*na* championships

şampuan sham·poo·*an* shampoo

şans shans chance • luck

şanslı shans·*luh* lucky

şapka shap·*ka* hat

şarap sha·*rap* wine
— **dükkanı** dewk·ka·*nuh* wine shop

şarkı shar·*kuh* song
— **söylemek** say·le·*mek* sing

şarkıcı shar·kuh·*juh* singer

şarküteri shar·ke·te·*ree* delicatessen

şehir she·*heer* city
— **dışı** duh·*shuh* countryside
— **merkezi** mer·ke·*zee* city centre
— **otobüsü** o·to·bew·*sew* city bus

şehirlerarası otobüs she·heer·*ler*·a·ra·*suh* o·to·*bews* intercity bus

şeker she·*ker* candy • lollies • sugar • sweets
— **hastalığı** has·ta·luh·*uh* diabetes

şelale she·la·*le* waterfall

şemsiye shem·see·*ye* umbrella

şımarık shuh·ma·*ruhk* spoilt (person)

şiddet yanlısı sheed·*det* yan·luh·*suh* activist

şiir shee·*eer* poetry

şikayet shee·ka·*yet* complaint
— **etmek** et·*mek* complain

şilte sheel·*te* mattress

şimdi sheem·*dee* now

şimdiki zaman sheem·dee·*kee* za·*man* present (time)

şirket sheer·*ket* company (firm)

şişe shee·*she* bottle n
— **açacağı** a·cha·ja·*uh* bottle opener

şişlik sheesh·*leek* swelling

şişman sheesh·*man* fat a

şort short shorts

Şubat shoo·*bat* February

şunu shoo·*noo* that (one)

T

taahhütlü posta ta·ah·hewt·*lew* pos·*ta* registered mail/post

tablo tab·*lo* painting (a work)

taciz ta·*jeez* harassment

tahmin etmek tah·*meen* et·*mek* guess v

takım ta·*kuhm* team n

takip etmek ta·*keep* et·*mek* follow

taksi durağı tak·*see* doo·ra·*uh* taxi rank

takvim tak·*veem* calendar

tam mesai tam me·sa·*ee* full-time

tam olarak tam o·la·*rak* exactly

tamir etmek ta·*meer* et·*mek* repair v

tanışmak ta·nuhsh·*mak* meet (first time) v

tanrı tan·*ruh* god (general)

tansiyon tan·see·*yon* blood pressure

tapa ta·*pa* plug (bath) n

tapınak ta·puh·*nak* shrine • temple

taraftar ta·raf·*tar* fan • supporter

tarak ta·*rak* comb n

tarım ta·*ruhm* agriculture

tarife ta·ree·*fe* timetable

tarih ta·*reeh* date (day) • history

tarihi ta·ree·*hee* ancient • historical

tartışmak tar·tuhsh·*mak* argue

tartmak tart·*mak* weigh

tarz tarz style n

taş tash stone n

taşımak ta·shuh·*mak* carry

tatil ta-teel holiday(s) • vacation
tatlı tat-luh dessert n • sweet a
tava ta-va pan
tavla tav-la backgammon
tavsiye tav-see-ye advice
— **etmek** et-mek recommend
tavşan tav-shan rabbit
taze ta-ze fresh
tebrikler teb-reek-ler congratulations
tecavüz te-ja-vewz rape n
— **etmek** et-mek rape v
teçhizat tech-hee-zat equipment
tehlikeli teh-lee-ke-lee dangerous • unsafe
tekel bayii te-kel ba-yee-ee liquor store
tekerlek te-ker-lek wheel
— **parmaklığı** par-mak-luh-uh spoke n
tekerlekli sandalye te-ker-lek-lee san-dal-ye wheelchair
tek kişilik oda tek kee-shee-leek o-da single room
tekmelemek tek-me-le-mek kick v
tekrar tek-rar again
tel tel wire n
teleferik te-le-fe-reek cable car
telefon te-le-fon telephone n
— **etmek** et-mek telephone v
— **konuşması** ko-noosh-ma-suh phone call n
— **kulübesi** koo-lew-be-see phone box
— **rehberi** reh-be-ree phone book
— **santralı** san-tra-luh telephone centre
telesiyej te-le-see-yezh chairlift (skiing)
telgraf tel-graf telegram n
tembel tem-bel lazy
temiz te-meez clean a
temizlemek te-meez-le-mek clean v
temizlik te-meez-leek cleaning
Temmuz tem-mooz July
teneke kutu te-ne-ke koo-too can • tin
tepe te-pe hill
tercih etmek ter-jeeh et-mek prefer
tercüman ter-jew-man interpreter
termofor ter-mo-for hot water bottle
terzi ter-zee tailor
teslim etmek tes-leem et-mek deliver
teşebbüs etmek te-sheb-bews et-mek try (attempt) v
teşekkür etmek te-shek-kewr et-mek thank v
teyit etmek te-yeet et-mek confirm (a booking) v
teyze tay-ze aunt
ticaret tee-ja-ret trade n

tıkalı tuh-ka-luh blocked
tıp tuhp medicine (study, profession)
tıraş kremi tuh-rash kre-mee shaving cream
tıraş olmak tuh-rash ol-mak shave v
tırmanmak tuhr-man-mak climb v
tirbüşon teer-bew-shon corkscrew
top top ball (sport) n
toplantı yeri top-lan-tuh ye-ree venue
toplum refahı top-loom re-fa-huh social welfare
toprak bastı top-rak bas-tuh airport tax
toprak kap top-rak kap pot (ceramics)
toprak parçası top-rak par-cha-suh land n
torun to-roon grandchild
trafik adası tra-feek a-da-suh roundabout
trafik ışığı tra-feek uh-shuh-uh traffic light
transit yolcu salonu tran-seet yol-joo sa-lo-noo transit lounge
traş losyonu trash los-yo-noo aftershave
traş makinesi trash ma-kee-ne-see razor
turuncu too-roon-joo orange (colour)
tutkal toot-kal glue n
tutucu too-too-joo conservative n
tutuklamak too-took-la-mak arrest v
tutulmuş too-tool-moosh booked out
tuvalet too-va-let toilet
— **kağıdı** ka-uh-duh toilet paper
tuz tooz salt
tüccar tewj-jar tradesperson
tükenmez kalem tew-ken-mez ka-lem ballpoint pen
tütün tew-tewn tobacco
tütüncü tew-tewn-jew tobacconist

U

ucuz oo-jooz cheap
uçak oo-chak airplane
uçmak ooch-mak fly v
uçurum oo-choo-room cliff
uçuş oo-choosh flight
ulaşım oo-la-shuhm transport n
ultrason ool-tra-son ultrasound
uluslararası oo-loos-lar-a-ra-suh international a
umumi telefon oo-moo-mee te-le-fon public telephone
umumi tuvalet oo-moo-mee too-va-let public toilet
unutmak oo-noot-mak forget
utangaç oo-tan-gach shy
uyandırmak oo-yan-duhr-mak wake up v

uyarmak oo·yar·mak warn
uygarlık tarihi ooy·gar·luhk ta·ree·hee humanities
uyku hapı ooy·koo ha·puh sleeping pills
uyku tulumu ooy·koo too·loo·moo sleeping bag
uykulu ooy·koo·loo sleepy
uyumak oo·yoo·mak sleep v
uyuşturucu oo·yoosh·too·roo·joo drug (illegal) n
— **alış-verişi** a·luhsh·ve·ree·shee drug trafficking
— **bağımlılığı** ba·uhm·luh·luh·uh drug addiction
— **bağımlısı** ba·uhm·luh·suh drug user
— **etkisi altında** et·kee·see al·tuhn·da stoned (drugged)
— **satıcısı** sa·tuh·juh·suh drug dealer
uzak oo·zak far · remote
uzaktan kumanda oo·zak·tan koo·man·da remote control
uzanmak oo·zan·mak lie (not stand) v
uzatma oo·zat·ma extension (visa)
uzay oo·zai space (universe)
uzman ooz·man specialist (medical) n
uzun oo·zoon long a
— **boylu** boy·loo tall (person)
— **yürüyüşe çıkmak** yew·rew·yew·she chuhk·mak hike v

Ü

ücretsiz ewj·ret·seez free (gratis)
üçüncü ew·chewn·jew third a
ülke ewl·ke country
— **haritası** ha·ree·ta·suh country map
ünlü ewn·lew famous
üretmek ew·ret·mek produce v
ürün ew·rewn crop (food) n
üşütmek ew·shewt·mek have a cold
ütü ew·tew iron (clothes) n
üye ew·ye member
üzgün ewz·gewn sad

V

vadi va·dee valley
vaftiz vaf·teez baptism
vapur va·poor boat
varmak var·mak arrive
vatandaşlık va·tan·dash·luhk citizenship
ve ve and
vergi ver·gee tax n
vermek ver·mek give

vestiyer ves·tee·yer cloakroom
veya ve·ya or
video kayıt cihazı vee·de·o ka·yuht jee·ha·zuh video recorder
vites kutusu vee·tes koo·too·soo gearbox
vücut vew·joot body

Y

yabancı ya·ban·juh foreign a · stranger n
yağ ya oil n
yağlayıcı madde ya·la·yuh·juh mad·de lubricant
yağmur ya·moor rain n
yağmurluk ya·moor·look raincoat
Yahudi ya·hoo·dee Jewish
yakacak odun ya·ka·jak o·doon firewood
yakın ya·kuhn close adv · nearby adj
— **zamanda** za·man·da recently
yakında ya·kuhn·da near · soon
yakışıklı ya·kuh·shuhk·luh handsome
yalan söylemek ya·lan say·le·mek lie (not tell the truth) v
yalancı ya·lan·juh liar
yalnız yal·nuhz alone
yangın yan·guhn fire (out of control)
yanık ya·nuhk burnt
yanında ya·nuhn·da beside · next to
yanlış yan·luhsh wrong
yanma yan·ma burn n
yapmak yap·mak do · make
yaprak yap·rak leaf n
yara ya·ra injury
— **bandı** ban·duh Band-Aid
yaralı ya·ra·luh injured
yararlı ya·rar·luh useful
yardım yar·duhm help n
— **etmek** et·mek help v
yargıç yar·guhch judge n
yarım ya·ruhm half
— **gün** gewn part-time a
yarın ya·ruhn tomorrow
— **akşam** ak·sham tomorrow evening
— **öğleden sonra** er·le·den son·ra tomorrow afternoon
— **sabah** sa·bah tomorrow morning
yarış ya·ruhsh race (sport) n
— **bisikleti** bee·seek·le·tee racing bike
— **pisti** pees·tee racetrack · track (sport)
yasal ya·sal legal
yasama ya·sa·ma legislation
yastık yas·tuhk pillow
— **kılıfı** kuh·luh·fuh pillowcase

Ü

yaşlı yash·*luh* old (person)
yaş yash *age* n
yatak ya·*tak* bed • sleeping berth
— odası o·da·*suh* bedroom
— takımı ta·kuh·*muh* bedding
yavaş ya·*vash* slow a
— koşu ko·shoo jogging
yavaşça ya·vash·*cha* slowly
yay yai spring (coil) n
yaya ya·*ya* pedestrian
— geçidi ge·chee·dee
pedestrian crossing
yaz yaz summer
yazar ya·*zar* writer
— kasa ka·sa cash register
yazı yazmak ya·zuh yaz·*mak* write
yemek ye·*mek* dish • meal
— listesi lees·te·see menu
— pişirme pee·sheer·me cooking
— yemek ye·*mek* eat
yeni ye·*nee* new
Yeni Yıl ye·nee yuhl New Year's Day
— arifesi a·ree·fe·see New Year's Eve
yeniden gözden geçirme ye·nee·*den*
gerz·den ge·cheer·me review n
yeniden kazanılabilir ye·nee·*den*
ka·za·nuh·*la*·bee·leer recyclable
yeniden kazanmak ye·nee·*den*
ka·zan·mak recycle
yer yer floor • place • seat • space • vacancy
yerel ye·*rel* local a
yönetmen yer·net·men director
yeryüzü yer·yew·zew Earth
yeşil ye·*sheel* green
yeterli ye·ter·lee enough
yetişkin ye·teesh·*keen* adult n
yıkamak yuh·ka·*mak* wash something v
yıkanmak yuh·kan·*mak* wash oneself v
yıl yuhl year
yılan yuh·*lan* snake
yıldız yuhl·*duhz* star
— falı fa·luh horoscope
(dört) yıldızlı (dert) yuhl·duhz·*luh*
(four·)star
yiyecek yee·ye·jek food
yoksulluk yok·sool·*look* poverty
yokuş aşağı yo·koosh a·sha·*uh* downhill
yokuş yukarı yo·koosh yoo·ka·*ruh* uphill
yol yol road • way
— haritası ha·ree·ta·suh road map
— parası pa·ra·suh fare
— yorgunluğu yor·goon·loo·oo jet lag
yolcu yol·*joo* passenger

yolculuk yol·joo·*look* journey n
yolculukta izlenecek yol yol·joo·look·*ta*
eez·le·ne·jek yol itinerary
yorgun yor·*goon* tired
yön yern direction
yönetim yer·ne·*teem* administration
yukarı yoo·ka·*ruh* up
yukarısında yoo·ka·ruh·suhn·*da* above
yumru yoom·*roo* lump
yumurta yoo·moor·*ta* egg
yumurtalık yoo·moor·ta·*luhk* ovary
— tümörü tew·mer·rew ovarian cyst
Yunanistan yoo·na·nees·*tan* Greece
yurt dışı yoort duh·*shuh* abroad • overseas
yuvarlak yoo·var·*lak* round a
yüksek yewk·*sek* high a
— ses ses loud
yükseklik yewk·sek·*leek* altitude
yün yewn wool
yürümek yew·rew·*mek* walk v
yürüyen merdiven yew·rew·*yen*
mer·dee·ven escalator
yürüyüş ayakkabısı yew·rew·*yewsh*
a·yak·ka·buh·suh hiking boots
yürüyüş güzergahı yew·rew·*yewsh*
gew·zer·ga·huh hiking route
yüz yewz face • hundred
— havlusu hav·loo·soo face cloth
yüzde yewz·*de* per cent
yüzme yewz·*me* swimming (sport)
— havuzu ha·voo·zoo swimming pool
yüzmek yewz·*mek* swim v
yüzük yew·*zewk* ring (on finger)

Z

zaman za·*man* time n
— farkı far·kuh time difference
zamanında za·ma·nuhn·*da* on time
zar zar dice n
zararlı atık za·rar·luh a·tuhk toxic waste
zarf zarf envelope n
zaten za·ten already
zayıf za·*yuhf* weak
zehirli ze·heer·lee poisonous
zengin zen·*geen* rich • wealthy
zincir zeen·jeer chain n
zirve zeer·ve peak (mountain)
ziyaret etmek zee·ya·ret et·mek visit v
zona zo·na shingles (illness)
zor zor difficult • hard
zührevi hastalık zewh·re·vee has·ta·*luhk*
venereal disease

What kind of traveller are you?

A. You're eating chicken for dinner *again* because it's the only word you know.

B. When no one understands what you say, you step closer and shout louder.

C. When the barman doesn't understand your order, you point frantically at the beer.

D. You're surrounded by locals, swapping jokes, email addresses and experiences – other travellers want to borrow your phrasebook or audio guide.

If you answered A, B, or C, you NEED Lonely Planet's language products ...

- **Lonely Planet Phrasebooks** – for every phrase you need in every language you want
- **Lonely Planet Language & Culture** – get behind the scenes of English as it's spoken around the world – learn and laugh
- **Lonely Planet Fast Talk & Fast Talk Audio** – essential phrases for short trips and weekends away – read, listen and talk like a local
- **Lonely Planet Small Talk** – 10 essential languages for city breaks
- **Lonely Planet Real Talk** – downloadable language audio guides from lonelyplanet.com to your MP3 player

... and this is why

- **Talk to everyone everywhere**
  Over 120 languages, more than any other publisher
- **The right words at the right time**
  Quick-reference colour sections, two-way dictionary, easy pronunciation, every possible subject – and audio to support it

Lonely Planet Offices

Australia
90 Maribyrnong St, Footscray,
Victoria 3011
☎ 03 8379 8000
fax 03 8379 8111
✉ talk2us@lonelyplanet.com.au

USA
150 Linden St, Oakland,
CA 94607
☎ 510 250 6400
fax 510 893 8572
✉ info@lonelyplanet.com

UK
2nd floor, 186 City Rd
London EC1V 2NT
☎ 020 7106 2100
fax 020 7106 2101
✉ go@lonelyplanet.co.uk

lonelyplanet.com